Praise for *Fierce Vulnerability*

"Kazu Haga's deep, nuanced, and principled commitment to nonviolence has challenged and inspired me and many others who've had the privilege of encountering his work."

—MICHELLE ALEXANDER, author of *The New Jim Crow*

"Kazu Haga has crafted a profound contemplation on the inseparable nature of inner healing and collective transformation. An inspired call to listen more deeply, *Fierce Vulnerability* invites all of us to live our way into a different future together."

—OREN JAY SOFER, author of *Your Heart Was Made for This*

"This is a reading experience for your heart, not to be missed. Once again, Kazu Haga has addressed the most contentious and difficult events of our time with humility, beauty, and exquisite care, opening the door to new possibilities in a world that often seems impossible."

—SARAH PEYTON, author of *Your Resonant Self*

"*Fierce Vulnerability* invites us into healing at scale and remembering what it is to be human. It calls us to rest our social justice movements in the truth of interdependence. We have a traumatizing collective history we long to transform—this is a different way."

—STACI K. HAINES, author of *The Politics of Trauma*

"Thought-provoking and healing, at times soul-searching and challenging, a must-read for anyone seeking meaningful change in these times."

—RIVERA SUN, author of *The Dandelion Insurrection*

"Don't miss this book if you're looking for new ways of being and doing together to confront the deeply interconnected, relational challenges we face in our world."

—JULIA ROIG, founder of Thᵣ

"Profound in all directions. Bravo."

—LARRY YANG, author of *Av*

T0370169

ALSO BY KAZU HAGA

Healing Resistance:
A Radically Different Response to Harm

Fierce Vulnerability

Healing
from Trauma,
Emerging
through Collapse

Kazu Haga

Foreword by Kaira Jewel Lingo

PARALLAX PRESS
BERKELEY, CALIFORNIA

Parallax Press
2236B Sixth Street
Berkeley, CA 94710
parallax.org

Parallax Press is the publishing division of Plum Village Community of
Engaged Buddhism, Inc.

Cover design by Katie Eberle
Interior design by Maureen Forys, Happenstance Type-O-Rama

Disclaimer: Please seek advice, such as from a doctor, physician, or mental
health worker or healer, to determine whether the exercises and advice
in this book are suitable for you. Do not rely on this information as a sub-
stitute for, or replacement of medical advice, diagnosis, or treatment. If
you experience mental or physical distress while reading this content or
engaging in any of these activities, stop immediately, and consult with an
appropriate health care worker.

Printed in Canada by Friesens on FSC-certified paper

Parallax Press's authorized European representative is SARL
Boutique La Bambouseraie Point UH, Le Pey, 24240 Thénac, France
europe@parallax.org

ISBN 978-1-946764-98-0
Ebook ISBN 978-1-946764-99-7

Library of Congress Control Number: 2024951467

1 2 3 4 5 FRIESENS 29 28 27 26 25

I have had the honor to learn from many great elders in my life and be in relationship with countless well-known teachers. And yet, it is the people closest to me who have taught me the most and made this book possible.

Shilpa Jain helped open the door for me and put me on my healing journey. Thank you and to the Jam community you helped to create for continuing to hold that door open.

Sonya Shah is the first person who showed me healing is possible even after the greatest harms. Thank you and the Ahimsa Collective for showing me what we are capable of.

Chris Moore-Backman could almost be a coauthor of this book. Thank you for your humility, wisdom, friendship, and for modeling fierce vulnerability.

Once the door of healing was opened, it is my partner, LiZhen Wang, who has supported and pushed me to grow more than anyone in my life. Thank you for showing me magic, for keeping me close to spirit, for the countless ways you support and inspire me.

Contents

Foreword

THIS IS NOT HYPERBOLE: the world has been waiting for this book, and its wisdom is desperately needed. Kazu Haga is a gifted surgeon-healer, skillfully addressing a core wound of our time: the delusion of separation. For too long, the realms of personal healing and systemic change have pulled in opposite directions, like a two-headed snake. Kazu tenderly stitches these realms together, offering a new vision for liberation that integrates our inner transformation with our work for justice

Drawing from the legacies of nonviolence and direct action, Kazu shows us what a truly liberatory movement can look like—one that includes not only activists but also healers, artists, and grief tenders. He reminds us that vulnerability is not a weakness but a fierce, transformative force capable of dismantling the walls built by trauma and oppression.

Kazu powerfully articulates the need for collective healing of trauma to stop perpetuating harm, including the destruction of the Earth that sustains us. I experienced a glimpse of what such collective healing might look like in 2007, traveling to Vietnam with my teacher, Thích Nhất Hạnh and the Plum Village community. Together, we organized three Grand Requiem Masses to honor those who died in the Vietnam War. These ceremonies—held publicly for the first time since the war ended—created space for grief, without discrimination.

In one ceremony, hundreds of us chanted through the night in a Buddha Hall as tens of thousands prayed and practiced alongside us. I was profoundly aware of the collective healing happening, as decades of unacknowledged loss were finally grieved and released through the power of our prayers. In that sacred space, my prayers extended beyond Vietnam to include the ungrieved losses of the Indigenous genocide in North America, those who perished in the Middle Passage and during centuries of slavery, and the women of wisdom burned in the witch hunts. I longed for such intentional ceremonies to be held in the United States, where systemic injustices remain stuck in our psyches, unhealed in a culture of historical amnesia.

Kazu's work points to the possibility of this deeper collective healing. He shows us that until we face and transform our trauma, we cannot create the liberated world we long for. This healing is not just a personal endeavor but a political necessity.

In a world teetering on the brink of ecological and social collapse, *Fierce Vulnerability* offers a vision grounded in courage, humility, and the radical power of healing. Kazu reminds us that healing personal and intergenerational trauma is inseparable from healing systemic injustice. This book is an essential guide for how we can embody this work together, whoever we are.

KAIRA JEWEL LINGO,
GARDEN CITY, DECEMBER 2024

Kaira Jewel Lingo is a teacher in the Plum Village Tradition of Engaged Buddhism and the Vipassana tradition through Spirit Rock Meditation Center. She is the author of *We Were Made for These Times: Ten Lessons on Moving Through Change, Loss, and Disruption* and coauthor of *Healing Our Way Home: Black Buddhist Teachings on Ancestors, Joy, and Liberation.*

Prelude

I DON'T KNOW what fierce vulnerability is.

This book is pretty much just me thinking out loud. It's my musings about my understanding of how to create change and bring more healing to our world. By the time you read this, I'll probably have more to say, and some of it may even be contradictory to what you read here. Fierce vulnerability evolves as I live into it.

This book is not about personal healing. In fact, I have come to believe the idea of personal healing and individual liberation is a delusion. There is no such thing as personal healing in an interdependent world. In order for any of us to be free, we must work for the liberation of all beings. This means that this book is also about collective healing and systemic change. Call it social justice, call it activism, call it movement building, call it whatever you'd like, but don't mistake this for some sort of self-help book.

The things we might call "personal healing" work—spiritual practice, healthy living, trauma healing—must be an integral part of systemic change work. We must embody the changes we want to see in the world; if we ask the world to heal, we have to be willing to do the hard work ourselves.

Trauma is the lingering impact of experiencing or witnessing something so distressing it overwhelms your body's ability to cope. While the impact of stress goes away relatively quickly, the impact of trauma can linger for years and lifetimes. When we experience something so scary we become paralyzed and feel like fight or flight is not an option, or when we are so scared it becomes impossible to feel our emotions, we shut down. The incredibly powerful energy of fear gets trapped inside of our bodies. When we aren't able to properly discharge it, this energy can become frozen in our bodies as trauma.

In an era of escalating climate catastrophes, nationalist and authoritarian regimes rising to power around the world, the impact of a 500-year legacy of racial oppression rising to the surface,* unprecedented wealth disparity, daily mass shootings, and political upheaval, healing ourselves is not enough. We are experiencing collective trauma, and that demands a collective response. The intention of our individual healing must be to remember our interdependence. We are at our strongest when we realize we depend on each other, not when we buy into the myth of independence.

The legacy of nonviolence has always been filled with people who work on personal transformation. For me, practices like meditation, yoga, healing workshops, and therapy have been some of *the hardest* things I've ever done in my life, and I consider them to be part of my nonviolence practice. I am purifying my own mind, body, and spirit of the violence I hold in my heart.

At the same time, we're living at a particular juncture in human history; if we don't make changes at the largest, systemic levels, we may not survive much longer. Luckily, the legacy of nonviolence has also been filled with fierce advocates who used strategies like direct action to push for change at the largest scales. The paradox is if we don't root that change in a commitment to personal transformation, I'm afraid the changes we need at the largest levels won't be possible. And if personal

---

* Globally and in the United States, the 2010s and 2020s have been an era of reckoning of hundreds of years of the effects of European colonialism and the invention of modern racial oppression, the North Atlantic slave trade, and the international nation-state system.

transformation doesn't extend to a commitment to justice, we will always be spinning our wheels.

The thoughts in this book are the results of the experiments and experiences of my life. I began my activist life in a Buddhist monastery. While I don't see Buddhism as a dogmatic religion, some of its essential teachings remain the first lens through which I see the world, so you'll see them scattered throughout this book. After my time in the monastery, I threw myself into movement spaces that were deeply disembodied, disconnected from the heart, and had little commitment to healing or reconciliation. Then, as I wrote about in *Healing Resistance*, through the teachings of Dr. Martin Luther King Jr., I found nonviolence. And that changed everything.

Exploring nonviolence led me to my own healing journey and into contact with people like Shilpa Jain and spaces like Jams.* They kicked my ass and made me realize how much I needed to heal. Facilitating nonviolence workshops brought me into working in prisons, which led me to restorative justice work, meeting people like Sonya Shah, and joining the Ahimsa Collective. These spaces shattered my mind and showed me the depth of healing of which we as a species are capable.

As I healed my own wounds, and as I sat in circles witnessing others heal theirs, I started to understand *healing* is what we need as a collective. Injustice is not a political thing. It is manifestations of collective pain. If we want to bring healing to the world, we need to learn from the spaces that have helped people heal through their personal traumas and work to bring these lessons to scale.

What that looks like is the key question of fierce vulnerability.

- - -

---

* See *www.yesworld.org*.

Almost twenty years ago, I visited the Anne Frank House in Amsterdam. To this day, it is among the most powerful places I've ever been. Walking around the house, knowing what happened up in that attic, and what happened to Anne afterward.... I was in tears by the end of the tour. There, on a large wall, was a written statement. It said the museum sometimes receives criticism for doing so much to tell the story of just one person when so many millions of people lost their lives. The museum responds by sharing that for them, the true scale of the Holocaust is too much to take in at once—it's simply too overwhelming. But through deeply understanding the story of one person, we begin to be able to touch the collective suffering of all.

Sometimes, the global, intergenerational violence of the world is too overwhelming. Thinking about climate collapse alone can shut someone down or put them into panic. While I've been learning about systemic violence for years, it wasn't until I started going through my own healing that I was able to truly let the grief of these "political" issues sink into my body and become personal. It was through understanding my own story and my own pain that I was able to develop a deeper understanding of our collective story and our collective pain.

In that depth and sometimes despair, I started to see glimmers of hope. You can't see the light of a candle until it's dark. Similarly, I didn't see the light of hope until I finally sank into my despair.

Fierce vulnerability is about trying to understand that dynamic and learning to extrapolate its lessons to larger and larger scales. It's about reimagining activism as healing work and organizing as a spiritual practice: imagining a social justice movement led not only by "activists" expert at shutting down highways, but also by healers, artists, grief tenders, and ceremony leaders expert at opening up our hearts. In this movement, we work not only on strategies that lead to revolution, but also on connections and healing that lead to liberation. This work is about transformation.

Fierce Vulnerability

The term "fierce vulnerability" came out of many years of conversation with my friend Chris Moore-Backman. Both of us were deeply committed practitioners of nonviolence and spent a big part of our lives facilitating nonviolence trainings. For us, a commitment to nonviolence meant a commitment to standing against violence and injustice in all forms and speaking truth to the forces of power that maintain violence and injustice. Yet we both felt that there were so many misunderstandings of the word "nonviolence" that it actually became a barrier. In many communities, as soon as we used the word, people lost interest and walked away.

"We just need to find a new word," we'd say to each other. "Once we get people in the room, we can talk about this thing that is so deeply important to us. But the word 'nonviolence' has become a hindrance."

About three years into our search for a new term, Chris attended a planning retreat for a network known at the time as the "Yet-To-Be-Named Network," or YTBN, envisioned as a national decentralized network of people deeply committed to nonviolence engaging in direct action* at the intersection of climate justice and racial healing. When Chris came back, he mentioned someone had uttered the term "fierce vulnerability."

"What do you think about 'fierce vulnerability' as the word?" he asked.

We kept sitting with it and talking to other advocates of nonviolence about our attempt to rebrand it. At the end of the day, we decided to stick with *nonviolence* and recommit to the process of reclaiming its revolutionary power. The word, as problematic as it may be, ties us to a lineage too important to give up.

---

* We will discuss the term "direct action"—and how my understanding of it has shifted over the years—much more later, but direct actions are typically forms of protest that fall outside of "sanctioned" ways of making change—at times involving breaking laws.

In the meantime, the words "fierce vulnerability" stuck. There was *something* different and powerful about the juxtaposition of these two words. We reached out to two friends, meditation teacher Anuttara Lakshmin Nath and Kingian Nonviolence trainer Sierra Pickett, and launched our first-ever two-day Fierce Vulnerability workshop in the fall of 2018.

The invitation read:

How do we stop injustice in its tracks while acknowledging the interconnectedness of all people? How do we protect ourselves while nurturing a relationship with our broken heartedness? How do we build a movement that can shut down a highway while creating a culture of opening up? How do we build a movement with the militancy to occupy a government building and the sensitivity to see it as an act of healing? How can we come to experience vulnerability as a strength, not a weakness?

Our world is in crisis. Our social systems are being torn apart, our economic systems have created historic levels of wealth disparity, and Earth's life support systems are on the brink of collapse. The need for a powerful direct action movement that nurtures a radical, fundamental transformation has never been greater. Despair seems to be in the air we breathe and can be felt in the depth of our hearts.

Yet our need is not only a transformation of systems and laws and policies. What we yearn for is a fundamental transformation of our hearts, our values, and our relationships—to ourselves, to each other, and to the Earth.

Fierce vulnerability is an attempt to build such a movement. A movement that understands the assertiveness needed to address the crises of our times. A movement that sees social change as a radical act of healing. A movement that knows each of us needs to heal as much as those we may feel compelled to blame. A movement that knows violence hurts all parties. A movement that will never see any individual as disposable, undeserving of dignity, or incapable of transformation.

Fierce vulnerability is born of the conviction that our vulnerability is our greatest strength. Vulnerability makes us whole, and that wholeness is the only thing that can undo generations of investment in plunder and exploitation.

Join us and let us explore together what it might look like to enter movement spaces with the courage to be our whole selves, sometimes courageous, sometimes fearful, sometimes clear, sometimes confused, sometimes joyous, sometimes grieving, often a mixture of it all. We seek to bring ourselves as we are, in service to life, growing in our capacity to be fierce in our vulnerability and vulnerable in our ferocity.

Registration for the workshop filled within forty-eight hours, and we knew we'd hit a nerve. Years later, YTBN decided to make the workshop the mandatory first step in onboarding into the network, and eventually voted to name the network the Fierce Vulnerability Network (FVN). I was opposed to this at first. I was already deep into writing this book, and I didn't want my name so prominently associated with the Network. I didn't want people to think I was the founder or some kind of leader when neither of those things were true. And yet, the stewards of the naming process ensured me they'd thought this through; they believed my writing this book could be supportive to the Network, and vice versa. Somewhat begrudgingly, I went along.

Around the same time, another unexpected thing happened. For years, leaders of the then-YTBN had been working on producing a network "DNA" as a practical handbook and we were offered an opportunity to have it published. Packed in the 300-page document are stories, practices, and strategies we consider critical in building this movement. Again, I was opposed. Our DNA is constantly evolving as we learn through experimentation, and I was afraid the moment it was published, it would become out of date. But again, I am but one voice out of so many contributing leaders, and the overwhelming momentum leaned toward publication. So, in the summer of 2022, *The FVN Handbook: The Principles and Practices of the Fierce Vulnerability Network* was published. It turned out beautifully. However, as the rate of change among activists has been rapid in recent years, it is only a snapshot in time, but this guidebook is still something I feel can be a contribution to movement spaces.*

So, there's me, and there's this book you're reading now. I am one person, and this is one book. Then there are the fierce vulnerability workshops, which have facilitators around the country creating their own versions. In addition, there is the Fierce Vulnerability Network and the accompanying *FVN Handbook*. The Network is many people, and the handbook was written by many individuals; I was just one contributor.

I don't own trademarks on the term "fierce vulnerability"; I didn't invent the concept, and while I am writing a book on it, I'm far from the only person who gets to define it. So many people have contributed to the understanding and practice of fierce vulnerability, including the broader Healing Justice movement. Like the word "nonviolence," there can be many different ways to speak about and understand fierce vulnerability. I believe all these different ways will contribute to our getting to where we need to go.

The Need for Healing

Social change work at its best is about healing. If we're not working toward healing ourselves and our relationships, I'm not sure

---

* Initially published by a small Oakland, California–based social justice publisher called Nomadic Press. In 2023, however, Nomadic sadly closed its doors, and the *FVN Handbook* is now published by Black Lawrence Press, another independent publishing company.

what it is we're doing. If we're not working toward healing and reconciliation, there will be endless conflict, endless forms of violence, and endless systems of oppression.

For me, a commitment to nonviolence is a commitment to healing ourselves and healing our relationships. And in order to heal, we need to be vulnerable. If you're injured and need surgery, you literally give a doctor permission to cut your body open! That's a scary thing. Most times, you're not even conscious for surgery. You are literally lying there unconscious on a table, while people you don't know cut you open. That's vulnerable. And it's necessary for healing.

When I was young, I was *deeply* lonely. When I was seven years old, a major rift in my family of origin resulted in my mother being disowned from her entire family and our leaving Japan. Because I was so young, my parents tried to shield me from the reality of what was happening. They simply told me we were coming to the United States on a vacation and never explained to me what was going on. While their intention was pure, this ultimately led to a lot of confusion for my young mind.

We constantly underestimate children. Even at a young age, with our parents doing their best to hide the pain of separation from us, I could feel something was deeply wrong. One day, I was in Japan living a "normal" life filled with loving and large family gatherings. Then, suddenly, we were living in a foreign country, not allowed to see or talk to any of our grandparents, aunts, uncles, or cousins. While my parents never uttered a negative word about any of them, I implicitly received the message they were suddenly "bad" people whom I was not allowed to love. There was an "us," and they were now a "them." We no longer belonged to each other.

Each year on our birthdays and Christmas, my aunt Shigeko and uncle Marcus sent me and my sisters presents—every year, without fail, through all those years our families were separated and no longer talking to each other. Whatever happened between them and my parents, they still loved us children. However, I absorbed the pain and anger my parents felt toward them, so receiving those presents became very confusing. I was a kid, and I loved presents. At the same time, my confused child-body told me these presents were coming from "them." Bad people. People who no longer loved us. So why would they send me presents? Were they trying to buy my love and turn me against my parents? I misinterpreted my aunt and uncle's acts of love as a hidden agenda.

I now see this planted a seed of desperate loneliness in my young body. Underneath all the toys, I was scared and confused. Looking back, I could feel in my body something was deeply wrong, but I couldn't make sense of it. Everyone pretended everything was normal, but my body told me something different. It was deeply confusing and disassociating.

On top of that, we moved to an almost all-white area of Massachusetts where we were the only Asian and immigrant family in the entire school district. I was too young to understand my own emotions, so I didn't realize how lonely I was. But I was completely frozen, drowning myself first in music and Japanese comic books* and later in drugs and alcohol. By the time I was fourteen, I only came out of my room to eat meals before locking myself back in—if I was even home at all. Sitting frozen in my room, my emotions froze with me. Throughout most of my early adult life, I carried years of loneliness like a heavy bag of bricks in the middle of my gut.

I realize now part of the healing work I need to do is to retroactively feel what I couldn't feel back then. I need to go back into those memories and allow myself to feel lonely and to cry so those frozen emotions can be acknowledged, released, and integrated into my life. Going back to those emotions is scary and

---

* Shoutout to *Dragonball* and *Rokudenashi Blues*! *Shonen Jump* life forever!

vulnerable. And it is necessary for healing. If I want to contribute to the healing of society, there's no better place to look for lessons on how to do that than in my own healing journey. Because I believe the process of healing looks the same, no matter the scale.

In the same way my personal healing work involves retroactively embodying the feelings of loneliness and shame I couldn't feel when I was younger, I believe every community and nation *collectively* has deep feelings of pain it has not acknowledged. We carry hundreds of years of frozen emotions, rooted in the legacies of violence experienced and perpetrated. We need to learn—collectively—how to retroactively embody these frozen emotions so they can be acknowledged, released, and integrated.

In the same way I need to have scary and courageous conversations with my inner child and with my family about my childhood trauma, groups, communities, and nations need to have scary and courageous conversations with themselves about their collective childhood traumas.

Quantum Organizing

Traditional organizing models—those of labor unions, community organizations, and many of the movements that have come before us—have brought us so many gains. Without them, we would still have child labor, only cis-men would have the right to vote, and white supremacy would still be explicitly written into the laws of the United States.

However, we're in a new era, facing challenges we've never confronted before. We are trying to call forth a level of transformation we have never experienced. While the essential truths fierce vulnerability is trying to uncover are timeless and universal, we've learned so much about trauma healing in the last several decades. Our understanding of trauma and the various modalities developed to heal it were simply not available to activists in the past.

Fierce vulnerability is the latest link in a chain dating back to the first moment our ancestors said no to violence and injustice. We must carry forth the lessons from previous movements. We're not starting something brand new and ignoring the reality that we stand on the shoulders of everyone who came before us. We're adding to their legacy. We will still have to shut down highways and construction sites, occupy government buildings and corporate offices, and march down Main Street and Wall Street. Fierce vulnerability simply infuses these actions with a different energy and gives birth to new forms of action.

In one FVN gathering in Oakland, my friend Katie Loncke said, "fierce vulnerability feels like quantum physics, whereas traditional models of organizing feel Newtonian." This resonated with me on so many levels, and we've since had a couple of conversations about what they meant by that. In Newtonian physics, reality makes sense to our intellectual minds. Matter behaves in the way we have always been taught. The world is predictable, structured, and linear. 1+1 will always equal 2. But in quantum physics, reality makes less sense to our intellect. Matter behaves in unexpected ways, and the world seems much more random and nonlinear. Adding up 1+1 might give us an apple. Particles can exist in multiple places simultaneously, or two particles can become entangled and interconnected in ways that defy logic.

In Newtonian organizing models, we can do a power analysis, figure out the right levers to pull, mobilize around the perfect point of intervention, and demand the one piece of legislation that will result in the change we want to see. So, what does quantum organizing look like? It may look like accessing a different kind of power than we are used to. It may look like understanding our interdependence: that the liberation of our "oppressors" is the key to our own freedom. It may look like an incredibly small response to the biggest crisis in our collective history. It may be that, as adrienne maree brown describes in *Emergent Strategy*, the smallest intervention can have the largest impact.

In traditional ways of thinking, the world is often viewed in a binary, black and white way. And in Newtonian organizing, movements usually operate from an "us" and "them" worldview. "We" are here to stop "them." But I believe this binary worldview is at the heart of what is destroying this planet. The "us" and "them" worldview relies on us believing in the delusion of separation—"we" are separate from "them." In the Newtonian world, that is the case. "I" am a separate individual self, and "you" are reading this book. But in the quantum world, the idea of a separate self becomes less clear. Countless ancient wisdom traditions have spoken of the delusion of separation and the reality of oneness.

Part of what makes the quantum world difficult for us is that we're all living in a state of panic. Part of this panic is a natural response to the compounding crises of our times. It's hard not to panic when you read the news every morning and the world is burning all around you. This is further amplified by the fact that the twenty-four-hour news cycle and social media bombard us with images of a world on fire. This constant bombardment of panicked energy is a perpetual trigger for our traumas. So many of us constantly and unwittingly operate from a panic-induced trauma response state.

When our traumas are triggered or when we're in panic, the world becomes black and white. Our brain starts to look for any signs of comfort and safety, and the simplicity of a black and white world is stabilizing. In times of uncertainty, we crave certainty. We see evidence of this all over society, from cancel culture (if you're not 100 percent good, then you *must* be bad) to conspiracy theories (Trump lost the 2020 election, and it *must* have been because the election was stolen) to political polarization (if you're not with us, you *must* be against us).

This is why fierce vulnerability emphasizes the importance of healing work and emotional regulation practices. The more grounded we are, the more we can be okay sitting in the uncertainty of the quantum realm.

Far too often, we engage in movement work from a trauma-tized and panicked place, so our ability to engage in deep healing work is compromised. My dream is to be part of a movement of people committed to their own healing, not just so they can find inner peace for themselves but so they can help build movements that see the work of political resistance as healing work happen-ing on a collective scale. This book, developed out of the Fierce Vulnerability workshops, infuses the lineage of nonviolent action with the science of trauma healing and the depth of spiri-tual practice I believe are necessary to create such a movement.

There is no "demand" we can come up with big enough to capture the transformation I want to see. The level of healing necessary in our world has never happened before. We've never defeated capitalism, unraveled the pain of patriarchy, or rid our-selves of nation-states. So, the idea that we can come up with a clearly articulated goal and strategy is a delusion.

This transformation is too big for our intellect to grasp. It's too complex for us to develop a work-plan for. I've been trained for years that you can't build a movement without being able to clearly articulate your goals, develop a clear strategy, and have good messaging. And I'm not saying all of those things don't have a role. But to me, they feel like window dressing. The changes fierce vulnerability is working toward require a spiritual practice, not only our intellect, to begin to understand.

My vision is not about electing a Democrat over a Repub-lican. It's not even about getting someone like Bernie Sanders elected. It's about abolishing the office of the presidency itself.

It's not about ending the war in the Ukraine. It's about ending war.

It's not about increasing the minimum wage. It's about erad-icating capitalism.

It's not about a free state for the Palestinian people. It's about letting go of the notion that nation-states, borders, and separa-tion will give anybody freedom.

It's not about reparations if we think the transfer of money alone will heal the legacy of white supremacy.

It's not about abolishing the Immigration and Customs Enforcement agency (ICE). It's about creating a world where people don't feel a need to risk their safety to move away from their ancestral homelands unless it is by choice.

To achieve this level of transformation, our traditional, linear, Newtonian way of thinking won't be enough. We have to operate on the quantum level, where less is understandable, but more is possible.

The Great Mystery

It's hard for me to imagine our society making the depth of transformation necessary in this time without some relationship with spirit. Let me explain what I mean. To me, engaging in "spiritual practice" has nothing to do with organized religion or blind faith in some dogma. At its core, spirituality is deep faith that we are part of something bigger than ourselves as individuals; it is accepting a great mystery that can never be fully understood by our intellect alone.

This could mean a belief in a God, or in many Gods. It could mean you feel guided by your ancestors. It could mean you have a deep commitment to the welfare of future generations. Perhaps you feel a deep connection to the beyond-human* world or an unwavering belief in interdependence. Even science can be a spiritual practice. When I read about cosmology, quantum physics, or about how trees use underground networks of mycelium to communicate with each other, I am filled with the same level of deep connection and awe at the complexity and vastness of our universe that I experience at a meditation retreat or

---

* I prefer this term over "natural world" because, aren't we as humans natural too?

in spiritual ceremony. That awe, humility, and inspiration—the realization that our world is so vast it can never truly be known—is what I mean when I use terms like "spirit."

I've had countless experiences outside of any traditional "spiritual" practice that I consider a bridge to the sacred. When I was eighteen, I took a bus ride through the Tibetan plateau on my way to Leh, the capital of Ladakh in current-day India. I'll always remember one specific moment when the bus turned a corner and the road opened up into the most expansive valley I had ever seen in my entire life. The mountains were ginormous. I remember feeling like I was on Mars, shocked at seeing an environment unlike anything I knew existed on this planet. Looking up at those gargantuan Himalayan mountains was among the most humbling experiences of my life; I had never felt so small, so insignificant.

I still remember my awe when my partner, LiZhen Wang, first took me to the Ancient Bristlecone Pine Forest in the Eastern Sierra. I learned the oldest tree in that forest was over 4,800 years old. This realization stunned me—this tree was well over 2,000 years old when the Buddha walked the Earth and almost 3,000 years old when Jesus lived. It puts things into perspective; it makes me realize the ridiculousness of a human-centric perspective on the world.

These moments, in the best way possible, remind me how insignificant I am. They're great practices for letting go of my ego. Spirit may give us breath, and yet somehow it exists most powerfully in the moments that take our breath away.

In other moments, human relationships become my pathway to the sacred: in circles with incarcerated people who have lived through so much pain and suffering, yet found the courage to be radically honest and vulnerable about their experiences and talk openly about their darkest secrets; when I stare deeply into the eyes of my child and feel like I can see the entire expansiveness of the galaxies; when I am broken, can accept I am broken, and allow myself to defenselessly wail into the arms of someone with whom I feel safe. These moments of shared humanity open me up to a depth of connection infinitely too large to be contained in a single human body or moment of time.

From experiences in nature to experiences of deep connection with others, there are countless access points to "spirit." Simply listening to the right song at the right moment can feel like a spiritual experience.* There's a reason songs have always been part of spiritual traditions from every corner of the world.

I consider any practice or experience that allows us to access that feeling of deep awe and connection a "spiritual practice." Meditation. Prayer. Ceremony and ritual. A walk among towering redwoods. Dancing in the rain. Watching the murmuration of starlings. Being in community, singing sacred songs, or having the fierceness to be seen in our vulnerability. Healing our wounds and holding space for others to heal theirs.

In my own healing, I sometimes sense deep, old emotions of sadness, grief, or fear in my body. Often, these feelings are easy to understand—they're directly connected to a story from my past. I feel grief from the loss of my father; I feel shame for not being there for my mother and sisters; I feel sadness about how lonely I was when I was young. Other times, the feelings are harder to connect to a specific story. My mind plays tricks on me and keeps me from accepting these feelings: "This feeling isn't real, because there's no story attached to it," it says. "It doesn't make sense." My first therapist, Angela, told me this is one of the challenges of healing intergenerational wounds. Our bodies sometimes feel the pain our ancestors weren't able to heal during their lifetimes. When we feel that pain in our own bodies, it "doesn't make sense" to our intellect, because we

---

* Stevie Ray Vaughn's version of "Little Wing," the Gypsy Kings's "A Mi Manera," or Michael Kiwanuka's "Cold Little Heart" transport me to another place.

don't remember the stories. We just feel the emotions. The more I get out of my mind, stop looking for the story, and accept the unknown, the more I'm able to see the truth of what exists in my body—that this is spiritual healing: I am healing something that "doesn't belong to me," yet is connected to me.

A similar thing happens when I think about collective pain. When I take a deep breath and try to feel the grief of our ecological collapse, sometimes my mind plays tricks on me. "It's sad there's ecological destruction, but I'm an independent being," it says. "I'm not actually feeling the pain of the Earth." It tries to keep the fear intellectual. It tries to tell me the Earth is this thing "out there" being destroyed, as opposed to acknowledging the deeper reality that as we destroy the Earth, we destroy ourselves.

Years ago, when I was thirteen, I was at home by myself eating a candy bar. When I finished, I carelessly threw the wrapper onto the table in front of me. And something strange happened. As I stared at this plastic wrapper in front of me, a wave of emotions hit me. I started crying. Like, *bawling*. Out of nowhere, I was filled with grief at the amount of trash we had accumulated in the world and terrified by how much of our planet had been destroyed, how we had taken this beautiful home and trashed it with so many plastic bottles, Styrofoam cups, and candy wrappers. . . . This was long before I became any sort of activist or learned to care about the Earth in the way I do today. As a young person, I was not having an intellectual experience, but a deeply embodied experience of grief—not *for* our planet, but *of* our planet.

Spiritual practice—or whatever you want to call it—helps us understand we are deeply impacted by things we cannot touch, see, or understand. It helps us accept that we can't know everything. It helps us see that even if we can't understand something, we can still know it is very real. And that's important, because I have very little interest in being part of movements that see changing legislation as their ultimate goal.* No matter how significant that legislation may be, it pales in comparison to the fundamental transformation I so desperately want to see in our world—that I believe our world so desperately needs.

In the Tao Te Ching, one of the spiritual texts I hold most important in my life, Lao Tzu teaches us:

Those who seek knowledge, collect something every day.
Those who seek the Way, let go of something every day.[1]

Many activist spaces seem to embody the opposite of this. Too often, we feel like we need to know everything, collect every piece of data, know all the woke lingo, understand all the analysis. There's a sense of urgency and competition. It feels like we're constantly in our heads.

The Way I want to feel into is something we'll never "understand" in the traditional sense. It's more like I can sense a direction I'm being pulled in. I can't articulate a clear destination, which makes it impossible to map out all the steps to get there. But the more I sit in silence, the more I spend time in nature, the more I learn to cry and be vulnerable, the more I get a sense of which direction to move toward. Of how and where to act.

It's a vulnerable practice, to move without having a clear sense of where we're going. But the very first verse of the Tao Te Ching also teaches us:

The Tao that can be described is not the eternal Tao.
The name that can be spoken is not the eternal name.

So perhaps, the goal that can be described is not the eternal goal. The strategy that can be developed is not the true way.

---

* You'll get sick of me saying this, but I can't say it enough.

Perhaps we need to accept the vulnerability of the unknown and let go of our usual ways of trying to create change.

Understanding the Questions

In Douglas Adams's classic novel *The Hitchhikers Guide to the Galaxy,* a group of scientists are determined to find the answer to the question: What is the meaning of life, the universe, and everything?

The scientists embark on an ambitious plan to build the world's smartest computer, named Deep Thought. It takes them 7.5 million years to build Deep Thought, and it takes Deep Thought 7.5 million years to compute the answer to their question. After a 15-million-year journey, the descendants of the original scientists are finally ready to hear the result.

"Do you have . . . er, that is . . ." After waiting lifetimes and lifetimes to hear the answer, you can understand how nervous they were to hear it.

"The answer for you?" Deep Thought interrupted. "Yes, I have."

The scientists were stunned and couldn't wait to hear it.

Deep Thought, however, added, "I don't think you're going to like it." It didn't matter. They just wanted to hear it.

"The Answer to the Great Question . . ."

"Yes . . . !"

"Of Life, the Universe and Everything . . . ," said Deep Thought.

"Yes . . . !"

"Is . . . " said Deep Thought, and paused.

"Yes . . . !"

"Is . . . "

"Yes . . . ! . . . ?"

"Forty-two," said Deep Thought, with infinite majesty and calm.

After 15 million years of waiting, they were finally ready to understand the meaning of life, the universe, and everything. The answer was forty-two. How could this be? That doesn't make any sense! Upset, they demanded an explanation. Deep Thought said the scientists never understood what they were asking. Once the scientists were able to understand the question, the answer would make sense.

I love this story. Too often, we spend so much time asking the wrong questions that we wouldn't even understand the answers if they smacked us in the face. Fierce vulnerability is about admitting we don't know the answers and not getting immobilized by this not knowing. It's about accepting the unknowable, asking the right questions, listening deeply, and taking one step in the direction of our intuition.

In the novel *The Left Hand of Darkness*, Ursula K. Le Guin writes of learning "the utter uselessness of knowing the answer to the wrong question." So, these days I'm asking myself a different set of questions, to which I don't know the answers.

What if instead of chanting, we cry?

What if instead of holding signs with demands, we tell stories?

What if instead of yelling, we sing songs?

What if instead of anger, we lead with heartbreak?

What if we stop trying to win and start trying to heal?

What if we build a movement where nobody, even those on the "other" side, ever think to question their sense of belonging?

What if we view nonviolent action as collective trauma healing?

What if instead of our goal being to "shut it down," we try to "open it up?" Open up our hearts and our opportunities for healing?

What if we mobilize the power needed to stop harm while cultivating the love necessary to heal it?

What would it take?

What if?

CHAPTER 1

The Power of Vulnerability

Water is fluid, soft and yielding. But water will wear away rock, which is rigid and cannot yield. As a rule, whatever is fluid, soft and yielding will overcome whatever is right and hard. This is another paradox: what is soft is strong.

LAO TZU

The strongest love is the love that can demonstrate its fragility.

PAULO COELHO

THE WORDS "fierce" and "vulnerability" may seem at odds. If you're fierce, you're not vulnerable. If you're vulnerable, you're not fierce. But there are different ways to think about "vulnerability."

The Merriam-Webster dictionary defines "vulnerability" as follows: capable of or susceptible to being wounded or hurt. "Vulnerability" is often understood as putting yourself in a position to be harmed. And that is one aspect of it. There is always a risk in being vulnerable. I learned the hard way that sometimes vulnerability is not met with compassion. That can be incredibly hurtful—even re-traumatizing. I'm beginning to understand that by engaging in our own healing, though, we can reduce these risks, enabling us to speak difficult and painful truths with more ease regardless of how they are received. This, in turn, can significantly contribute to the healing of all.

Back in 2012, I attended a weeklong experience called a "Jam." Jams are healing and transformative gatherings for change-makers organized by a group called YES!* I was invited by my friend Shilpa Jain, who at the time served as YES!'s executive director. Back then, I was pretty closed off, and being vulnerable around others was not something I did much of. I remember jokingly challenging Shilpa to make me cry in the opening circle.

Little did I know Shilpa is a *master* at helping people open up; of course, I ended up being one of the first people in our group of thirty to break down in tears. It was during an activity where those of us who identified as male sat in an inner circle talking about our experiences as men while others sat in an outer circle simply listening. I decided to share some childhood experiences I'd been thinking about.

When I was young, my sisters and I had had a stepfather who brought a lot of harm into our home. In a few short years, the dynamics in my home completely shifted, and I witnessed shouting, screaming, crying, and arguing on a nightly basis. These were by far the most tumultuous years of my early life. I didn't know then all the details of the violence going on in my home, but I saw and heard enough to shut down. I started to act out in school, I stopped coming home, I started drinking and getting high.

Decades later, I began to uncover more of the truth of what had happened. As stories of abuse started to emerge, so did feelings of shame: shame I hadn't been there for my mother and my sisters. Shame I had essentially run away. Shame I drank and got high while my family experienced so much harm. Shame I couldn't protect them. Shame I wasn't enough. At the same time, I told myself these experiences happened twenty years ago. I'd gotten over them. I told myself it wasn't a big deal.

And then I spoke about it out loud in that circle for the first time.

---

* Unrelated to the magazine of the same name.

There's something magical about saying things out loud. It's like popping the cap off a shaken soda can. The pressure's been building, but from the outside you have no idea the can is about to explode. Trauma is very good at hiding.

In that circle, I started speaking about the shame I felt, and the moment the words began to fall out of my mouth, I went straight into panic and completely broke down. I could barely get a breath in, never mind find the right words. I had no idea: no idea that for twenty years, I'd been carrying such a heavy burden of shame. It didn't matter that my intellect told me it wasn't my fault. My brain understood I was just twelve when all of this started, and there was probably little I could have done. Running away and turning to substances to drown out the violence in my home was a coping strategy I had used to survive. But none of that mattered to the deeply entrenched, unspoken shame in my body. Trauma doesn't live in the brain, it lives in our bodies, so it didn't matter that my intellect could tell me it wasn't my fault. I cried and I cried and I cried, held tightly in the arms of Shilpa's husband, Austin.*

From that moment on, I knew having this conversation with my family, expressing my sorrow for the hurt they experienced, and apologizing for not being there was perhaps the most important conversation I needed to have in my life. And I was scared out of my mind. Out. Of. My. Mind. It felt like the holy grail of healing, this *one* conversation I needed to have with my family would open so many avenues for healing—for myself as well as in our relationships with each other. I was deeply saddened those

---

* In addition to the realization that I was holding so much shame, this was another huge learning for me: my patriarchal conditioning had always told me I could watch sports with other men but not cry in their arms, because that would be "gay," *and oh-my-god you don't want to be that.* I realized at that moment how good—how safe—it felt to cry in the arms of another man. It taught me how much I needed that kind of relationship with other men, and how much patriarchy has taken away.

difficult years had fractured our family, and we were never as close after that as I wanted to be—as I now know we all wanted to be. I knew I had to get there. And I had no idea how. I had never felt so lost, so scared about any conversation in my life.

It took me eight years. Eight years of meditation, therapy, journaling, processing in group spaces, attending healing workshops and more Jams, and confiding in trusted friends. It wasn't an easy path, nor was it a linear process. There were times I opened up to people I trusted—took that risk of being vulnerable—and was shut down or dropped in re-traumatizing ways. Whether because my story triggered something in the other person or simply a lack of skill on their part, there were times I told myself I would never speak of these experiences again.

In a lot of the work I do in prisons, we invite participants to write letters. These letters might be letters of harm—a letter to someone who harmed them or to someone they harmed. They might be forgiveness letters—letters asking for or offering forgiveness. The point isn't necessarily to send the letter. The purpose is personal healing. Participants write their letters, then read them out loud in the group to be seen, supported, and, hopefully, to help them let go a little bit and find healing.

I decided I needed to write my family a letter. I had no idea how to start a conversation without completely breaking down. Reading a letter would give me just enough support, just enough structure to communicate everything in my heart. One night, alone in a quiet cabin in the woods, I grabbed a pen and notepad, sat down by an oil lantern, and started to write.* It was the hardest letter I had ever written. I cried the entire way through and had to stop several times to catch my breath. By the time I

---

* There is something about writing by hand under natural light that feels different than flicking on a light switch and typing away on my computer. It feels like a more direct path from my heart. Though to be honest, I am typing these exact words on my laptop at a Starbucks. It was the only café I could find on the road. But I promise they're from my heart!

finished, the letter was soaked in my own tears, but I committed
to reading it to my family in person.

It took another six months before I actually did. In those six
months, I told several friends about my plan—I think I needed to
give myself some accountability. I also got a chance to read the
letter out loud to the core members of the Ahimsa Collective, the
group with which I facilitate restorative justice work in prison,
and for whose support I will always be grateful. And then, eight
years after that fateful circle at the Jam, as we gathered together
for New Years, I cried and cried as I read my letter in front of my
mother and two sisters.

It turns out healing isn't a one-time thing you do and then it's
over.˙ Our family still has a lot to heal, but that experience opened
up conversations about things we had never talked about before.

Throughout my life, I've gotten into fights, gotten beat up,
had a gun pulled on me, broken up fights among strangers, participated in civil disobedience, been arrested, pepper sprayed,
and tear gassed. But nothing took more courage than crying in
front of my own family. Nothing took more courage than talking
about the truth of the harms we experienced as children. Nothing took more courage than showing all of my heart.

Vulnerability is as fierce as anything we can do with our
bodies. It has the potential to break down the walls put up by
trauma. If healing is our goal, vulnerability may be among our
most powerful tools.

Sources of Trauma

Trauma is not something that happens only to people who have
experienced extreme violence. When we think of trauma, most
people think of "acute" trauma: the kind of trauma that results

---

˙ Damn it!

from a single incident—a car accident, a natural disaster, or a violent crime, for example.

Someone who experiences multiple traumatic incidents over an extended time can develop "chronic" trauma. A child being bullied at school once may not result in trauma. But if the child is bullied repeatedly, the stress from each incident could accumulate and result in chronic trauma. Chronic trauma is common in survivors of abuse, domestic violence, or war, circumstances where the traumatic incident doesn't stop after one occasion. Chronic trauma doesn't have to be the accumulation of the same kind of stress factor, though: someone could experience the loss of a loved one, then have their car get stolen, then survive a natural disaster, all in a short time span. Any one of those things alone might not have caused trauma, but their accumulation could.

"Insidious" trauma is another type of trauma that can be hard to diagnose. It's similar to chronic trauma, but usually results from the long-term accumulation of more minor but constant stressful experiences. It could be the result of growing up in poverty or a lifetime of oppression and marginalization based on your race, ethnicity, sex, gender identity, sexual orientation, or other intrinsic identities.

Sometimes, we validate the kinds of trauma that have an obvious and blatant cause—usually involving physical violence—as the only "real" kinds of trauma. This is not only false, but dangerous. In one healing group I was a part of, a participant expressed feeling guilty for having a seat at the table because he came from a relatively privileged background. His parents never beat him, nor did he ever lose a friend to the streets. Unlike the other men in the group, he'd never experienced any physical violence that could result in trauma. While he may never have experienced one single incident that resulted in trauma, he had experienced a lifetime of "complex" trauma, a trauma often rooted in neglect or abuse from a caretaker at a young age. This doesn't always manifest as physical abuse, so it may be harder to name, but in this man's case it was pretty glaring: he once spoke about his father refusing to utter a single word to him for over six months because he failed one of his classes. That kind of disapproval and neglect—especially early on in life—can easily impact you for years.

Just because you haven't experienced any major traumatic incidents doesn't mean you don't have trauma. The accumulation of minor incidents can be just as dangerous.

"Indirect" trauma is another type of harder-to-see trauma that is just as real and can have consequences just as devastating as experiencing something directly. For example, many Americans experienced indirect trauma after witnessing the World Trade Center collapse on September 11, 2001—even if they just watched on TV and didn't know anyone directly impacted. Constant news reports about mass shootings can also result in indirect trauma, even if we don't know a single person who has been shot.

"Vicarious" trauma is a form of indirect trauma common among counselors, therapists, healers, and anyone who works with or has close, regular contact with trauma survivors. It's the result of long-term exposure to traumatic stories, and its impact can be as heavy as the stories the person listens to.

Then there's the 1,800-pound elephant in the room: intergenerational and collective trauma. On an individual level, this can be hard to notice—it lives as deeply embedded memories in our bodies. We don't know exactly what our ancestors lived through and what they have passed down to us, but multiple studies show trauma can indeed alter our DNA and be passed down from generation to generation.* When viewed collectively,

---

* As I wrote in *Healing Resistance*, the topic of intergenerational trauma is so huge that instead of going deeply into it here, I will simply recommend you check out books like Professor Joy DeGruy's *Post Traumatic Slave Syndrome*, Resmaa Menakem's *My Grandmother's Hands*, or Eduardo Duran's *Healing the Soul Wound*, as well as scientific studies by Brian Dias and Kerry Ressler, Rachel Yehuda and Amy Lehrner, or Dora L. Costa, Noelle Yetter, and Heather DeSomer.

intergenerational trauma can be easier to spot. It's hard to know about the centuries of state violence and systemic oppression against Black and Indigenous people and not think there must be deep impacts on the collective psyche of people with those heritages.

Given the context of this book, it's also worth noting that, sadly, being in movement spaces can be deeply traumatic. I cannot tell you how many people I've talked to who have left social justice work because of traumatizing experiences. Part of it is the never-ending stress of the work itself: if you're working in marginalized communities, you constantly hear and witness stories of loss, oppression, and the day-to-day dehumanization so many folks have to tolerate to survive. Of course, these experiences are mixed with the joy of being in community, the celebrations of campaign victories, and the inspiration of working with deeply empowered people. But if we don't tend to the difficult moments, vicarious trauma can be rampant.

Another cause of trauma in movement spaces is that activist communities—especially those doing direct action work—constantly face state violence. Spending so much time in physical confrontation, getting tear gassed, and perhaps jailed or beaten can be traumatic. Frontline direct action work can be an extremely pressurized environment with a nonstop pace, little sleep, and constant high levels of tension.

Activists also tend to be buried knee deep in studying, reading about, and analyzing the worst forms of oppression. After some time, it feels like we become the sum of all the ways we're oppressed. We forget to laugh, we forget to sing, we forget to cry—all things that help us release traumatic stress. If all we do is talk about the worst aspects of humanity, that can easily lead to trauma.

Finally—let's be real for a second here—a lot of activists are assholes. I don't really mean that. But I sort of do. Okay, a lot of activists *act like* assholes. Many people in social justice movements—because we're advocates of social justice—like to think we've got it all figured out: the problem, the violence, the oppression is *out there;* we stop challenging ourselves and stop working on ourselves *in here.* This includes not working on healing our own traumas or the ways we've internalized oppression.

Many of us come from a traumatic background, and we join movements to find belonging. But because not everyone is working on healing those traumas, we all bring our shit into our movements. And we take our shit out on each other, because hurt people hurt people. Since the punitive criminal justice system is the main model we know for responding to harm, despite the fact that our values may not align with it, when harm happens in our communities we often turn to similar tactics of punishing, shaming, and isolating each other to "hold each other accountable."[*]

When acting from a place of trauma, we tighten up and try to protect ourselves by running as far from vulnerability as we can. Unfortunately, vulnerability not only helps us heal from that trauma, but builds a movement culture grounded in the kinds of trusting relationships necessary for healing. It is imperative we learn more about how trauma works so we can learn strategies to address it in our own lives, in movement spaces, and in society.

Choice and Agency

This isn't to say vulnerability is *always* healing.

Some people have been hurt so much and their pain never validated that they end up walking around pouring their vulnerability out to anyone who will listen. When you share your vulnerability, it is a gift. But not everyone is capable of holding that gift with care. Some people may get triggered themselves while listening to your story. Others may be too hurt and closed off to hold your story. Sometimes a person simply does not have the

---

[*] I put this in quotations because I believe punishing, shaming, and isolating do the opposite. More in chapter 5.

skills to be present in such an intimate moment. Or it may simply not be the appropriate time or place to share.

I once heard a group agreement from the Bay Area Transformative Justice Collective (BATJC): "This is not a place for healing, though healing may happen here." This is an acknowledgment that healing can happen in any place at any moment, but that not all places (like a business meeting or a workshop about a specific topic) are designed to hold traumatic stories. While it's inspiring to see so many communities operate with some awareness of trauma these days, it's not always skillful to center trauma in every gathering. Centering trauma is not the *only* thing we have to do. Part of the fierceness of fierce vulnerability is about clear discernment: learning to access our vulnerability with choice and agency, skillfully and with consistent purpose and intention.

The valve on a faucet controls the pressure of the water coming out of it. If the valve becomes loose, small amounts of water could leak out. Or maybe the valve is broken, and you turn the faucet just a little bit but a huge flood of water bursts out. Letting out emotions when you don't intend to, feeling "flooded" or overwhelmed, and expressing more than is wise may cause harm to yourself or others. Part of the work of healing is to develop more control over when and how much we let out; to repair and learn to close our faucets back up when necessary. It's as if we strengthen our muscles of vulnerability—we strengthen that valve so we can have more choice and agency.

Capacity Building for Greater Agency with Strong Emotions

The work of building agency with your "emotional valve" is ultimately about interacting skillfully with some of your deepest shadows in service of healing. This is long-term work, and not recommended to try alone. Try to find supportive friends or community, or reach out to people with experience in supporting others—therapists, healers, counselors, elders, etc. Once you're ready to begin training in emotional awareness, here are some practices you can explore.

PRACTICES FOR ACCESSING VULNERABILITY

- Do you remember the last time you grieved? Even if it was decades ago, when was the last time you allowed yourself to express sadness and mourning? Think back to that moment. Try to think about every little detail you can remember. What happened? How did you feel? How did you grieve? What did it feel like to grieve? Who was there for you, or who needed to be there for you? Perhaps you'd like to journal about it. Writing down and articulating your experience can be a helpful way to process it.

- You may be used to experiencing something hurtful or unenjoyable, brushing it off, and moving on with your day. Try to take note of these experiences. Write them down if it helps. Then at the end of the day, take a look at the list and do some journaling. Bring yourself back to that moment and ask yourself—why did this incident cause me discomfort?

- Next time you notice vulnerability emerging—whether in response to a current event, a sad movie, or something else—pause. Try to feel it in your body. Where is it? Don't feel a need to name, analyze, or interpret it. Just notice the sensation in your body and try to be with it for three to five breaths.

- As you notice moments of vulnerability, ask yourself: Does a pattern emerge? Perhaps some things make you more vulnerable than others. What are they? Why might these things bring up more vulnerability? Are they rooted in old memories?

PRACTICES FOR DEVELOPING AGENCY

- Next time a difficult emotion is triggered, try utilizing the acronym STOP. *Stop, Take a breath, Observe, then Proceed.* You can still express what you want to express, but taking a brief pause, observing what is coming up for you, and consciously *choosing* to express your emotion (or not) gives you more agency.

- Create a morning ritual of imagining building a protective bubble around yourself. Throughout the day, remember you are protected by this bubble—you don't have to let external triggers pierce through.

- Notice each time you draw a boundary and don't share something you may habitually share. Celebrate those moments!

- Take care of yourself! Engaging in practices that nourish you, surrounding yourself with supportive community, and having time for rest resources your body and gives you more agency.

Vulnerability that stems from unprocessed, unconscious trauma can be harmful. Thinking about the difference between vulnerability driven by trauma versus vulnerability rooted in speaking our truth has helped me navigate this rocky terrain. In *My Grandmother's Hands*, therapist and author Resmaa Menakem describes the difference between "clean pain" and "dirty pain." Clean pain is "pain that mends and can build your capacity for growth." It's the pain you feel when you face your fears and take actions that you know will lead to healing or growth, despite how difficult they may be. Dirty pain, on the other hand, "is the pain of avoidance, blame, and denial." It is the pain that comes from suppressing what you know to be true. It can manifest as withdrawal or as acts of violence against others. When you deny yourself the space to process your hurt, you may end up acting out of that place of hurt and causing harm to yourself or others. Dirty pain may say things like, "You're an asshole." But if we look closely, there is a deeper truth beneath. It might sound something like, "You're hurting me." But even that is actually an accusation. Deeper than that might be the truth, "I am hurting." This statement is not about something someone else is doing; it is a statement about your truth and experience. In this expression of clean pain, healing is possible.

When we release vulnerability rooted in unprocessed trauma, it often manifests as dirty pain. Unprocessed trauma overrides our choice and agency about how and when it comes out. It's not you choosing to speak to your trauma, it's the trauma speaking in your place. This kind of vulnerability puts us at higher risk of getting injured or re-traumatized and can harm those it touches.

Of course, we all have unprocessed traumas in our lives, especially when we first begin to turn toward healing. Unprocessed trauma is not "bad"; we shouldn't be ashamed to have it. We just need to be conscious about where it is safe to bring it out. To muddy the waters, though, unintentionally releasing unprocessed trauma isn't always or only harmful. As BATJC's group agreement states, "healing may happen here." Healing is available in every moment if the right conditions are present. Choice and intention just make healing more likely.

In the context of systemic violence and historical trauma, entire communities have experienced harm on an unimaginable scale for generations. In many cases, their traditional healing modalities have been ripped away from them. Countless people hold so much pain in their bodies that it constantly leaks out. This is not due to some lack of capacity on their part; it is the result of centuries of systemic violence from which some communities have never had a single day off.

Without any judgment, I simply want to acknowledge that it can be dangerous if we don't build a relationship with our own vulnerability valve and instead allow external triggers to have more control over our expression than we do. It is important for each of us to begin to discern where our unprocessed traumas lie and to find safe containers where they can be seen, processed, and integrated. Our communities need to create more and more resources for this kind of healing.

When we're able to process our trauma, we can touch into the vulnerability rooted in a deep truth. *I am hurt. I need help. I am scared. I am sorry.* It may still be scary to speak these words. But we'll have more choice and agency about what we do with them. They may even hurt to voice out loud, but the pain will be clean.

From my late teens to that fateful Jam in 2012, I thought my life was pretty well put together. I thought I had a healthy relationship with my family. We almost never argued and there was never any visible conflict. I had a meaningful job doing something I cared about. I had healthy relationships with friends. But I was hurting in ways not so visible. I struggled with an inability to build intimacy in romantic and platonic relationships, ongoing addiction (mostly to marijuana), and at times depression. I wouldn't have been able to name those things out loud then.

I knew, but I didn't know, you know? My body knew something was wrong, even if my brain refused to acknowledge it.

Years later, my therapist helped me see that when I left home at seventeen, I completely cut off my old life and all the trauma that came with it. I hit reset and started from scratch. I went from living in a broken home in Massachusetts to a Buddhist monastery in Nepal, thousands of miles from anyone I knew and anything associated with my traumatic upbringing. My life couldn't have been more different.* I came back from that experience a

---

* Here's an inappropriately short summary of a life-changing experience, which I've also shared in my first book. I was a seventeen-year-old high school dropout stoner kid. I met a group of Japanese Buddhist monastics who brought me under their wing. I walked from Massachusetts to New Orleans with them, learning about the legacy of slavery, then ended up living in their monasteries in South Asia for a year.

new person: Kazu 2.0. In my mind, I had "gotten over it." My time in monasteries, traveling the world, and engaging in meaningful work had "healed" me. "That was years ago," I told myself. "Those early years were hard, but aren't I glad they're over?"

While having space away was helpful, I didn't actually "heal" anything. I just left my wounds behind and started over. But you can't just leave the past behind and not think about it. It follows you. Trauma doesn't let you off the hook that easily. Maybe you live your entire life ignoring it; but you haven't "moved on"—you've learned to bury the pain and suppress the truth. And there is always a cost.

The pain of unhealed trauma weighs on you and finds ways to seep out. It's "dirty pain." It may seep out through addiction, workaholism, anger issues, depression, anxiety, a lack of intimacy, or any number of physical, emotional, or spiritual ailments. On its surface, it may seem like these difficulties have nothing to do with that traumatic experience. But our bodies can't simply hold onto such pain without finding some avenue of release.

For the longest time, my body knew a truth my brain refused to acknowledge: I was hurting. I was lonely. I needed to heal from my past. I needed to talk to my family. Like, *really* talk to them. It takes an enormous amount of spiritual energy to suppress a truth your body knows to be true. It saps you. It may be a slow process, especially at first, but it's constant. It saps you of your creativity, joy, intimacy, of spaciousness, lightness, freedom, of life energy.

Think about what we could do with all that energy if we weren't busy trying to suppress that truth. What would it feel like to free yourself from the heavy, constant work of hiding? How much creativity would be in your life? How much hope? Faith? Love?

Sinking into the grief of "clean pain" and learning to integrate past experiences is probably going to be a long, scary, horrible, amazing, liberating, inspiring, intimidating, ultimately never-ending process that will create an unimaginably enormous amount of space in your life. At least that has been, and continues to be, my journey.*

The Practice of Vulnerability

For some people, accessing vulnerability flows naturally. For others, accessing vulnerability is a struggle. The valve on that faucet can get so rusty it becomes stuck and impossible to open. The water gets blocked up, and the pressure builds until it explodes. While I'm getting better at it, I count myself among those who struggle with opening up the vulnerability valve. Building a relationship with my vulnerability has been a constant practice for me.

In the summer of 2016, I attended the weeklong Nonviolent Leadership for Social Change retreat organized by leaders within the Nonviolent Communication (NVC) community. It's one of the only NVC gatherings where most of the facilitators and participants are people of color and NVC is used to tackle issues of power and privilege. The agenda gave us a lot of space to explore racism, including how dynamics around race are often held unskillfully in NVC communities. However, the agenda left very little space to talk explicitly about issues of gender and patriarchy. And of course, those issues are always pervasive; if we don't talk about them explicitly, we end up allowing dominant patterns to creep into our spaces.

During the first few days of the gathering, people—almost always women and nonbinary people—raised the issue several

---

* I'm talking about this as if I'm now "healed," as if this process doesn't continue to be scary, horrible, amazing, liberating, inspiring, and intimidating for me. That is *definitely* not the case.

times. But there wasn't time on the agenda to dive into it. So, at one point, one of the women called an informal lunchtime gathering to discuss gender and patriarchy more fully. By that point, enough conversation about the wounds we all carry from the deep legacy of patriarchy made it clear some feelings were percolating inside of me. I went to the informal conversation and stood at the edge of the table with my plate of food, listening to others share. At one point, the young woman who called the meeting spoke about how patriarchy has also hurt men— how it has scarred us as well, how we're not whole because of it.

It's not that I'd never heard that before. I know any violent and oppressive system is ultimately harmful to all people. But for some reason, when this young woman made that comment at that table at that moment, it hit me like a ton of bricks. A huge surge of emotions rose inside of me. The valve on my faucet began to rattle. But I didn't feel safe enough to cry in front of a bunch of people during an informal conversation over lunch, so I left. I cleaned my plate and walked into the woods by myself. I reached a spot with a beautiful view, sat down, and did something I had never tried to do before in my entire life. I *tried* to cry.

It wasn't hard. The moment I sat down, a tsunami of tears poured out. Unknowingly, the pressure had been building for so long, and now the valve opened wide. I wasn't even sure what I was crying about. But it was a huge flood.

And then something funny happened. After about thirty seconds, I stopped. I found myself wondering how NBA star Kevin Durant, who'd just signed a contract with the Golden State Warriors basketball team, might fit in with them next season. But I could sense I wasn't done; There was more that needed to come out. I took a breath and refocused my attention on my body. Immediately, the tears started to flow. And then again, about thirty seconds later, I found myself thinking about what would happen in the next season of the TV show *Game of Thrones*.

Over and over, I observed myself in this strange dance of crying, stopping to notice my mind had drifted off into the most random thought, realizing I had more I needed to release, and starting to cry again, only to find myself getting distracted once again. I was deep enough into my meditation practice by then to at least be aware of what was happening. As I observed myself doing this dance, I noticed myself starting to get angry.

Crying, one of the most basic tools humans have to release our pain, a sacred medicine, had been ripped away from me by the system of patriarchy and the concurrent doctrine of toxic masculinity. I had been told my entire life to "suck it up." All those messages about how "boys don't cry" had made me forget how to cry, how to release these toxins in my body.

I would later learn what was happening wasn't all bad. Partly, the innate wisdom of my body was helping me to pendulate—to move back and forth between immense grief and something totally random—as a way to help me slowly release and integrate that grief a little bit at a time, in pieces I could chew. Since then, I've walked an active, at times bumpy and slow path to reclaiming my own tears and building a relationship with my own vulnerability. I still struggle to notice when I'm not doing okay or to ask for help.

Accessing vulnerability is an ongoing *practice*. Vulnerability is a sacred gift. It opens up so much for us. One of my favorite things in the world is the feeling of laughter after a good cry. It's the purest laughter, like bright, warm sunshine after a hard storm. Like a large glass of water when your throat is parched. Like the first warm day of spring after a long winter.

Now, imagine how good it would feel if we—as a nation, as a species—learned to cry collectively. To release all we've been holding onto for so long. To learn to be vulnerable together and then to share in that pure laughter, together. How good would that feel?

Facing Truth

Now let's zoom out a little bit.

From the realm of talking about personal trauma, I want to talk about the United States. This nation is founded on violence. We can try to justify it if we want, but there's no denying it. The legacy of the nation-state known as the United States of America* begins with the genocide of Indigenous peoples and the enslavement of African peoples and quickly moves through the oppression of almost all people at some point—including other "white" peoples such as the Irish, German, Jewish, and Italian people who faced harsh discrimination early in their migration story.

We don't like to talk about it much. We like to pretend we're "over it." "That was hundreds of years ago," we say. "Yeah, those times were brutal, aren't we glad they're over?" I get why many Americans don't want to dig into that history. It's a really ugly, painful history. To heal from such deep wounds will require a really, really deep excavation of the darkest moments of our collective history. That's not fun, and I can empathize with the fear that leads someone to pretend "everything's okay," to want to "keep the past in the past."

But I believe the memories of those tragedies live inside of our collective bodies, and that dirty pain is seeping out all over our society. I believe so many challenges today are rooted in the fact that we have collective, unresolved trauma we never integrated. As nations are composed of individual human beings, it's not surprising they carry traumas and behave in very human ways. The experience of a society isn't that different from my own experience.

---

* Of course, the history of this land, also known as Turtle Island, does not start there. There is a long, rich history of community, joy, culture, songs, dance, science, civilization, life, and death of countless Indigenous peoples, told in many stories, including Charles C. Mann's book *1491*.

The reality that the choices we have made are responsible for the extinction of countless species, the destruction of unimaginable beauty, and the devastation of our one and only home are really scary and shameful things to face. The reality that the ongoing choices we make today may be contributing to the next great extinction and the destruction of life as we know it is even scarier. So, we keep ourselves busy with distractions. Our collective brain has gotten so good at devising hoops and obstacles that keep us from facing this truth. In the same way my mind kept going to basketball analysis and *Game of Thrones*, we as a society constantly think about our bills, TV shows, our Amazon wish lists, the newest gadgets, the latest celebrity gossip, and meaningless political arguments.

There is a deep spiritual cost to this.

For years now, Chris has been talking about writing an article titled "Climate Honesty as Spiritual Practice" that would point out it actually takes a certain maturity of spiritual practice to see through these delusions, to accept the data for what it is, and to truly grapple with the reality we face, all without breaking down. This is no easy feat. It is an embodied practice that requires the vulnerability of acknowledging feeling scared, lost, perhaps even hopeless. It also demands the fierceness to not shut down, to sit with difficult emotions and face them head-on, to see more suffering is likely coming and not look away.

Not everyone has read the reports and knows the climate crisis data. But even without the data, I believe that as creatures of this Earth, each one of us can *feel* it. In our own way, we all know something is *deeply* wrong; we are hurting as the Earth is hurting.

I used to wonder how our ancestors figured out what's edible and what's poisonous, which plants are medicinal and which cure what ailments. Was it purely trial and error? Did they wait until someone ate something and died to realize it was poisonous? But then one day on a walk, my dog started devouring grass like she was a hungry goat who had retired to greener pastures and was planning to overthrow the local cows. I got curious, so I did some research, and many studies suggest dogs eat grass because of a deficiency in certain nutrients. It got me thinking—how the hell did my little Wasa know that? No one taught her; she just knew.

Then I realized animals in the wild know what to eat and what not to eat.* Not only that, there's an entire field of science dedicated to the study of how animals in the wild self-medicate!† From apes eating aspilia leaves to fight off parasites to birds seeking out specific medicinal plants (some of the same ones used by humans, like yarrow and lavender) to build their nests to raise their young, the examples are endless. These animals never attended a class on herbal medicine. They just . . . know. It's the kind of intergenerational wisdom that lives in their bodies. As beings who are a part of nature, they're in relationship to their environment; they can sense what they need and where to get it.

Human beings are no different. We've come a long way, and now we tend to see ourselves as somehow separate from the natural world. But we're of the Earth as much as any other species. And this helps me understand how our ancestors might have discerned what was safe to eat and what plants offered medicine for what ailments. We *knew* in our bodies, just like Wasa knew she needed to feast on some grass that day.

Our ancestors' close relationship with their environment allowed them to communicate with the beyond-human world in a way most of us have forgotten. To me, this isn't some spiritual-West-Coast-hippy-pseudoscience BS. We see animals do it in the wild every day.

---

* Key word being in the *wild*. Poor Wasa was not a wild creature and ate anything off the street, often leading to stomach problems. Often, looking at Wasa, this tiny, sweet, adorable little Jack Russell, I am in awe she is a descendent of a wild wolf.

† It's called zoopharmacognosy, which sounds like a made-up word. But then again, I suppose all words are made up.

When I was thirteen years old and crying over the candy wrapper, I couldn't quite explain why I was crying. For whatever reason, at that moment, I tapped into a grief I believe we may all carry. Since that time, the pace of destruction has only increased exponentially. The science on the climate crisis is clear. We are running out of time.[*] And it's not just the climate. In this interdependent world, we feel the suffering of so many in our bodies. When our educational systems fail our children, when our medical industrial complex makes us sick, when 25,000 people die every day from starvation, when sexual violence is normalized, when millions of people are kept in cages and entire communities are caught in an inescapable cycle of generational poverty, we can feel in our bodies that *something is not right*.

In the movie *The Matrix*, Neo *knew* something was wrong, right?[†] He couldn't understand it intellectually, but he knew he was living in the Matrix. He knew in his body that he was not free.[‡] And that deep, *felt* knowing sapped him; he was not happy, joyful, or spacious.

To dig out of this polycrisis we're in, we need to be at our best. When so much of our energy is sapped by denying what's right in front of us, we don't have the spaciousness needed to move forward. There are many deep, scary truths we suppress and pretend aren't there, as individuals, as nations, and as a species. But if we're to free ourselves from the cycles of violence, we need to have the courage and vulnerability to face them.

---

[*] I'm no expert on the science of climate crisis, nor is this a book specifically about any one issue. There are countless resources on the climate crisis and I encourage everyone to read books like *This Changes Everything* and *The End of Ice*.

[†] It's been over twenty years. If you still haven't seen *The Matrix*, I can't help you. Just go watch it.

[‡] Okay, fine, that was mean. If you haven't seen it, you can fast forward to chapter 7 for a brief synopsis.

CHAPTER 2

The Compassion of Fierceness

And that visibility which makes us most vulnerable is that which also is the source of our greatest strength.

AUDRE LORDE

Our spiritual practice is meant to make us dangerous, to temper us like steel into the cogs that grind the wheels of injustice to a halt.

NICHOLA TORBETT

VULNERABILITY ALONE is not enough. A common misnomer about nonviolence is that it's about flowers, scented candles, and white doves; if we just love our opponents hard enough, they will magically transform and stop causing harm. If we love enough of those people, we can turn this whole thing around.

Yeah, no.

My commitment to nonviolence comes from the lineage of one of the fiercest leaders this country has ever seen, a leader who wanted to build a nonviolent movement "as disruptive [and] as attention-getting as the riots," who demanded billions of dollars a year from the federal government to address poverty and was willing to cripple the infrastructure of Washington DC to do so, who described white moderates as "more devoted to order than to justice" and as a greater stumbling block in Black people's stride toward freedom than the KKK, who called riots the "language of the unheard," who said it would "be morally irresponsible for me to [condemn riots] without, at the same time, condemning the contingent, intolerable conditions that exist in our society ... that cause individuals to feel that they have no other alternative than to engage in violent rebellions to get attention."

That person, of course, is Dr. King, the same person the federal government loves to parade around every January as a symbol of this country's supposed morals. Dr. King was fierce. He was powerful. His brilliance was that he combined fierceness with an unending commitment to love. He never let his eyes wander from the ultimate goal of Beloved Community—a fully reconciled world.

Being "fierce" can look like refusal to allow a pattern of harm to continue. It can look like speaking your truth, no matter the consequences. It can be refusing to have your personal dignity diminished, committing to showing up as your true self even if that means putting yourself in danger. It can look like holding someone accountable for harm they cause. In the same way vulnerability is largely about accessing your heart, part of fierceness is accessing your intellect to develop sharp analysis and an airtight strategy for engagement in conflict. Fierceness is the discernment and clarity to know your deepest, most vulnerable truths and the courage to say these truths out loud; it's engaging in conversation with those you need to heal with or putting up strong boundaries; it's trusting your truth and speaking directly to the collective pain that drives our movements; it's the courage to use escalated forms of direct action, to put your body in harm's way to honor, protect, and serve life. The history of nonviolence is filled with people who risked their lives for what they believed was right. People have been arrested, beaten, disappeared, and assassinated in the name of nonviolence.

I often wonder how ready I would be to make some of those same sacrifices. I've been leading trainings for years and have been in many tense situations during protests, but if it came down to it, would I have the courage to take a beating? To go into an action where my life was literally in danger? How would it feel to, like the student leaders on the Freedom Rides in 1961, sign over my will before heading into an action?

I'm going to share a slightly vulnerable truth here, which is that I'm sometimes disappointed by advocates of nonviolence, and the nonviolent movement overall. Myself included. In the summer of 2017, Chris and I attended a counter-demonstration in Berkeley, California, organized in response to a planned rally by a group of white supremacists. When we arrived, several hundred Antifa* activists, all dressed in black, were roving around as a block. At times, they got into violent confrontations with the few white supremacists who actually showed up. Later that day, Chris and I debriefed our experience. He admitted to a tinge of jealousy—Antifa had mobilized hundreds of people, all wearing the same colors, all on the front lines, all risking bodily injury for what they believed was right. While our values around how we want to show up in the world may differ from theirs, he couldn't help but look at what they had and ask, "Where are our people?"

Of course, many of "our" people *were* in the streets that day. Most of them joined the main counter demonstration: a march of thousands of people who peacefully walked through the streets and didn't come into direct confrontation with the white supremacists. I'm not criticizing the march. It's important to always build in tactics accessible to a wide range of people; the movement against white supremacy has to have a place for children, elders, and everyday people who may not consider

* Short for "anti-fascists," Antifa is a decentralized movement and philosophy that draws its roots in early-twentieth-century antifascist movements in Europe. The movement gained momentum in the United States after the 2016 election of Donald Trump. While most of the actions led by activists associated with Antifa don't involve physical violence, they're not afraid to get into violent confrontations with their political "opponents." They are closely associated with the Black Bloc movements active in the late 1990s and 2000s.

themselves activists. At the same time, I wonder if a peaceful march that doesn't engage directly with the forces of violence or disrupt business as usual will ultimately bring systemic change.

I want to be clear about a couple things here. One is that I'm not suggesting *everyone* needs to be on the front lines, engaging in nonviolent action. We need to create a movement where every single person's vocation and gifts are engaged and honored. Movements like Standing Rock and Occupy Wall Street offered beautiful examples of what this could look like: therapists and healers offered their services to those on the front lines; spiritual teachers and elders provided guidance, led ceremonies before or after actions, and offered prayers during them; artists infused immense beauty into our work; cooks and farmers fed countless organizers; builders helped construct encampments; teachers and childcare workers created children's programming; poets and musicians wrote the songs of our movements; herbalists, acupuncturists, and health-care workers of all kinds treated the sick and injured. There is no shortage of ways for people to lead with *their* vocational gifts in service to the great changes we're facing.

However, we also need to acknowledge the scale of destruction we're witnessing on our planet right now—its severity means we need to create a movement with the power to meet that intensity of systemic destruction. Secondly, I want to state the obvious: there have always been, and continue to be, people deeply committed to the fierce legacy of nonviolence fighting for systemic change, people taking risks and sacrificing their bodies in the name of justice. They are just few and far between.

I believe we are fooling ourselves if we think we can transform the world simply by individual life choices. "If we all buy organic produce, drive electric cars, meditate, and do yoga every day, are kind to our neighbors, and commit to the vulnerable work of healing ourselves, the world will change. One heart, one mind, one person at a time." This is a dangerous worldview. Putting more money into the pockets of billionaires like Jeff Bezos and Elon Musk, spending thousands of dollars going to fancy meditation retreats, and being a "nice" person does not challenge the status quo. For many, it *is* the status quo.

The belief that we can change the world one person at a time severely underestimates the active and powerful systems in place that perpetuate violence and injustice at a rate much higher than we can possibly imagine. For too long, advocates of nonviolence have failed in creating a movement that has the power to go toe to toe with those forces. Many advocates of nonviolence—often due to privilege—have been relatively comfortable organizing peaceful, risk-free vigils and permitted marches, running campaigns to ban plastic grocery bags, and working in schools to bring about a culture of peace.

Again, all of those things are important! In fact, I've been doing those things as well. For the majority of the last ten years of my life, I've been working in schools and prisons leading nonviolence trainings and facilitating restorative justice dialogues, working to transform a culture of violence within those larger institutions. I am proud of the work I have done, and I regret none of it. I know our work has had a direct impact on the lives of countless people, and I will continue to do that work. Much of the insights in this book were gained in that work.

I'm also aware, however, that the momentum toward violence in our large institutions is so strong that if a new school principal or prison warden came in and shut down our programs, the culture of violence would sweep back in a heartbeat. No matter how deep the healing has been for those who have participated in our programs, there are still millions of students and incarcerated people who have never had access to programs like these, with more on the way every day. So, what kind of *systemic* change are we really making?

Yes, we need more healing spaces and more bridge-building work. But that's not all we need. We're dealing with systems of harm that have been growing for thousands of years, and if we only deal with harm and healing on an interpersonal level, it will never be enough. Against the forces of violence and injustice, we need more fierceness. We cannot simply ask nicely for injustice to go away.

I once heard a leader in the Movement for Black Lives say, "We are asked to heal collective wounds as individuals." So much of our wounding comes from generations of systemic violence. Yet we are asked to do our healing in private, with an individual therapist, talking about our individual lives.

Systems of violence require a fierce, systemic response. At some point, we need the power to change systems on a fundamental level. And for that, I believe we need powerful forms of nonviolent action. The nonviolent movement—people who hold an unwavering commitment to healing and refuse to disregard the dignity of any human being—needs to reclaim fierceness.

Power and Purpose

Throughout my life, conversations about nonviolence have been a real struggle in frontline activist spaces engaging in resistance work. More than once, I've been booed out of rooms for suggesting we hold empathy for our "enemy." At the same time, when I find myself in communities where conversations about healing, reconciliation, loving our enemies, and all that beautiful jazz feel like second nature, I come up against a wall when I start talking about resistance, building power, and engaging in direct action. People sometimes assume this is contrary to loving all people and working toward healing—that when we engage in resistance work, we create conflict rather than lifting existing conflict into the open.

We are in a crisis. We cannot be afraid to harness power. We need to harness an incredible amount of power, rather quickly. But we also need to be clear about the intention behind our desire for power and what we mean when we say we need power. Semantics matter when we talk about concepts as important as power.

Dr. King once defined power as "the ability to achieve purpose." While I will never have the chance to talk to him about it, I wonder what he meant by the word "purpose." When I think about purpose, I think about short-term goals like my purpose in writing this book as well as a larger context, like our purpose in life. Not just my purpose, but that of life itself. What is life's purpose? Roughly 14 billion years ago, our universe was born in an explosive moment of chaos. Since the Big Bang, the universe has continued to dance between chaos and order. The laws of physics as we know them had yet to be defined, matter scattered in all directions, and the entire universe burned with unimaginable heat. But as time flowed, gasses began to form a semblance of order as they gathered and collapsed under their own gravity. Intense heat forged gases together, causing chemical reactions that created the first glimmers of light.

These were the first stars that shone in the darkness of our early universe. In the core of these early stars, intense heat fused gases together to create the heavier elements that make up the building blocks of everything that exists today. The intensity of this fusion caused many of these stars to explode, scattering elements into space until they found order again in the formation of new stars, planets, solar systems, and galaxies. At some point, this rhythm of chaos and order, expansion and contraction, destruction and creation produced life as we know it. It created us.

Every time chaos dances with order, every time destruction gives way to creation, something new is born. Light. Matter. Planets. Life. Life's ability to love. Love's ability to create new life. It feels like the purpose of our universe is to continue this constant dance between chaos and order, creating beauty and life along the way. So, what is life's purpose? Perhaps it's to be agents for balance and midwives for beauty. Power, at its best, is what helps us fulfill this purpose.

Traditionally, even in nonviolent movements, campaigns and direct actions are organized with the intention of gaining power, but a kind of power based on a limited understanding of the word. If we can harness enough of this power, the understanding goes, we can achieve our stated purpose. And while I'm not afraid of power, this dynamic feels like the same old zero-sum struggle humanity has been playing for countless millennia—it's ultimately about seeing which side can gain more power to enforce their will. It's a *power-over* dynamic. This understanding of power—as something we can use to enforce our will —has been abused time and time again. It's not the kind of power I want, and it's not the kind of power fierce vulnerability seeks to tap into. What I intend isn't about "creating" power, forcing it down someone's throat, or taking it away from someone else. It's about acknowledging a deeper power that already exists in every corner of the universe—the power created out of the balance of chaos and order, the power that continues to create life: the power of beauty, creativity, and belonging.

We may not know the exact things that need to happen to bring healing to the world. But the cosmos knows, because it's been doing it forever. We just need to listen. If I think back to the moments in my life when I felt most "powerful," they're when I've connected to my deepest, most authentic self. They're when I've been reminded I'm part of something so much larger than this being called "Kazu." I feel most powerful when I don't even think to question my sense of belonging, because there's no doubt about my interdependence with the rest of existence.

In these moments, I don't need external validation of my worth. No one can give me validation, nor can they take it away from me because it's innate. There is no power struggle because I have tapped into the infinite power of the universe. From this place, I certainly don't feel a need to take power from anyone else.

Steven Wineman, in *Power-Under: Trauma and Nonviolent Social Change*, discusses how violence most often happens as a result of unhealed trauma. The dynamic of lashing out from unprocessed trauma happens unconsciously. And because this is an unconscious process, people don't have power over it. In fact, their trauma has power over them. When I talk to people who have caused harm and slow down enough to truly unpack their story, it becomes clear simply saying "Well, they *chose* to pull the trigger" is far from complete. After a lifetime of experiencing violence, poverty, and oppression, ideas like "choice" and "agency" become overrated. On some level, it's true we all make choices in our lives. But often, the choices we have access to are limited by our circumstance. And too often in the exact moment choices are made, we're in panic; our trauma has taken over our ability to think through our choices and make decisions consciously.*

If your choices are limited by a lifetime of violence, and unhealed trauma has put you into panic and taken away your ability to connect, this is not a moment of "power." It's what Wineman calls a "power-under" dynamic: your trauma forces you to "choose" violence. True power, or what NVC teacher Miki Kashtan calls internal power, is about understanding our own value and dignity and aligning with our purpose in life. I don't believe anyone's truest purpose is to abuse another person. If someone is being abusive, they're not living into their true purpose. They are, therefore, acting in the *absence* of power. When people commit violence, they're not exercising power. They're exercising abuse. Their lack of *inner* power makes them turn to sources of *external* power to cause harm.

---

* More on this later.

> ### In the World
>
> *Think about someone like Donald Trump. In one sense, he's clearly a powerful person. But really, if we think about it, is he? He certainly has access to a lot of external, structural power, but is he really powerful, in the truest sense of the word? Do you see him as someone with inner resources, dignity, and a deep sense of belonging?*
>
> *The fact that he has access to so much external power gives him—and the rest of us—the delusion that he is powerful. But with an understanding of the power-under dynamic and the difference between internal and external power, we can argue he is actually powerless. No amount of votes will meet his need for validation. No amount of media coverage will make him feel truly seen as a human being.*

When people lack internal power, they often try to fill the gap by amassing as much external power as possible. Our world has taught us our entire lives that power comes from weapons, titles, physical strength, political office—external factors that can be wielded in an abusive, power-over dynamic. Of course, when someone has external power and uses it to cause harm, we need "power" to stop them. But rather than trying to "take power away" from them, can we move with an understanding of infinite universal power and nudge the person causing harm closer to their true, internal power by reminding them they are sacred and they belong? Rather than "taking power away," can we actually give it back to them?

The Two Hands of Nonviolence

The novelist F. Scott Fitzgerald once said, "The test of a first-rate intelligence is the ability to hold two opposed ideas in mind at the same time and still retain the ability to function." In many ways, I believe the heart of nonviolence tries to balance two seemingly opposing ideas. In one hand is fierceness, assertiveness, at times even militancy, the ability to say no—to refuse to allow injustice to continue and to demand change. In the other hand is vulnerability, understanding, and unwavering compassion for all beings—the refusal to disregard anyone's inherent dignity.

In *Revolution & Equilibrium*, activist Barbara Deming wrote:

With one hand we say to one who is angry, or to an oppressor, or to an unjust system, "Stop what you are doing. I refuse to honor the role you are choosing to play. I refuse to obey you. I refuse to cooperate with your demands. I refuse to build the walls and the bombs. I refuse to pay for the guns. With this hand I will even interfere with the wrong you are doing. I want to disrupt the easy pattern of your life."

But then the advocate of nonviolence raises the other hand. It is raised outstretched—maybe with love and sympathy, maybe not—but always outstretched.... With this hand we say, "I won't let go of you or cast you out of the human race. I have faith that you can make a better choice than you are making now, and I'll be here when you are ready. Like it or not, we are part of one another."[2]

Nonviolent direct action is one of the most powerful ways the fierce hand that says "no" manifests in our movements. One modern community that has contributed greatly to the legacy of nonviolent direct action is the Ruckus Society, which has trained countless activists in direct action. The Fierce Vulnerability Network borrowed and added to their definition of direct action to offer the following in our handbook:

[Direct action] The strategic use of immediately effective, disobedient acts to achieve a political or social goal and

challenge an unjust power dynamic. This happens at points of intervention through embodied practice of nonviolence.*

The FVN Handbook goes on to explain:

This is where our private heartbreak becomes our public witness, and our unseen power is released. When we stand in front of 10,000 tons of coal traveling by train or between militarized police and a targeted community, when we defy laws to see the homeless housed and the undocumented protected, we are telling the truth about the world around us in powerfully disobedient ways—challenging the assumption that "that's just the way things are." Direct action is our deliberate engagement in constructive conflict, putting our bodies into action to clear the way for the fullest expression of our humanity and for the building up of the nonviolent society we long to inhabit.

In the legacy of nonviolence, the power of the "no" hand can at times be as fierce as any form of violence. During the Indian independence movement in 1930, poet and activist Sarojini Naidu led a march of 2,500 people to the Dharasana Salt Works to protest the British tax on salt. When they arrived, police beat them with steel-tipped batons that cracked skulls and bones. Because of their training and fierce commitment to nonviolence, the marchers didn't even raise their arms in self-defense. Images of their commitment to nonviolence garnered international attention and exposed the violence of British rule.

---

* Points of Intervention is a tool used to select strategic targets of direct actions. Originally developed by Patrick Reinsborough and the smartMeme Strategy and Training Project (later renamed the Center for Story Based Organizing), it is one of the most important tools when organizing actions. Check out *https://beautifultrouble.org/toolbox/tool/points-of-intervention* for more.

The student leaders of the Freedom Rides—a group of Black and white students who traveled on interstate buses to challenge segregated bus terminals—knew they would likely be beaten along their trip. Each one filled out their will before leaving, knowing they were risking their lives. Throughout their journey, they were violently beaten multiple times; the bus they rode was stopped and firebombed by a mob outside Anniston, Alabama. They were beaten again as they escaped the burning bus.

Thích Quảng Đức, a Vietnamese Buddhist monk, self-immolated in 1963 to protest the South Vietnamese government's persecution of Buddhists. Witnesses—including members of his Sangha—say he lit himself on fire and sat in meditation until he passed. He didn't scream. He didn't move. Motivated by his commitment to his people and supported by decades of spiritual practice, his act was not one of desperation. It was a pre-planned action made in consultation with his spiritual community, a deeply spiritual and symbolic gesture. It was an offering and a sacrifice—made in the fiercest way possible.

The White Rose movement of young Germans printed and distributed pamphlets openly criticizing the Nazi regime in the early 1940s, knowing the consequence of being caught would be death. Most leaders were eventually arrested and executed, but even during their trial and incarceration, they stood by their morals and continued to openly condemn the regime.

There are countless examples of such fierceness shown by nonviolent activists throughout the world. The movement for justice requires each generation to add to the legacy and create new expressions of the struggle. Offering fierce vulnerability as our own contribution, I am grateful for these reminders from our elders and ancestors that nonviolence can be as fierce as violence.

> At the same time, as powerful and necessary as direct action is, we must be careful how we utilize it to avoid certain pitfalls. Too

> often, when we engage in direct action we focus exclusively on the
> "no" hand. We extend the "yes" hand to the communities we view
> as on "our side," but wave a fist at those we perceive as the enemy.

Other times when we practice nonviolence, we extend the "yes" hand to all people only in a superficial way that ignores the real power dynamics that cause suffering. We talk about the importance of "loving our enemy" but don't have the courage to build movements with the power to say "no," to disrupt business as usual, and to challenge those inflicting harm. True nonviolence—and fierce vulnerability—is about extending both hands simultaneously.

The Intention of Spiritual Practice

For me, spiritual practice is a fierce practice. Its intention is to cultivate the courage necessary to face reality as it is and to give us the audacity to fight for the liberation of all life. I can't help but feel it's critical in the work of fierce vulnerability.

The main form of meditation I practice is called *vipassana*, which means "to see things as they truly are," not as we want them to be. Spiritual practice has helped me to cut through the delusions I hold, to see and accept reality for what it is. For us to truly accept the reality of the climate crisis—and many other forms of systemic harm—is no easy task. But it's the reality in front of us, and until we can fully accept it, we won't be able to move forward with the appropriate focus and capacity. Seeing the climate crisis for what it is goes beyond reading reports and understanding data. It includes accepting and embodying the fear, grief, and anxiety that may emerge as we sit with the depth of this crisis.

My friend Kritee Kanko is a part-time Zen priest, part-time climate scientist, and full-time spiritual activist. As a climate scientist who has done a lot of grief work, she can not only summon the data but can also understand the gravity of our situation in her body. Years ago, we were talking about why more of her climate scientist peers, who understand the depth of the crisis better than anyone, aren't engaged in activist work. Why aren't they up in arms? Why aren't they throwing their bodies onto the front lines to try to mitigate this disaster?

She told me when she asks other climate scientists, "How do you *feel* about this data?" many of them enter a state of panic and respond along the lines of "Don't even ask me that, I can't go there." They don't have the emotional or spiritual space in their bodies to allow their feelings to sink in. They understand the data intellectually, but not somatically. They cannot embody it. It's a survival mechanism that allows them to keep the fear at a distance and continue living as if we aren't in an urgent crisis. They're not alone. Alarming, nightmare-inducing climate data has been out there for decades now, yet society refuses to accept the existential severity of the crisis. We watch documentaries, read books, or attend lectures about the environment, human trafficking, our broken educational system, or any number of crises, and we are genuinely appalled. And then we go on living our lives as if we don't need to change anything.

I remember when the movie *Don't Look Up* came out in 2021, satirizing humanity's incapacity to form a meaningful response to its impending annihilation. For a short time, *everyone* was talking about it, how we need to have more urgency around the climate crisis. Then the new *Top Gun* movie with Tom Cruise came out, and we went back to our regularly scheduled program.

There's dissonance. Our intellect recognizes these problems, but our emotional bodies shut down and block us from processing the feelings that arise. As a result, we're unable to move in the direction of change. In unconsciously seeking to protect ourselves from this fear, we endanger the very foundation of our survival. This is why we need to work on strengthening our emotional capacities by engaging in healing modalities, spiritual practices, and vulnerable conversations to create more space for ourselves to feel. To be vulnerable enough to fully experience our fear without breaking requires a fierce spiritual practice.

The more we stretch in these ways, the more we can see things for what they are—see and feel not just how scary the issues are, but how *scared we are*. On the other side of accepting our vulnerability and the enormity of the task in front of us lies the fierceness to move forward with our entire hearts and minds.

While I emphasize the importance of spiritual practice, I sometimes find myself disheartened at the lack of fierceness I feel in many spiritual spaces. Often, I experience communities engaging in spiritual practices in ways that don't have an analysis of collective liberation and systemic change. Many people, for example, pay thousands of dollars to attend fancy retreats that focus only on their own healing. The multi-billion-dollar "wellness" industry, which touts the benefits of mediation, yoga, and vegan, raw, macrobiotic, whatever diets, puts the emphasis on the individual. The message is: if you meditate enough, exercise, and eat a healthy diet, you will be healthy and happy. An analysis of broader, systemic factors at the root of disease and depression is notably absent. This industry does not challenge the status quo; the wellness industry and all its pseudo-spiritual apps and self-help retreats *are part of the status quo*.

This cannot be where we stop. Healing and spiritual practice aren't individual practices. They're relational, collective experiences. If spiritual practice is about understanding we are part of something bigger, it's impossible to practice solely at the individual level. If you're truly deepening into a worldview of interdependence, it's only natural to work for the liberation of others who are suffering. I'm afraid many communities use "spiritual" practices as a form of spiritual bypassing—convincing themselves they are "healing" and becoming more "enlightened" while ignoring the hard work of looking at their own shadows and understanding our complicity in systems of violence.

Practices like meditation and yoga can help us overcome stress and anxiety, which is always a good thing. However, the danger is that these practices teach people to be complacent about injustice. Accepting reality doesn't mean being complacent about it; acceptance can be the foundation of seeing clearly and lead to dedicated, unwavering engagement with injustice. There is a world of difference between accepting the reality of our world and committing to changing it or accepting the reality of our world and using spiritual practice to make our complicity with it a little easier to live with. Practices used to decompress from the stresses of living in a capitalist economy so you can go back into it and continue to earn wealth from a system that causes so much harm aren't liberatory, for you or for anyone else.

We're all doing the best we can, and I don't want to shame anybody for their practices. I simply see the crisis we're in and know that collectively, we need to be doing so much more. Myself included.

Countless communities use spiritual practice to bring genuine healing to the world. Here are some considerations that may support you in finding them:

- Has leadership from your community encouraged members to participate in world events happening outside of your community?

- Have they offered or encouraged practices that support people looking at their own shadows? This could include unconscious privilege or unhealed traumas.

- Does your community work to facilitate building authentic relationships with each other?

- Do the teachers and elders in your community support you in building resiliency to *be* with the crises of our times rather than suppressing the emotions?

- Is your community willing to take public stances on controversial issues?

- Have you experienced or witnessed open engagement with conflict in your community, or is conflict discouraged and shoved under the rug? Have you experienced leadership taking accountability when they fall short?

- Does your community take proactive steps to include and lift up members who may have marginalized identities? Do they create spaces for them to feel safe, seen, and supported?

- Is your community accessible to those without financial resources?

The Gifts of Anger

A common myth about nonviolence is that if you're expressing anger, you're not practicing nonviolence. Anger is often seen as the motivating fuel of violence and injustice. Therefore, the myth goes, we can't be "angry" if we want to transform these dynamics, because we can't fight fire with fire. It's actually not true that you can't fight fire with fire. When firefighters fight a forest fire, they often use controlled fires to burn a strip between the raging inferno and the lands they're trying to protect. This strategy, called "back-burning," creates a space with no fuel for the fire to burn so when the forest fire gets there, it's unable to continue its movement.

Our relationship to anger has to start with an acknowledgement that anger is a natural and appropriate response to injustice. People are right to be pissed off. Just as wildfires are a natural and inevitable part of our ecosystem,* anger is a natural and inevitable response to injustice. Once we can acknowledge anger is legitimate and inevitable, we can talk about what to do with it. What is the strategic response to the fact that we live in a society where people are filled with righteous anger? Because, as with the use of backfires, there are skillful uses of anger—and even rage.

Rage is a *strong*, powerful emotion. This is one of the reasons why movements that have come from marginalized people have been so powerful. Part of what drives them is righteous rage, whether a movement is nonviolent or not. The Black Panther Party emerged out of the rage of Black communities and figured out a way to skillfully channel it. Their rage wasn't an unprocessed, uncontrollable wildfire burning down everything in its path. It was an organized, disciplined rage.

Often when the first spark of rage enters our hearts, it seeks a target. And because our own hurts are usually caused by those who look like us, we tend to attack targets who look the same. But if we slow down and create space to witness and honor our rage, we can begin to create some separation between the anger and the hatred that accompanies it. We can see we aren't actually motivated by hatred. Often, rage is driven by grief, sadness, or disconnect. And if we dig even deeper, we see it is perhaps rooted in a desire to protect ourselves or the people, places, and things we love.

Even though the Black Panther Party is often remembered for their willingness to shoot back, they gained support from their community because of the love they offered. Their free breakfast programs, medical services, free schools, and so much more were their sources of power, not their guns. They organized because they loved their people.

---

* Forest fires have certainly been exacerbated by climate change and other human-made issues but remain a natural phenomenon.

Sometimes, a fire becomes so powerful all we can do is to create a container around it and let it burn into an inferno. If we can let it burn on its own, the inferno will eventually turn into a charcoal. Likewise, sometimes our emotions are so powerful that the best we can do is create a safe container to let them burn. To yell, to scream, to let out all the anger and hurt so it can eventually burn down into a charcoal. That charcoal is the fuel we carry into direct action. That charcoal can still connect us with our righteous indignation. But it's now safe enough to hold and easier for us to channel. It's focused. It's concentrated. And it sometimes requires that blaze to create.

I envision a movement of charcoals. A movement of individuals who have honored our rage and removed the poison of hatred so it becomes a powerful and disciplined energy: one that blazes a path toward healing rather than destruction.

In the World

On the morning of August 6, 1945, an inferno raged in Hiroshima as an atom bomb was dropped on a civilian population for the first time. Tatsuo Yamamoto, then a young soldier, survived the bombing and went out to look for his uncle, Yasuke, who owned a local bookstore. When Tatsuo arrived at the store, he found it flattened with no sign of Yasuke. Flames still burned in the remains where the store once stood.

Tatsuo used that flame to light his portable charcoal warmer—something commonly used in Japan at the time to stay warm during cold nights. He took that charcoal back to his home village of Hoshino, where he kept the flame alive for decades before the community found out about it and used it to light an eternal flame that still burns to this day as a prayer for world peace.

Tatsuo's son Takudou, a monk and now the keeper of the flame, says his father's dying words were: "It's time to end the foolish practice of killing one another."

In 2002, Jun-San[*] led the Hiroshima Flame Peace Walk, a prayer walk across the United States. A small ragtag group of peace activists carried with them a hand warmer, much like the one used by Tatsuo. Inside, it contained a charcoal lit by the eternal flame in Hoshino. I joined this walk for a few days. I still remember the moment when one of the leaders of the walk asked if I wanted to hold the charcoal warmer for a little while. I vividly remember the feeling I had the moment that pouch was placed in my hand. I was holding the Hiroshima flame. The same flame that, as a burning inferno, tore through Hiroshima, killing Yasuke and 140,000 others. The same flame that had been prayed over in the name of peace for close to sixty years.

In the first few years Tatsuo kept feeding this flame, it was an embodiment of his anger. The physical flame had become controlled, but the inferno still raged in his heart. But as time went on, with the help of an actual flame to represent his rage, the meaning of the flame slowly transformed into a charcoal for peace. This is what can happen when we create space for our rage to be honored. After the flames of the inferno burn down, we realize there is something different underneath. Love for our people. A desire for peace. A commitment to reconciliation.

When we remove the poison of hatred from our rage, we can find the gift. Rage tells us something is deeply wrong. It reminds us what matters to us. It energizes us to protect. When

---

[*] Jun-san is a nun from the Japanese order Nipponzan Myohoji. She has walked across this country on prayer walks close to a half a dozen times. Beat that, Forrest Gump!

we choose not to be afraid of our rage, it can become a powerful force moving us into skillful action. It's risky work—proactively choosing to create space for our rage. But not ignoring it is an important practice of fierceness.

Sides of the Same Coin

It's possible to be both fierce and vulnerable at the same time. In fact, I'm convinced transformative change in the face of injustice is possible when we can see these powerful energies as two sides of the same coin.

In the final days of the Nonviolent Leadership for Social Change retreat I wrote about, I found myself on the floor in one of several piles of people holding each other amidst a cascade of tears and cries. I'd been in many spaces without a single dry eye. And yet, this may have been the only time I experienced almost every person crumpled on the floor, *wailing out loud* for what felt like an hour. There was no talking, just crying.

Rewind to a few minutes before we became this sobbing heap: we'd again been discussing the painful legacy of patriarchy. A woman stood up, tears flowing from her eyes. She slowly walked around the entire circle, pausing in front of each and every male-identified person in the room and *demanding* we look into her tearful eyes.

"Look at me! Can you see my pain?" she asked. "This is what you did to me, to all of us . . ."

It broke me. Through her tears, she was almost yelling at us. It was excruciating. And it was an incredible gift to each person in the room.

There's no way for me to say she was being either fierce *or* vulnerable. It wasn't one or the other. She deeply embodied both energies. It was one of the fiercest expressions of vulnerability I'd ever witnessed. This woman was deeply connected to her story, unafraid to feel her pain or express her rage. Yet her intention wasn't vengeance or to release unresolved, unprocessed pain. Her emotions were powerful, yet expressed with the sharp clarity that only comes from years of healing. They weren't used as a weapon but offered as medicine.

This ability to offer our pain as medicine without giving up the power of demanding accountability is fierce vulnerability. That day, that woman shattered the false sense of composure we so often hide behind. She reduced a gathering of grown adults into a crumpled mass on the floor, interlocked in embraces and consumed by inconsolable cries. Her pain and her rage emanated from the depths of her gaze yet were expressed with a grace that shielded me from defensiveness. Instead of shutting down and building a wall, my heart opened. That moment, I imagine, took an incredible amount of emotional labor for her. But she chose to give it, because she understood we're dependent on one other for our liberation. While we all received her expression as a sacred gift, she also understood it was necessary for her own healing—it was an investment in our collective liberation.

How can we imagine extrapolating her example to larger scales of change? What would it look like to plan public, nonviolent actions with the same spirit? What would we need to do to prepare ourselves for such an action? These are some of the explorations of fierce vulnerability.

CHAPTER 3

Panic and Trauma

Between stimulus and response, there is a space. In that space lies our freedom and our power to choose our response. In our response lies our growth and our happiness.

ALEX PATTAKOS (SORT OF)[*]

If we don't transform pain, we will transmit it.

FATHER RICHARD ROHR

EDUCATOR KARL ROHNKE developed a model I find helpful when discussing how our bodies dysregulate when we're distressed: the comfort-stretch-panic zones. Most of us spend our days in what Rohnke calls the "comfort zone." The comfort zone is where our emotions are well regulated, where we can breathe slowly and think about complex problems—we're simply going about our day without a lot of stress. It's where creativity happens, where we're best able to solve problems, and where we feel

---

[*] I'm a stickler for giving credit and sourcing where wisdom comes from. This quote is famously attributed to the Austrian psychiatrist, author, and holocaust survivor Viktor Frankl. But I never found this quote in anything of his I read, so I did some research. According to the Viktor Frankl Institute, this quote comes from the book *Prisoners of Our Thoughts* by Alex Pattakos, a book about Frankl's teachings. Pattakos read this quote in a library once and thought it described Frankl's work well, so he quoted it in his book. However, he never shared the name of the book or its author.

deeply connected to others. It's a good place to be. But it's not where growth happens.

Growth happens when we are challenged and end up in the "stretch zone." Perhaps you are in a conflict with somebody or are challenged by a new and different perspective. You're pushed, pulled, challenged, but still able to listen. You can take in new information, consider differing perspectives, and remain in dialogue with others. You're able to open up and speak vulnerable truths, to explore parts of yourself that may be uncomfortable. It's not always a fun place to be, but growth, healing, and transformation are largely possible in this zone.

If you're working out at the gym and aren't at least a little bit uncomfortable, you're not getting stronger. But it's also possible to go to the gym, work out too hard, and pull a muscle. That's the "panic zone." In the panic zone, your survival instincts take over and you enter fight or flight. In extreme cases, you may freeze. In panic, you're unable to take in new information or listen to different perspectives; everything becomes black and white, and your emotions are no longer regulated.

Comfort Zone, Stretch Zone, and Panic Zone.
Artwork by Ayse Gokce Bo

We can get into panic when something scary happens, like a car accident or violence. But we can also enter the panic zone because of something relatively minor, like watching the Boston Celtics lose an important game.*

Sometimes, the signs of someone being in panic are clear. They scream or engage in physical violence. But other times, the signs are very subtle. Often, if I'm in an argument with LiZhen, I'm in my panic zone but unable to realize it until I'm fully back in my comfort zone. My panic doesn't *look* like panic. I never raise my voice, and I certainly don't engage in physical violence. But when I look back at my behavior from the comfort of the comfort zone, I realize I was unable to see her perspective. I notice the binarism of my view—I was right, she was wrong.

The zones aren't three distinct buckets—they exist on a spectrum and blend into each other. You can be *a little* stretched but still pretty comfortable or *really* stretched and on the verge of panic. You can be *a little* panicked and not able to take in a different perspective but have a regulated heartbeat or *really* panicked and completely out of control. The zones are also dynamic. Something that puts you into panic one day may barely register the next. Not sleeping well the night before or being hungry can impact your movement through the zones.

Also, the panic zone isn't a *bad* thing. It's just that the panic zone serves a very specific function, which has a lot to do with survival. The panic zone is really good at keeping us safe from harm, but not so good at helping us learn and grow. In panic, we lose sight of things like our values and our ability for connection, because we can only focus on the immediate threat (or perceived threat) in front of us. If our intention is to heal, it's important to track when we might be in the panic zone and learn to bring

---

* I would argue this is not a minor thing. It amazes me, after all these years of working on myself, that my emotions still get so dysregulated by whether or not a group of grown men can put a ball into a basket.

ourselves back into stretch and comfort. If we're working on our own healing, we want to be in the stretch zone. If we're supporting others in their healing, it may be best to situate ourselves in the comfort zone.

A trauma response almost always happens in the panic zone, though not all panic zone responses are rooted in trauma. Sometimes you can get thrown into panic by seeing a cockroach, but the stress of that moment isn't related to any older trauma, nor does it linger beyond the initial moment of fear. For someone else, though, a minor incident like seeing a cockroach could bring up traumatic memories that put someone *way* into their panic zone and keep them there longer than if they were just reacting to the cockroach alone. Perhaps a cockroach reminds someone of the generational poverty they lived through and brings back difficult and traumatic childhood memories.

Unprocessed trauma makes it easier for someone to go into panic. Trauma can result in someone having very little capacity to be in their stretch zone; they might go from their comfort zone *straight* into panic due to a relatively minor incident. Unhealed trauma can look like someone who is in a constant state of panic. The good news: the stretch zone is like a muscle—we can work it out and make it bigger.

How to Tell: Regulated and Dysregulated Nervous Systems

REGULATED	DYSREGULATED
Your breathing is slow and even	Your breath speeds up, or you find yourself holding your breath
Your body is relaxed	Your muscles tense up
You're able to stay present	You're easily distracted by stress or anxiety
You're able to take in new, different, or complex information	Everything becomes black and white and you lose the ability to see nuance

REGULATED	DYSREGULATED
You're able to experience a wealth of emotions	Your emotions feel overwhelming
You feel safe, can trust others and maintain connection	You feel threatened and are on alert for the next source of danger

Back in 2012 when I attended that first Jam, I was a relatively regulated person, by which I mean I was reliably able to breathe well, connect to others, and explore nuanced perspectives. I had been practicing nonviolence for many years, been in countless escalated action situations where tensions were high, and had learned to stay calm even in the midst of chaos. My capacity to be in the stretch zone was pretty high, or so I thought. It turned out, though, that when it came to my old family trauma, I had almost no ability to be in the stretch zone. I went from comfort *right* into panic.

The moment I started to share my story, my heart rate increased, my vision got blurred, I lost awareness of who was around me, and I could barely get a breath in. I've worked hard on that over the years and am now in a place where I can talk about my past without going into panic. It still puts me into stretch—but I'm able to remain present, remain in dialogue, and use those moments to continue to learn, to heal, and to integrate my past. In the same way lifting a 200 pound weight gets easier every time you do it, my story gets easier every time I explore it.

So, it's possible for someone to generally be regulated but have very little capacity to stretch themselves when it comes to a certain topic. Just because you can bench press 200 pounds doesn't mean you can do the same on a leg press. Someone may feel very comfortable in, say, physical confrontations, but go into panic anytime emotions are brought in, or vice versa. For example, the United States seems to be very comfortable going to war but goes into panic when the conversation turns to racial healing.

Panic can also put you into a freeze state, shutting down your ability to enter the stretch zone altogether. I've worked with people who have lived through horrific events and seem to be incredibly calm all the time. While it may not look like it, this can be akin to settling into a default state of panic. It's easy to assume someone has integrated their traumas and found peace, but getting to know them a bit more may make it clear they have actually completely shut down their ability to be vulnerable.

In the World

Years ago, I worked with a soft-spoken incarcerated man who had a perpetual aura of calm. Each time we invited him to share his story, he talked about the most horrific acts of violence he experienced as a child and later committed as a young man without an ounce of emotion; it was as if he were sharing a story he'd read in the newspaper. He said he felt no anger, no sadness, no anything. Then one day I asked him, "When was the last time you felt genuine joy?" He thought about it for a while and replied, "I guess I can't remember the last time I felt happy."

That's the trick with emotions—they come as a package. When you shut down your body's ability to feel grief, you also cut off your ability to feel joy.

The practice of shutting down his vulnerability helped this man survive when he was younger. However, in the absence of a full understanding of how his trauma affected him, those same survival mechanisms had become so deeply ingrained he began to mistake them for his personality. Quiet. Calm. Stoic. The mechanisms that had protected him earlier in life now prevented him from experiencing life's fullness.

Our Triune Brain

Our beautifully rich and diverse planet is filled with tens of millions of species of which we are only one. Each species has unique shapes, sizes, and characteristics. We are vastly different from one another. Some can fly, others live underwater. Some never stop moving. Koalas and sloths sleep as much as twenty-two hours a day.* Mayflies live only twenty-four hours; a French woman named Jeanne Calment lived for 122 years and 164 days, and . . . well, just read the footnote.†

And yet, if we go back far enough, we all share common ancestry. We all evolved out of the same single-celled organism way back in the day. It's a thought that still fills me with awe. A lot of the things we take for granted—our ability to breathe oxygen, our opposable thumbs, our ability to walk upright on two feet—were developed by our non-human ancestors and gifted to us through evolution. Our human brain is one of those things. Human beings didn't develop the brain; hundreds of millions of years of evolution did. Since our brain has so much to do with how we respond to panic and trauma, some basic understanding of the brain's physiology is helpful to keep in mind. So, forgive me as this briefly becomes a science book. I promise it's important!

The triune model of the brain, developed in the 1960s by neuroscientist Paul MacLean, is in some ways outdated. As researchers learn more and more about the makeup of the brain, they discover many details and intricacies MacLean missed. However,

* In my next life, perhaps I'll be lucky enough to be reborn as a koala.

† A giant tortoise living in a zoo in India died in 2006 at 255 years old. Glass sponges (which are considered animals) in the East China Sea can live for more than 10,000 years. And in July 2020, marine biologists discovered some microorganisms hundreds of feet beneath the ocean floor in "quasi-suspended animation" that were up to 101.5 million years old. That's one hundred and one point five million years old. That's 101,500,000 years old. You can't even write that in Roman numerals! Which is another amazing fact I learned when researching this footnote. The world is full of mystery and surprises.

the triune model is still commonly used to give a very broad over-view, so let us borrow it here. Roughly 500 million years ago, a part of the brain began to develop that helped our very non-human ancestors survive the harsh conditions of their lives. This part of the brain was so effective at keeping them alive that it got passed down from generation to generation, even as some of these creatures began to evolve into mammals, then apes, and eventually into *Homo sapiens*. This part of the brain, the basal ganglia, more commonly known as the reptilian complex or the lizard brain, is the oldest part of the human brain. It's responsi-ble for many unconscious actions, including many of our motor functions. It regulates our most basic survival instincts.

If you're walking down the street and you slip on a banana peel and begin to fall to the ground, your hand may instinctively reach out to grab onto a railing. That's your reptilian complex at work. No conscious thought, no logical process: your brain didn't stop to say, "Oh, shoot, I'm falling, and if I do then I might get hurt, but oh, look, there's a railing, if I reach out and grab it, it may keep me from falling, so let's do that." The reptilian complex can't engage in such a complex series of thoughts. It simply senses danger and reacts.

Though this ability clearly supports survival, life wouldn't be so exciting if all we did was go about our days reacting to everything around us. Luckily, our non-human ancestors came through for us yet again. About 150 million years ago, the paleo-mammalian brain began to develop in small mammals. The limbic system, a key component of this part of the brain, lies on top of the reptilian complex and is made up of many smaller com-ponents like the hippocampus (largely responsible for memory) and the amygdala (largely responsible for processing, filtering, and regulating emotions). The limbic system gives us the ability to feel deeper emotions and form complex social relationships. It's sometimes referred to as the emotional center of our brain. And yet, our ability to hold nuance or solve complex problems didn't come until much later.

While evidence suggests the neo-mammalian complex, otherwise known as the neocortex, existed in small mammals as early as 200 million years ago, something strange happened to the neocortex of our early primate ancestors about 2.5 million years ago. For reasons we still don't fully understand, the neocortex in these primates began to expand in size at a rapid rate. This continued until the first *Homo sapiens* began to roam the Earth some 300,000 years ago. This rapid growth of the neocortex ultimately gave our early ancestors the ability to develop language, create art, tell stories, and plan for the future in a way no other species had before. The neocortex is sometimes called the "human brain," though other animals, including primates, dolphins, and elephants, have it as well.

At the very front of the neocortex is the frontal lobe, and within the frontal lobe is the prefrontal cortex. This is where we think about philosophy, morality, and ethics. It's where nuance and complexity are held. It's where we think about solutions to our problems with things like logic and reason. It's where we create stories and imagine the future. The prefrontal cortex is the last part of our brains to develop, not only as a species but as individuals—most of us don't have a fully functioning prefrontal cortex until our mid-twenties. This is why children can't have nuanced discussions about philosophy and why teens and young adults don't always think about the consequences of their actions. It's the most evolved part of our brain, responsible for its highest executive functions.

Our society may rely on this part of our brain a bit too much, but you have to admit, it's a pretty helpful little tool.* So, what does this have to do with anything? Well, another

---

* Again, that was a *very* simplified description of some of the main components of our brain. In reality, the brain is too complex to lay out in neat, clean sections. All the parts of the brain interact with each other in incredibly complex ways; it's almost impossible to tell, for example, where the limbic system ends and the neocortex begins. But this is not a neuroscience book, so we'll leave it here for now.

way of thinking about our panic zones is what psychologist Daniel Goleman calls the "amygdala hijacking." When our brain receives sensory inputs (like a dog chasing you, someone making an offensive comment on social media, watching the Los Angeles Lakers beating the Boston Celtics),* it has a choice to make. Should the response be dictated by your prefrontal cortex or by your amygdala?

Prefrontal cortex responses are likely to happen in the comfort or stretch zones. The prefrontal cortex takes its time to assess how dangerous something is or isn't and chooses an appropriate response based on reason. Unfortunately, the amygdala makes decisions just slightly quicker than the prefrontal cortex—the amygdala doesn't process detailed information; it just reacts based on limited context. When the amygdala perceives danger, it automatically overrides the prefrontal cortex and activates the fight or flight response of the reptilian complex. When this happens, your amygdala's hijacked your brain, and you're off and running in your panic zone.

The problem is after centuries of developing our capacity to survive alongside say, saber-tooth tigers, we no longer live in a world where wild animals waiting to kill us lurk around every corner. Yes, there remain many actual threats to our lives today, especially if you live in a war-torn country or an impoverished neighborhood. But compared to 200,000 years ago, a large number of us live in relative physical safety. These days, instead of going into our panic zones because we're being chased by a wild animal, we go into our panic zones because we see something on social media with which we disagree. If someone makes a comment that triggers a feeling that I don't belong, it may *feel* like the end of the world—in more primitive times, if you were banished from your village, it probably was the end for you. This

---

* Luckily, as of 2024, I won't have to worry about this happening for at least a decade. Yes, I said it. Shots fired.

is why, when I only have access to the part of my brain that sees in black and white, an offensive comment on social media feels like a threat to my existence.

Responses to modern day conflicts that come out of our panic zones are often not appropriate. Your emotions may escalate, your actions and words may be illogical or irrational, and you may see things in an oversimplified way. This is not your fault. Your amygdala has hijacked your brain's capacity for things like regulating emotions, logic, and seeing nuance and complexity. The more unhealed trauma somebody has, the more sensitive their amygdala becomes. When you experience a traumatic event, that event creates an impression on your mind and body. The memory of that fear, pain, or danger hides out in your body until you can process that event and integrate it in your system. Part of the job of the amygdala is to protect you from harm, and the more harm you're still holding in your body, the more likely it is to see new stimuli as threatening.

Let's say you were attacked by a dog when you were young. That can be a traumatic experience with a lot of escalated emotions. Remember how I said the amygdala is responsible for filtering emotions and something called the hippocampus is responsible for memory? Well, the amygdala will take the emotions from that incident, and because they're so strong, will decide to store not only the *memory* of what happened but the *feeling* of fear in the long-term memory bank of the hippocampus. If you never had a chance to fully process and integrate that experience, the *emotional memory*—the pain, the fear, the danger—stays with you. This is a distinction between a stressful event and a traumatic one. With stress, the memory is a story of the incident—the story stays in that moment as something that happened to you in the past. With trauma, the memory is of the feeling. And that feeling stays with you, following you into the present.

Now, twenty years later, when you see a dog running toward you, it no longer matters that this is a small friendly dog with its tail wagging wildly because it wants to have its belly rubbed. The amygdala sees the sensory input, matches it with an old memory of fear in your hippocampus, hijacks your prefrontal cortex, and puts you in your panic zone. And now you're running away from a friendly little chihuahua named Tinkers. Your rational mind could tell Tinkers is not a threat. But your rational mind isn't accessible at that moment—you're experiencing an amygdala hijack, aka the panic zone. The lower functioning parts of your mind don't realize this fear is from twenty years ago; it thinks the trigger of that fear is happening *now*.

Amygdala, hippocampus, prefrontal cortex, reptilian complex, *mumbo jumbo*. It's not important you remember these scientific terms, but it *is* important we understand the basic functions and processes related to panic and trauma. Understanding lays the foundation for healing.

Our Autonomic Nervous System

It's not just in your brain either. The panic zone is experienced throughout your entire body. When your amygdala senses danger, it sends a signal through the command center of our brain, the hypothalamus,* which then activates something called the Sympathetic Nervous System, or SNS. This in turn floods your entire body with two stress hormones: adrenaline and cortisol. These chemicals give your body superhuman strengths as it prepares for fight or flight. Your airways open to allow you to take in more oxygen, your heartbeat increases so more blood can flow into your muscles, muscles tighten to prepare for rapid movements, your pupils dilate so you can see better, and your blood sugar increases so you can burn more energy. The SNS also shuts down your digestive systems, lowers your immune system, and

---

* Again, feel free to ignore all these terms!

disables your learning processes—all things that require a great deal of energy—as it focuses your resources into the systems needed for immediate survival.* This isn't a conscious choice you make. It's not voluntary. Your amygdala makes the choice for you, hence the SNS is part of the *autonomic* nervous system.

The SNS isn't a bad thing either. In fact, the SNS isn't only triggered by our amygdala telling us something scary is happening. It also kicks in when we exercise, make love, give birth, or watch an exciting superhero movie. Athletes train themselves and create rituals to activate their SNS before going into games or matches. However, if it's unconsciously triggered by your amygdala, it's possible you may overreact. In these cases, we need to learn to access our Parasympathetic Nervous System, or PNS. As you might have guessed, the PNS regulates things like slow breathing, muscle relaxation, cell replacement, digestion, concentration, and learning. It's what tells the amygdala things are okay and welcomes back our prefrontal cortex.

Emotional Regulation

As we build awareness about when we're unnecessarily in our panic zone, we can learn to get out of it by kick-starting our PNS. Try a few of these simple tools and see what you notice in your body:

* Take a few deep, slow breaths: start by recognizing all the sensations associated with your breath you weren't aware of until you read this sentence. The rise and fall of your chest, the expansion and contraction of your belly, the air entering and existing your nostrils. Go ahead, take a second ...

---

* Seriously, isn't our body amazing?

- Notice the pace of your breathing. Are you taking long, deep breaths or short, shallow breaths?

- Invite yourself to take long, deep inhales. It can be helpful to rest your hands gently on your belly to feel the air making its way in and out of your body.

- Exhale for as long as you can. Sigh aloud as you exhale. It's in the deep *exhale* that our PNS—the part of our nervous system that slows things down—is activated. Often when we're in panic and we try to take deep breaths, we're able to take in a long inhale, but we exhale everything out in one short burst. If we're not *practicing* long, deep exhales in our comfort zones, we may unwittingly activate the SNS, which is regulated by our inhales and could keep us in panic.

- Intentionally relax your body, one muscle group at a time. This helps bring your awareness back to your body and to what is real in the present moment. You can actually try tightening a muscle group in your body so you can really feel it, then observe it relaxing slowly with a deep exhale.

- Take a small sip of water or eat a snack slowly enough to notice its tastes and textures. Because the SNS shuts down our digestive system, we can kick the PNS into gear by giving our body something to digest. Awareness of the sensations (the taste, texture, temperature) can also bring us back to the present moment.

See that? You just practiced a number of emotional regulation tools, and hopefully you're a bit more connected to that neocortex. As simple as something like breathing or taking a sip of water is, the more you practice doing these things with mindful awareness, the more beneficial these acts can become.

The Dangers of Panic, the Impact of Healing

When trauma is triggered, we go into our panic zones. And because our panic responses were written into our DNA at a time when our ancestors' immediate survival was constantly under threat, they're often not appropriate responses to the triggers of modern-day life.

LiZhen is a long-time practitioner of Re-evaluation Counseling (RC), sometimes called co-counseling. It's a modality in which we don't need to be experts or licensed therapists to hold space for each other's healing. One day, she told me one of the basic principles of RC is that most of the time when we feel distress and enter our panic zone, it's because an older memory is being triggered.

When our early ancestors felt danger, chances are, it really was dangerous. It wasn't just that saber-toothed tiger—if they felt cold, they might freeze; if they felt hungry, they might starve. Their brains developed to see things in black and white. Life is either in balance or it's endangered. But these days, our modern world is mostly safe in comparison. We have developed a prefrontal cortex that allows us to take in nuanced information and assess if something is a real threat or not. But in a world filled with pandemics and climate catastrophes, our amygdala works overtime to figure out if we're safe. This, combined with language and awareness about trauma becoming more commonplace, can lead to presumptions that *everything* is traumatizing, or every moment of discomfort must be a trauma response.

It's a careful balance. We need to normalize talking about trauma and acknowledge it's something we all experience. At the same time, telling someone everything is traumatic can reinforce trauma. There's a real danger in the way I've heard trauma discussed, especially in some progressive spaces. Our well-intentioned attempts to normalize and validate trauma can lead to an overuse of the word, which in turn can paralyze people and communities, who end up swimming in a constant state of traumatic response.

Not everything uncomfortable is a trauma response—though you may be in the panic zone. The more we think everything is traumatic, the more we'll be in our panic zones. Part of the process of healing from trauma is to recognize when something is rooted in trauma and when it's not. Sometimes, a comment someone made might trigger discomfort, but it's not causing you trauma. Sometimes, a cockroach is just a cockroach.

I once heard Rev. angel kyodo williams ask, "Did I traumatize you, or did I bump into your trauma?" If I'm experiencing a trauma response, what does it matter if you caused it or not? In the moment, it may not feel like there's much of a difference. But there is a world of difference—a very important difference—between something traumatizing you and something bumping into your trauma. If you don't understand the source of something, it's hard to heal.

The more time you spend in your panic zone, the more the effects start to trickle into all areas of your life. This means even when you're in your comfort or stretch zones, you begin to have difficulties seeing nuance, taking in different perspectives, or regulating your emotions. As Menakem writes, our "trauma responses can begin to look like our personalities."[3]

We now know long-term exposure to stress and elevated levels of cortisol—one of the chemicals released in your body when the SNS kicks in—can actually change your brain structure. A 2006 study by Dr. Douglas Bremnar found that your hippocampus can actually decrease in size.[4] Since part of the role of the hippocampus is to store and organize memory, this results in a diminished ability to distinguish between past memories and present experiences. This is why when that chihuahua chases you down for belly rubs, your body feels the fear it felt twenty years ago when you were attacked by a dog.

That same study also showed long-term exposure to trauma can increase activity in the amygdala, making it more likely to trigger the panic zone and release even more cortisol into your system. This is hypervigilance: you're always looking out for the next threat, the next danger, the next thing that might harm you. And the way our psychology works is that if we're constantly looking for something, we're bound to start seeing it.

Part of our work is about learning to gain some amount of agency over our reactions to external stimuli. Yes, seeing a racial slur in the comments section of some online article *could* bring back traumatic memories for people of marginalized identities. But with practice, we can also learn to *choose* our response to external stimuli and stay in our comfort or stretch zones. We can recognize when we're not in real danger and have more agency and choice over what we do next.

How does this impact our movements?

Earlier in my life, every time I thought about my former stepfather, my mind jumped to the upper limits of my stretch zone, heading into panic. My perspective was very black and white. He was the bad guy, period, end of story. There was no room in my mind for nuance or complexity. Over the years, partially thanks to the medicine of time and partially due to the work I've done, I've gained the ability to see things differently. These days when I think about him, I see a deeply broken man. I'd always heard whispers about the violence, abuse, and discrimination he faced growing up, as well as the shame he felt about his Indigenous identity in his younger life. Knowing what I now know about trauma responses, it's very obvious he was a deeply traumatized man who didn't know what to do with his own pain and released it on us. I can have compassion for that and pray for his healing. And I have not forgotten the things he did. I have not forgotten the pain my family still lives with.

But here's a key lesson I've learned along the way—compassion isn't a zero-sum game. Cultivating compassion for him doesn't mean I have less for myself or my family. It doesn't mean I want less accountability from him. The well of love is infinite, and I just need to tap into it a little bit more. It's not going to run out.

Unprocessed trauma has obvious relational costs, including frequent conflicts or inability to build trust and intimacy. If I'm filled with unhealed, unprocessed trauma, I'm less likely to be able to practice nonviolence with myself, within movements, and with the world at large. I'm going to bring my brokenness into these spaces. If we're trying to build a world that centers relationship and healing, we have to embody those things in the process. Social change work is long-term work. It's the work of generations, not five-year strategic plans, grant periods, and election cycles. Long-term thinking and strategy happen in the prefrontal cortex—in the comfort zone. The more we're in a place of panic, the less strategic and visionary we will be.

> But perhaps one of the biggest impacts is this: *when we're in our panic zones, we lose our ability to heal and practice nonviolence*, our ability to see nuance, to hold multiple perspectives, to have compassion or at least curiosity about our "opponents," to think about concepts like interdependence, to reconsider our past as we continue toward healing.

The more brokenness there is within a movement, the more fractured we're going to be. We'll have more conflicts we won't be able to reconcile, we'll cause harm to one another and create more trauma. And the more fractured we are in our movements, the less we'll be able to bring healing to the world. A fractured and traumatized movement cannot help us heal from legacies such as genocide and enslavement.

Deep, Dark Legacies

Having real conversations about racial healing is a scary thing. But it's not life-threatening. However, because a country such as the United States has not had a chance to heal from its past as a collective body and integrate the traumatic memory of genocide and enslavement, every time the conversation is brought up, we go into panic:

- We start screaming at each other.
- The political left accuses everyone who isn't on "their side" of being white supremacists.
- The political right accuses anyone calling for reparations of trying to erase white people.

This is because the traumatic *emotional* memory triggered is from a time when dynamics of race and difference led to people being killed in greater numbers than they are today. Back in the day when these traumatic memories first entered our collective bodies, the enslavement of Black people was the norm in the US South and elsewhere.

- In the US and other colonial legal systems, the life of a Black person was worth less than that of a white person.
- There were groups of white supremacists running around slaughtering Black people without accountability.
- White people were afraid of being killed in response, because they knew their treatment of Black folks could elicit that sort of response.

We can't have a conversation about racial healing if we're screaming at each other. We can't heal if our traumatic memory tells us others are trying to kill us. We can't heal if all sides of the discussion are in the panic zone.

While wealthy white politicians may not have had a traumatic upbringing themselves, we all end up embodying the collective culture of our country. Because we don't have enough healed bodies in the United States, we haven't been able to create a collective culture and nervous system that allows for having deep, scary conversations while staying in our comfort and stretch zones.

This dynamic becomes even more important if we believe direct actions may play a role in our collective healing.* Direct action spaces are really tense environments with lots of stressful sensory inputs. People scream and chant, police in riot gear threaten arrests or tear gas, people throw objects. It's an environment made for the panic zone that requires serious training and preparation to breathe deeply through. Chances are, you're not going to get killed at a protest in the United States.† But your amygdala may play tricks on you, and you may feel that way—especially if you come from a marginalized identity. But we have to remember hypervigilance is a sign of trauma, and trauma responses aren't always accurate.

Luckily, it turns out our brains are much more resilient than previously thought. Neuroplasticity, the ability of our brain's neural networks to change, grow, and reorganize, was until recently thought only to be possible in childhood. It was believed that once we're grown up, if our brains become damaged, that's it for us. We now know that's not true. Western modalities such as cognitive behavioral therapy, functional electrical stimulation therapy, and even virtual reality immersion therapy have all shown signs of stimulating neuroplasticity. Science is also just

---

* Spoiler: I do.

† Multiple activists have been killed in protests in the last several years. However, protesting in the United States or other democratic countries today is still a relatively safe thing to do relative to the past or in countries ruled by a dictatorship today.

starting to catch up to the wisdom of Eastern spiritual teachers and Indigenous healers. Recent studies have shown the effectiveness of meditation, spiritual rituals, and the use of plant medicine in promoting neuroplasticity. Like all living systems, our nervous systems have a chance to grow and adapt throughout our lives.

The more each of us can commit to healing, the healthier our movement spaces will become. And the healthier our movement spaces become, the more healing we'll be able to facilitate, on larger and larger scales.

CHAPTER 4

The Fractal Nature of Trauma and Healing

Trauma decontextualized in a person looks like personality. Trauma decontextualized in a family looks like family traits. Trauma decontextualized in people looks like culture.

RESMAA MENAKEM

Fractals aren't just mathematics; they're also beautiful art, as they allow us to see the unseeable and express the inexpressible.

BENOIT MANDELBROT, THE MATHEMATICIAN
WHO COINED THE TERM "FRACTAL"

A FRACTAL is a pattern or design that looks the same no matter how far you zoom in or out: the pattern repeats itself, over and over and over again. We see examples of fractals throughout nature, from snowflakes to nautilus seashells to Romanesco broccoli.

I once heard mathematician Steven Strogatz say, "As we deepen our understanding of the natural world, we realize fractals . . . appear in the fabric of reality itself." An example: Have you ever found yourself driving down a highway in some dry, rural area and seen what looks like a tiny little tornado? Those things are called "dust devils," and they form because of hot air rising from the surface interacting with cool air above. Zoom out a little bit, and you see a tornado creates the same shape. Now zoom out even more, and picture how a hurricane circles around the eye of a storm. It creates a similar pattern, just at a different scale. Zoom out again, even more this time, and picture the planets in our solar system rotating around our sun—a similar pattern presenting itself at a much larger scale. Zoom out even more and you'll see our galaxy circling its center. From the smallest to the largest scale, we're all governed by the same laws of the universe. Therefore, we see the same pattern over and over again.

The idea that change is fractal isn't a new concept. adrienne maree brown talked about this in *Emergent Strategy*,[5] and before her, Gandhi and others talked about the inseparability of internal and external work. For Gandhi, the work of personal healing, community building, and systemic change were all just different scales of the same work.

Fractal patterns in nature

Core Trauma

You may be asking, *What do fractals have to do with trauma and healing?* There's a person in my life we'll call "Ursula." Ursula has a lifetime of unhealed trauma. It lives deep inside of her and impacts her life in myriad ways. For years, I have tried to support her through all the ways this trauma manifests in her life. I listened, counseled, and simply sat with her through challenges in her intimate relationships, finances, struggles at work, relationships with her children, and substance abuse.

Each time I felt she made a breakthrough, a new crisis popped up. It was like a never-ending game of whack-a-mole. She'd find a new job, then immediately blow her entire paycheck on some unnecessary impulse purchase. I'd mediate a conflict between her and her brother only for her to get into a huge argument with her daughter. At some point, I realized all these issues were just surface-level manifestations of a deeper, core childhood trauma. We'd be dealing with this trauma's 10,000 ways of manifesting until she healed it. It *was* an endless game of whack-a-mole.

Most of us experience things early in childhood that create an imprint in our bodies: our "core trauma." These experiences can happen at such an early age we may not even recollect the events. While the severity can vary greatly from person to person, it's very common for these experiences to have lifelong ramifications that manifest as various insecurities, trust issues, or anxiety, all of which may affect our reactivity and how easily we jump into our panic zone. All these effects may result in the perpetuation of harm and cause more trauma. Unhealed wounds tend to manifest in ways that constantly put self and other in difficult, unhealthy, or dangerous situations.

But back to fractals. Let's take Ursula's story and zoom out one level.

Years ago, I volunteered with an organization that does incredible work supporting the healing of people who come from marginalized communities. Let's call this organization "URSULA Inc."* As powerful as their work was, the organization had a seemingly never-ending pattern of conflicts and scandals—constant staff turnover, volunteers leaving on bad terms, lawsuits, questionable use of funding, lack of clear communication. During the organization's early years, unhealthy practices and patterns became embedded as the organizational culture. For example, early leaders had a very hierarchical way of making decisions with little communication or care for the people who would be impacted.

URSULA Inc.'s early life also had major blind spots around race. As an organization dedicated to social justice, they believed the culture of white supremacy didn't apply to them. As a result, the leadership refused to address concerns brought to them by their staff and volunteers of color.

Harm happened, and it never healed. It just got stuck—core trauma.

Now, years later, despite having a completely different board and new leadership, that toxic culture has outlived the individuals and become institutionalized. And because this history and its repercussions on URSULA Inc.'s organizational culture have never been addressed, they continue to deal with conflict after conflict, like a never-ending game of whack-a-mole.

Now, let's zoom out one more level. The United States of America.† Home of the free, land of the brave. The beacon of freedom, the symbol of liberty, the greatest democracy in the world. And yet, the US has one of the highest rates of incarceration in the world. There are over 650,000 homeless people as

---

* United for Restorative Solutions to Unjust Laws and Actions. Not bad huh?

† Get it? UrSulA? USA? I was proud of that one. I thought of it days after reading *Harry Potter and the Chamber of Secrets*, where we find out the name Voldemort is actually an anagram—perhaps I was inspired.

of this book's writing.[6] It's one of the few "developed" nations to not guarantee its citizens health care, with medical expenses being the most common reason for bankruptcy despite paying more per capita for health care than any other nation on Earth. We have a corrupt electoral system, a broken educational system, mass shootings daily,* a mental health crisis, an opioid crisis.... It's as if we're playing a never-ending game of whack-a-mole.

Sound familiar? Perhaps it is because we—*collectively*—hold some core trauma that, like Ursula's and URSULA, Inc.'s core trauma, has never been healed and therefore continues to perpetuate new harms. As a nation-state, our history starts with the genocide of Indigenous peoples and the enslavement of African peoples—two of the greatest acts of systemic violence in human history.

These are *traumatic* experiences this country went through early in its formation—in its childhood. Our core trauma. Not just for Indigenous and African peoples, but for the white settlers so far removed from their own sense of humanity and the truth of interdependence they were able to commit such gross acts of violence against people while pretending their souls weren't also being traumatized.

Let's come back down to the interpersonal scale of the fractal. For a long time, my family never talked about the traumatic years of my childhood. Sure, in small, hidden ways there were whispers of it. I shared my story with friends. My sisters might mention something to each other in passing. There were murmurs,

---

* According to Gun Violence Archives, a nonprofit organization that tracks gun violence, in 2022 alone there were 695 mass shootings in the United States (mass shootings being defined as incidents where at least four people are shot, not including the shooter). In case you forgot, there are 365 days in a year. During a 4.5 day stretch over the Fourth of July weekend of 2023, the US experienced 22 mass shootings. At least 20 people were killed, and 126 injured.

rumors shared one-on-one. But as a family, we never dove into it. Thus, the trauma we all experienced got frozen and stuck.

Now let's move back up to a larger scale of the fractal. As a nation, we have never talked about the traumatic years of our collective childhood. Sure, in some small, hidden ways there are whispers of it. We talk about it in activist spaces. Radicals read books about it and have healing rituals. Murmurs and rumors are spoken in progressive circles. But as a nation, we've never dived into it. Thus, the trauma we all experienced got frozen and stuck. We, as a country—collectively—are traumatized. Some wounds can heal on their own through the medicine of time. Others linger in our bodies as traumatic memories and need more explicit healing modalities. The trauma from things as severe as genocide and enslavement doesn't just goes away on its own.

As a nation, this core trauma has led to generations of cycles of harm. The enslavement of African peoples gave way to the convict leasing system, which gave way to Jim Crow, which gave way to mass incarceration. The physical genocide of Indigenous peoples gave way to cultural genocide through boarding schools, spiritual genocide through the destruction of sacred land, and economic genocide through the reservations system. Issues ranging from racial microaggressions and the killings of unarmed Black people to the Standing Rock protests and efforts to change racist names and mascots of sports teams all stem from these contexts.

Education. Criminal Justice. Health care. Voter rights. These are surface-level manifestations of our country's core trauma. And until we can go all the way back in our history and address it, we'll always be spinning our wheels, trying to whack the newest mole.

To be fair, the United States is not alone. It is, I fear, an experience shared by our entire species. Whether we're talking about the atrocities committed by my Japanese ancestors during World War II, the 1994 Rwandan genocide, the Chinese Cultural Revolution, the Middle East being a constant pawn in attempts by Western nations to control its oil, the horrors of the Spanish Inquisition, or the slaughters committed by the ancient Indian emperor Ashoka before his conversion to Buddhism, all our ancestors have traumas that need healing. Even more universal is the reality of the brutal, violent lives lived by our hunter and gatherer ancestors;* the loss of the sacred feminine most of our cultures experienced thousands of years ago; and the violent disconnection from nature driven by the industrial revolution, the separation growing wider with each generation.

Because we live in a fractal world and because we're governed by the same universal laws, trauma impacts Ursula, URSULA, Inc., and the USA all the same.

Awakening Collective Trauma

When I look out at the world in the last several years, I see more and more signs of collective panic. It feels like our collective trauma is being triggered left and right. Take the United States's suppressed trauma around race. While the trauma never went away, for some time we did a good job repressing it. During the Civil Rights era, the movement brought some of those issues to the surface and urged us to deal with them. Rosa Parks's mugshot following her arrest, the image of Emmett Till's mangled face after his lynching, the students who were murdered in Mississippi for registering Black voters, and scenes of young children getting attacked by fire hoses in Birmingham filled the airwaves, forcing a conversation the nation tried to ignore.

In some ways, this wasn't that different from me reading my letter to my family. Both interventions forced old traumas to

---

* We oftentimes romanticize these simpler times. And in many ways, I believe our hunter-gatherer ancestors lived a lifestyle closer to our true essence— living in small villages in relationship with the land, the sky, the seasons. Yet we sometimes forget how violent and brutal their lives were.

the table so they could be discussed. Both disrupted business as usual.

The resulting concessions from the state—the Civil Rights Act, the Voting Rights Act, etc.—did make significant improvements in the lives of millions of Americans. But they also pacified our nation by placing an even larger Band-Aid over the still gaping wound of slavery. These Band-Aids were not enough: they sought to make things easier for Black people moving forward but did nothing to heal the 350-year legacy of white supremacy and its ensuing trauma—no reparations, no truth and reconciliation commissions, nothing to address the hundreds of years of pain. So, the wound festered and continued to seep out through race riots, poverty, and the war on drugs. New Band-Aids like mass incarceration continued to try to suppress the issue and convince the public "We've healed that wound."

While decades of hard organizing from the grassroots made incremental changes in everything from education to prison reform, the Black Lives Matter Movement broke open the floodgates once again. Images of the killings of Oscar Grant, Trayvon Martin, Michael Brown, Tamir Rice, Sandra Bland, Breonna Taylor, George Floyd, and countless others had the same effect of the Civil Rights Movement filling the airwaves with the violence of white supremacy. They ripped open the bandage and exposed trauma that had never fully healed.

Every time a wound is opened up, it has an opportunity to heal. A surgeon, after all, has to cut someone open before they can operate on them. But there's also danger, because now you have a wide-open wound. You're closer than ever to healing, but you're also more vulnerable than ever.

The success of the Movement for Black Lives cannot be overstated. Before the movement took off, we weren't having conversations about defunding police or police abolition in mainstream spaces. At the same time, I fear the movement's rise may have caused a painful side effect, particularly for Black folks who were reminded over and over again that, in the eyes of law enforcement, their lives don't matter. It wasn't just the videos, nor was the trauma just for Black people. The constant, escalated battles against police—the tear gas, the arrests, the violence—were traumatizing for all involved: the police, the protesters who were in the streets following each killing, as well as everyone witnessing. Though so much healing and empowerment happened within movement spaces and major cultural shifts were won, there was never any real accountability from the state or efforts at national healing. I'm afraid a scalpel was used to open up an old wound, we dug around carelessly inside of it, and then barely patched it back up.

The forceful surfacing of old wounds also had an impact on white, mainstream America. The majority of white Americans had and still have little to no idea about the true history of violence against Black people in this country or about the impact of intergenerational trauma. Because of this, the outpouring of grief and rage into the streets wasn't understood in the proper context. That ignorance, combined with the media's portrayal of these uprisings as "violent riots," stoked fear and triggered the collective trauma of many white people as well. In this context, Donald Trump was elected president in 2016, and again in 2024—further triggers of collective trauma.

As someone who has worked a lot with trauma, it's very obvious to me Trump is a deeply traumatized man. It's written all over his face, his words, and his actions. With everything he does and says, every battle he has with the media, every tweet he sends out, he tries to fill some gaping hole in his heart. I believe witnessing someone operate so clearly from a place of trauma in such a public space may have triggered the trauma of an entire nation. I look at all the people "inspired" by him, and I have to wonder if it was inspiration or some form of trauma bonding—emotionally entangled dynamics rooted in shared traumatic experiences.

In so many ways, I believe Trump's trauma mirrors America's collective trauma, especially for white men who see themselves reflected in his image. When people see Trump, they identify with him, with his trauma, and with his responses to his trauma—his fear of those who look different, his scarcity mindset, his violent outbursts, his holding on to a delusion of the "good old days" that served as the foundation for his *Make America Great Again* slogan. It feels familiar to them, so it's incredibly relatable. Consciously or not, Trump spoke directly to people's traumas and their fears—two of our greatest motivators. In a trauma-bonded dynamic, the emotions of one person can be projected and felt by the other. So, the anger and fear Trump constantly projects is felt by his supporters as their own repressed anger and fear.

Let's summarize: the protesters in the streets are traumatized. The police are traumatized. The counter-protesters are traumatized. The folks sitting at home watching this all play out on the news are traumatized. The left is traumatized. The right is traumatized. Apolitical people are traumatized. Marginalized people are traumatized. And in that context, we experienced a global pandemic. . . . And *all of that* is happening within the context of the escalating climate crisis . . . sigh . . .

This is an era of social, political, and ecological collapse.

Collectively, there are constant triggers and stress points in our lives. As a species, that's always been the case, but I can't help but feel these have been escalating exponentially over the last ten years. The result is our *collective* trauma awakening at unprecedented levels, putting us into a collective panic zone. When so many traumatized people meet up in the real world, it's trauma meeting trauma, panic meeting panic. That is not a space conducive to healing.

Trauma Responses at Scale

If our collective traumas are constantly triggered, we must also be experiencing collective trauma responses. And, as it turns out in this fractal universe, collective trauma responses look a lot like individual trauma responses. Have you noticed in recent years we've been—culturally and collectively—more on edge, that people everywhere are having oversized reactions that don't always feel appropriate? Whether it's people freaking out and getting kicked out of stores for refusing to wear a mask during the pandemic or the mere presence of a red baseball cap* setting emotions ablaze, it's as if our collective nervous system is afflicted.

When we panic, our long-term thinking goes out the window. We get into tunnel vision, and we can only focus on what's immediately in front of us. Many of our political battles these days, whether in grassroots communities or national politics, seem incredibly short-sighted. Another sign we're in panic is the inability to hold complexity and nuance. When we zoom out, who can argue we're not living in some of the most extremely polarized times in generations? In our public political discourse, you're either a white supremacist or a Marxist.

When you're in your panic zone, you lose the ability to take in, process, and interpret information accurately. Zooming out to look at society, we see a culture that refuses to accept information, no matter how much scientific consensus there is. Whether it's the resurgence of a movement of flat-earthers,† climate change deniers, or people who refuse to believe the coronavirus pandemic was real, more and more people are unwilling to accept viewpoints that differ from theirs, despite overwhelming evidence.

---

* The bright red "Make America Great Again" caps have become a symbol for Donald Trump's supporters.

† Not long ago, I did a deep dive and watched countless hours of videos and read endless articles on this. Did you know there is an international movement of people who believe the Earth is flat and a global conspiracy brainwashes us into thinking we live on a globe? These people have conferences and everything. I'm so fascinated by this phenomenon.

Even among my friends, I see articles and memes shared on social media that contain headlines so obviously not true, a quick thirty-second Google search could easily disprove them. Yet because we're so set in our beliefs and refuse to take in new information, we see a meme and share it immediately and impulsively without questioning it.* Another way our inability to take in information manifests at scale is in how we interpret nonverbal communication or tone. When in panic, you can see a neutral face as aggressive or a scared face as angry. This may contribute to seeing so many people as the enemy and the uptick in protester versus counter-protester violence. Our collective hypervigilance, which of course is another sign of trauma, is evident in a culture of constantly assessing each other as a potential threat. In movement spaces, there are constant accusations of infiltration, of selling out, or of someone not being "woke" enough.

As individuals, when we enter our panic zones, we get dissociated. The adrenaline in our bodies may prevent us from noticing we're hurt, physically or otherwise. We may not be aware of our own needs. We may be slowly killing ourselves through unhealthy lifestyles or by sabotaging relationships but unable to see it. When we enter our collective panic zones, the same things happen on a collective level. The adrenaline running through our collective body may prevent us from noticing we are hurting or that we are hurting each other. We may not be aware of our collective needs. We may be slowly destroying our family or community, but unable to see it.

Luckily, it doesn't have to be this way.

---

* This is pet peeve of mine. If you see a meme or an article with a headline that seems hard to believe, *please* take thirty seconds and do a quick search before sharing it. Sites like Snopes, Politifact, or FactCheck can be helpful. I've also seen people repost articles from years ago in response to current events, which can cause confusion. There's too much misinformation out there, so let's all try to take a deep breath and not be so impulsive with our social media triggers.

CHAPTER 5

Healing in a Fractal World

You are not a drop in the ocean. You are the entire ocean in a drop.

RUMI

I have seen that we cannot fully create effective movements for social change if individuals struggling for that change are not also self-actualized or working toward that end. When wounded individuals come together in groups to make change, our collective struggle is often undermined by all that has not been dealt with emotionally.

BELL HOOKS

JUST AS HARM and trauma exist in fractals, patterns repeating themselves at all scales, so does healing. Whatever healing is possible at the smallest scale is also possible at the largest scale.

In 2018, I had the privilege to meet Cynthia, an Indigenous mother living in Northern California. Almost twenty years prior, Cynthia had experienced the most tragic thing a mother could: the brutal murder of her beloved fourteen-year-old son Mitchell, a young man who loved to play baseball. After years of healing, she reached out to the California Department of Corrections and Rehabilitation (CDCR), who put her in touch with the Ahimsa Collective. Cynthia was interested in a Victim Offender

Dialogue, or VOD,* a chance to meet face-to-face with the men who killed her son.

I don't know what kind of spiritual strength is required to go through what Cynthia endured and emerge as strong and loving as she is. Of course, it hasn't been easy for her, and it's not like the healing process is "over." That's not how healing works. There are good days and there are bad days. But her strength and resolve, for which she credits her family as well as her Choctaw spiritual and cultural practices, were obvious from the first time my co-facilitator Bonnie and I made the 2.5-hour drive up from Oakland to meet her.

Preparations for VODs aren't always easy or straightforward. Sometimes the person who committed the harm isn't open to having a dialogue. Sometimes the facilitators feel the person may not be ready to take full accountability for their crime and bringing the two sides together may actually be retraumatizing for the survivor. Any number of things can go wrong. A dialogue may take years to plan or may not happen at all.

Shortly after our first meeting with Cynthia, Bonnie and I traveled to Old Folsom Prison to meet with Richard, one of the two men convicted of Mitchell's murder. You never know with these things, but after meeting him, we both felt a dialogue between Richard and Cynthia could have happened that day. Not only had Cynthia spent the past twenty years doing the hard work of healing; Richard had also been working on repair.

About six months later, Cynthia, Bonnie, and I traveled back to the prison for the dialogue. It's a day I'll never forget. I remember getting Cynthia settled into the room where the dialogue would take place, leaving her with Bonnie, and going around

---

* It's an unfortunate name for an incredibly powerful program. Because it's officially run out of CDCR's Office of Victim and Survivor Rights and Services, they got to name the program, despite efforts in the Restorative Justice world to move away from divisive labels like "victim" and "offender."

the corner to the holding tank to get Richard. He was shaking. I gently put a hand on his shoulder and talked to him for a while. At some point, I asked if he was ready. I immediately realized how silly the question was. How do you ever get "ready" to have a conversation with the mother of the person you murdered? Despite this impossible question, he told me he was "As ready as I'll ever be," got up, and slowly walked around the corner.

As soon as he saw Cynthia, he broke down. I watched Cynthia gently stand up, open her arms, and embrace Richard as he collapsed into her. They embraced for what felt like an eternity. For the next six hours, they talked. In one moment, Cynthia took Richard's hands in hers and told him, "I dreamt I had to hold your hands, because these are the hands that took my son's life, and I need to have a different relationship with them." Throughout the day, I asked myself what I did to earn the honor of watching this magic.

In the mid 1980s, Cynthia had moved to a Tribal Ranchería* in Northern California to be closer to family. She settled in the small town where Richard grew up. He and Mitchell, who were about the same age, used to play baseball together. Cynthia mentioned driving Mitchell to all of those practices and always seeing Richard walking by himself. She told Richard she felt bad for him— she knew he came from a broken home and there was no one to drive him to practice. Richard said during those difficult years, he felt like no one saw him, no one cared. And now, to hear from the mother of the person he killed that *she* had seen him, *she* had cared.... Through his tears, he managed to say, "You saying that just now helped me heal something I've been holding for thirty years."

Healing is a complex thing. Cynthia wasn't there to promise Richard forgiveness, nor that she would advocate for his

---

* Rancherías are small rural communities of Indigenous peoples located throughout California.

release at his next parole hearing. But it was clear big things were moving in the direction of healing.

With both of their permission, I share just a small piece of their story, because I need us to remember that even after unimaginable tragedy, healing is possible. I need all of us to know that no matter how great the harm, healing is always an option. It's never guaranteed. And it may be a really messy process. It will most likely take a long time and a lot of hard, gut-wrenching work. It will also take a level of fierceness and lots of vulnerability. But it's always possible.

If healing between two individuals whose lives are brought together by such deep tragedy is possible, healing wounds and divides at any scale—healing between races, genders, and species—is possible because . . . fractals. What is possible at the smallest scale is possible at the largest scale. So much of our pain is rooted in collective experiences, from the climate crisis to oppression. If the harm happens in relationship and in community, the healing must also take place in relationship and in community.

One of the most powerful examples of collective healing I've heard about happened on December 4, 2016. In the midst of the battle against the Dakota Access Pipeline, where soldiers from the National Guard assisted police agencies in quashing protests, hundreds of US veterans lined up in formation and got down on their knees to apologize and ask for forgiveness in front of a group of Indigenous elders.

Wesley Clark Jr., who led the veterans, spoke these words:

Many of us, me particularly, are from the units that have hurt you over the many years. We came. We fought you. We took your land. We signed treaties that we broke. We stole minerals from your sacred hills. We blasted the faces of our presidents onto your sacred mountain. Then we took still more land and then we took your children and then we tried

to take your language and we tried to eliminate your lan-
guage that God gave you, the Creator gave you. We didn't
respect you, we polluted your Earth, we've hurt you in so
many ways, but we've come to say we are sorry. We are at
your service, and we beg for your forgiveness.

The veterans weren't necessarily apologizing for things they
personally did. Most of them had spent their time in service
overseas. But they recognized they were part of a system that
had caused untold harm to Indigenous communities and that
continues to do so. This was powerful not only because of the
vulnerability of the apology. The veterans also brought fierceness: they participated in the protests and direct actions to
defend Indigenous land and stop the ongoing desecration of
their home.

This is collective, generational healing.

Our Work First

Imagine if Cynthia went into that room pointing her finger, calling Richard a murderer and trying to shame him. She might be
justified, but it wouldn't have created space for healing. If anything, Richard was in his panic zone, and it was Cynthia who
helped bring him back into his stretch zone so they could engage
in dialogue. Cynthia took deep breaths, humanized Richard, vulnerably shared her story, and listened deeply to his. She didn't go
in with an attitude of "I was the one who was hurt, so you need to
listen to me. I don't care about your story."

In order for the possibility of healing to scale up, the principles, the spirit, and the strategy that guides healing work at
small, interpersonal levels must be used at the largest scales of
change. What happened between Cynthia and Richard and what
happened between those veterans and Indigenous leaders is the
same process, just happening at different scales.

I am often frustrated by activist communities who, at least in theory, believe in principles of restorative justice. Many of us are committed to using these practices within our movements* because we have some sense they can bring about healing and transformation. But when it comes to organizing protests, demonstrations, and direct actions to address systemic power, we turn to tactics that create a clear division between "us" and "them" and begin shaming, name-calling, and trying to beat "them" into submission. We don't make the connection that when we use tactics grounded in the "us versus them" worldview with a desire to shame and punish, we use the frameworks at the foundation of the carceral systems of "justice" we're organizing against. If those worldviews don't work to transform relationships at the interpersonal level, they won't be effective at the systemic level either. Because, you know, fractals.

How do we build resistance movements grounded in unwavering belonging? How do we initiate conversations about traumatic events without putting people into panic?

Ultimately, the work of social transformation is about asking society to have the hardest conversations it has ever had. What does it mean for us to zoom out of the fractal from Cynthia and Richard's relationship and imagine a collective movement having that same conversation, preparing ourselves in the way they prepared for their dialogue? The two of them did an incredible amount of emotional labor ahead of what may have been the hardest conversation of their lives. I wonder if we've fully accepted the grandeur of our undertaking. Has it really sunk in, what we're trying to do? If we're asking society to heal its deepest wounds, we'd better have done our own work first. How can

---

* And let's be real here—a lot of us aren't. A lot of us give lip service to things like restorative and transformative justice, but then tear each other to bits when there is harm within movement spaces. We just sit in a circle and use a talking stick as we shame each other.

we ask society to open up and transform its deepest legacies of violence if we're not willing to look at our own shadows?

I have my doubts Donald Trump will experience such personal transformation in this lifetime. But when I engage in movements that oppose his policies, I still try to hold him as a human being capable of healing and deserving of dignity. I see him for what he is—a hurt, lonely, and traumatized person far removed from his own sense of humanity. My compassion for him may never change him, *but it does something to me.* It matters to *me.* It reminds me that even he is part of the interwoven web of humanity. And if he's part of that web, I must be also. Having compassion for him isn't about some unrealistic fantasy that loving him will change his behaviors—it's about reminding me of my own sense of belonging.

There's not much we can do to control other people and how they show up in the world. The best we can do is control how we show up, be intentional about what we're contributing to a conflict, and hope we can impact the moment in a skillful and constructive way. The necessity of our doing our own work isn't just so we're in integrity with what we ask of the world. It's also for pragmatic reasons: the more escalated a conflict is, the more likely it is *someone* is going to end up in panic. The more we open up discussions about trauma, the more likely it is we may inadvertently *put* someone in their panic zone. This, in turn, makes it more likely panicked energy will put us into our panic zone.

As we prepare to respond to escalated harm, we need to escalate the healing we're doing ourselves. We need to be more grounded than we've ever been—ready to be in the midst of chaos and crisis, to be in the midst of a possible collapse of our ecological and social systems, engaging in national and global conversations about the history of violence and the future of our species, all while remembering to breathe.

That takes practice and preparation.

In the World

For myself, a lot of the practice and preparation started at home. One of the reasons it took me so long to begin to have healing conversations with my family is because I knew I had to do enough of my own healing first. After my own breakdown/breakthrough moment at my first Jam, I started taking more and more baby steps. I started meditating more. Reading about other people's experiences. Then, when I was ready, I began to escalate a tad bit more. Journaling about my experience. Talking to a therapist or trusted friend. Slowly starting to remember what those moments felt like and creating space in my body to feel those feelings again. As my muscles began to build, I began to escalate even more. Talking about it in group spaces. Attempting to write that first letter to my family. Not being afraid to break down, knowing I have the strength to build myself back up.

If I'd approached my family and begun opening these wounds before I was ready, it's very possible I might have thrown everyone—including myself—into our panic zones. All four of us being panicked and trying to have the most difficult conversation of our lives would not have gone well. I knew I had to do enough of my own work to speak to these deep wounds while staying in my stretch zone. Not only so I could be present enough to help facilitate the conversation, but also to model some level of balance between vulnerable emotions and a fierce groundedness.

When we experience traumatic events, the emotions associated with them are so scary we often banish them from our memory. We push them down into the depths of our unconscious mind so we don't have to think about them. In doing so, we fracture and fragment our own story. We deny a part of our own experience. Healing from these events means bringing those banished memories into our conscious minds and beginning to talk about and process these experiences out loud—often for the first time in years or decades. To create space for something you've ignored for so long. It means building a relationship with that experience, accepting that it happened, and allowing yourself to feel all the suppressed emotions. This creates space for the experience in our bodies. We can accept that those things happened and that, as hard as they were to go through, we are now safe.

This is what it means to "integrate" traumatic experiences on a personal level. It's accepting all of who you are and all of what you've gone through. It's carrying that traumatic experience as a part of you as you move forward. It's becoming whole again. At the collective level, in our traumatized world, we are incredibly fragmented. There's an "us," and so many groups of "them." Healing at this scale is also about integrating all of who we are and becoming whole again. The more I heal from and integrate my own traumatic experiences, the more I stay grounded in the midst of other people's panic. I don't engage in my own healing just to benefit myself and my family. I'm also preparing to engage with the trauma of those around me.

It took me eight years to read that letter to my family. So how long before we're able to build a movement that can open up such a discussion at a global scale? The leaders of the Nashville lunch counter sit-ins during the Civil Rights Movement trained for almost six months before embarking on direct action. Gandhi's Shanti Sena lived in an ashram together for fifteen years before embarking on the Salt March.* Unfortunately, we're in the midst of the largest crisis our species has ever faced. We might not have fifteen years.

---

* Loosely translated as "Peace Army," Gandhi tasked seventy-eight of his most dedicated followers to initiate the Salt March.

Ideally, as we engage in these challenging conversations, all sides will have regulated nervous systems. But because of the urgency of the crisis, fierce vulnerability suggests we may need to *push* these discussions into our public discourse. The legacy of nonviolence has always been about forcing issues to the table. Forcing the truth about the need for racial reconciliation or the reality of the climate crisis will put a lot of people into panic. If we're prepared for it, that isn't necessarily a bad thing. While we may not have been living in an ashram together for the last fifteen years preparing for this moment, many of us have been individually engaged in these practices for decades. Together, we can hold space.

Accountability in Healing

When harm happens, accountability is a prerequisite to healing a relationship. Truth and reconciliation commissions create space for survivors to tell their story and perhaps even for the people who caused the harm to open up about theirs. While I'm no expert in national truth and reconciliation efforts like those that took place in South Africa and Rwanda, I've heard from those involved that accountability can be a crucial missing ingredient. In these cases, such efforts seem to create space for the vulnerability of personal stories but lack the fierceness to demand accountability and reparations. The Grassroots Reparations Campaign says, "reparations are the midpoint between truth and reconciliation."

Dr. King once said: "Power without love is reckless and abusive, and love without power is sentimental and anemic."[7] The fierceness of accountability is essential in any movement that works toward healing and justice. Only with this element can we respond to systems and institutions that have caused—and continue to cause—untold harm. And yet, because "accountability" is often conflated with concepts like "punishment" and "consequences," movements for justice often harness the fierceness to make concrete demands but lack the vulnerability of healing dialogues.

If we make demands of those who cause harm but aren't willing to share our heartbreak and hear their story, we practice fierceness and skip vulnerability. But if we only make space for the two sides to share their story and lack a process of accountability, we practice vulnerability without fierceness.

Because movements often use tactics like direct action to create accountability, it's important we have a shared understanding of what we mean by the term. I wrote a little bit about this in *Healing Resistance,* but I continue to grapple with the concept myself, so bear with me. Right now, the formula I use is: Insight + Remorse + Amends = Accountability.

Insight

When I talk about "insight," I mean our ability to see things for what they truly are, beyond the assumptions we make, beyond our subjective interpretations of an event, and without any lens of unprocessed trauma in front of our eyes. In the Buddhist tradition, the word *vipassana* can be translated as "the insight that comes from seeing things as they truly are."

Thích Nhất Hạnh, in relaying the teachings of the Buddha, teaches all things are impermanent and can't exist in isolation.* Without these two truths, a seed couldn't become a plant. For a seed to become a plant, it undergoes countless changes. Nothing about the seed is static, or else it wouldn't grow into a plant. It couldn't transform into a plant without integrating the nutrients from the soil, the rays of the sun, the labor of the farmer. The

---

* This comes out of a core Buddhist teaching on the "three marks of existence": all things that exist have the characteristics of unsatisfactory-ness (*dukkha*), impermanence (*anicca*) and non-self (*anatta*).

transformation doesn't happen on its own, but in deep interdependence (or "interbeing" in Thích Nhất Hạnh's words) with
everything else that is.

In one of his most famous teachings, Thích Nhất Hạnh
explains a piece of paper is actually a cloud: without cloud there
is no rain, and without rain there are no trees, and without trees
there's no paper. If it weren't for the cloud, the paper couldn't
exist. In fact, the "paper" is made up entirely of "non-paper elements." My own body wouldn't exist without the food I've consumed that has turned into new cells in my body. And that food
wouldn't exist without all the natural elements and human hands
that grew it, harvested it, packed it, transported it, and prepared
the meal.

It's not just "good" things that are interdependent. Everything is, including suffering and trauma. This book wouldn't
exist without the computer I am typing on, which couldn't
exist without the minerals used to make the microchip, which
wouldn't exist without the wars that fuel the mining of those
minerals, the labor of the factory workers, and all the exploitation along the way.[*]

If it weren't for my former stepfather, I wouldn't be who I am
today.

My trauma is deeply interdependent with my stepfather's
own unprocessed trauma. This means the person I am today is
deeply influenced by every person who ever hurt my stepfather.
I may have never met them, but their experiences impacted me in
a very real way. This means my traumas are interdependent with
the traumas of countless individuals I will never meet. If we're
not aware of all of the factors from which conflict blooms, we see
a mirage—a delusion. We're not seeing what truly is. Without

---

[*] Of course, there *is* a way for us to access these minerals without war and
exploitation. But in the world as it is, access to these minerals and the violence that comes with it are inextricably linked.

insight into the true nature of reality, we're unlikely to be able to heal ourselves or our relationships. In Kingian Nonviolence, we're taught every conflict has history. We usually only see the exact moment a conflict erupts into violence; we rarely examine the conflict carefully enough to unpack its history. Without understanding the history, we cannot see the truth of the present moment.

Accountability is not something you can force down someone's throat. Holding space for people to gain insight into the harms they have caused, though, can kickstart the development of a sense of accountability.

In the World

Several years ago, I met David, a man serving a life sentence for a homicide. Twenty years prior, when he committed his offense, he was living on the streets and struggling with addiction. He often stole cars to sleep inside. One night, he went to the parking lot of a fast food restaurant and pointed his gun in the face of the driver in a parked car. He demanded the person get out. They hesitated, and the hesitation led to tragedy. David fired the gun and killed the driver.

For years, if you asked David what happened, he could recount the events of the story in great detail. He could even provide some explanation of what was going on for him at that moment: "I was cold and tired. I had been sleeping outside for a few nights and wanted a roof over my head. I hadn't gotten high for a while, so I was agitated. When the driver hesitated, I got frightened and thought he was about to attack me, so I fired the gun."

He was incredibly remorseful and had dedicated his life to trying to make amends, but his story didn't have the insight that would lead to full accountability; he couldn't see the full scope of what had actually happened. Over the two-plus years I had the honor to know David, he began to develop more and more insight. He learned to speak about the traumatic experiences in his own childhood and understand how they shaped him. He learned to tap into the vulnerability of his own mourning, sadness, and loneliness. He saw how the traumas his parents held led to abuses in his household that deeply impacted him. More and more, he recognized the nutrients (or toxins) that contributed to the blossoming of the moment he pulled the trigger. He saw the interbeing of the events that came to define his life. He saw the moment he took somebody else's life was the culmination of his own lifetime of pain. He understood his core trauma.

He began to have more compassion for himself, which allowed him to lower his defenses, which then allowed him to have more compassion for his victim and move into a different level of remorse and making amends. Self-compassion wasn't meant to evade his own responsibility, but to honor his full story.

Insight requires deep introspection; introspection requires space. When we conflate accountability with punishment and use tactics of shame or isolation to "hold someone accountable," that person ends up too defensive and busy trying to fend off attacks to have space for introspection.

Let's remember though, that fierce vulnerability is not just about individual accountability, but about extrapolating the lessons from personal transformation to larger scales. Once we have a systemic analysis, it's impossible to divorce David and his experience as a Black man from the centuries of state violence against descendants of African slaves. Thanks to the teachings of interbeing, we know David and his traumas didn't emerge in isolation. His life and the moment he pulled that trigger didn't develop in a vacuum. All of it was the result of a deep interdependence with generations of state violence. The fact that David grew up in an impoverished neighborhood had everything to do with policies like redlining, the coordinated racially discriminatory withholding of financing for home ownership. The fact that he ended up addicted to drugs had everything to do with the war on drugs. The fact that his parents were traumatized had everything to do with them growing up in the Jim Crow South. Once we begin to develop this level of insight, we see that for David to go through a full process of accountability also requires accountability for generations of harm inflicted on him and his community by forces much larger than him and his victim.

While David's story is directly interdependent with much larger systems of violence, it's still a story between two individuals. Let's take the lens of insight and look at a larger social issue. In recent years, several high-profile cases have surfaced of police killing unarmed Black people and later swearing they thought they were reaching for their taser instead of their gun. This is usually followed by a flood of articles and social media posts expressing outrage and disbelief. Many people, particularly those of us on the left, cannot imagine it's possible for an officer to mistake a gun for a taser. The outrage is natural and righteous. But I usually find myself biting my tongue—I believe, with more insight into the situation, it's *very* possible for an officer to mistake their gun and their taser.

Memes shared on social media clearly show a taser is typically bright yellow and is shaped differently than a gun. Tasers are also much lighter than a handgun. In addition, guns are typically holstered on the side of the officers' dominant hand, while tasers are on the other hip. But what factors are interdependent with the moment the gun was pulled?

For one, we overestimate how well-trained police officers are in the United States. The state of California requires 664 hours of training to become an officer. For comparison, California requires 1,500 hours of training to become a barber. In those 664 hours, officers are expected to learn 43 different subjects, including ethics, the structure of the criminal justice system, evidence handling, report writing, vehicle training, arrest procedures, use of force policies, crowd control, traffic enforcement, first aid, firearms training, and criminal law including property crimes, domestic violence, controlled substance, sex crimes, crimes against children, and juvenile law—all in less than half the amount of time it takes to become a barber. And California's training is considered the gold standard across the nation. In countries like Norway and Finland, recruits go through trainings that can last three years before being handed a police badge. Many of them don't carry guns daily.

The second factor I want us to consider is the fact that police officers have the same psychology and nervous system as you and I. Their uniforms, badges, and riot gear don't protect their brains from experiencing the panic zone. I remember a protest at Occupy Oakland years ago: a small group of five or six police officers moved into a large crowd to make an arrest. All of a sudden, this group of police officers found themselves surrounded on all sides by an angry mob of protesters. The officers had formed a ring with the person they had just arrested in the middle. The protesters tried to free their comrade. I remember the yelling and the screaming. I remember bottles being thrown. Someone threw a water balloon filled with blue paint. At that moment, I looked directly into the eyes of one officer: they were so obviously filled with fear.

It may have been hard to see through his body armor, helmet, and face shield, but it was written all over his face. He was scared, most likely in his panic zone, fearing for his life. Was his life in actual danger? No, of course not. But is that what his body felt? Most likely. Imagine being surrounded by a mob of over a hundred people, all yelling and screaming in your direction. How many of us wouldn't go into panic in a situation like that?

Police at Occupy Oakland, 2011

We want to hold officers to a higher standard because they're "trained professionals." And that's nice in theory, but in practice they are severely undertrained. They definitely don't participate in fierce vulnerability workshops or other modalities that may prepare people to stay grounded in tense situations. If anything, they are trained in the opposite. I've written previously about things like the Bulletproof Warrior Training law enforcement goes through, which essentially trains them to be more trigger happy, more afraid, and more likely to enter panic. The fact that a gun weighs more, is a different color than a taser, and is holstered on the other side of their hip are all sensory inputs that happen at the cognitive level. After only 664 hours of training—an incredibly small amount of which is actual weapons training—that kind of thing may not be hardwired into their body. Somatic teacher and author of *The Politics of Trauma* Staci Haines once told me it takes practicing something 300 times to turn it into muscle memory and 3,000 times to embody it.[8]

We overestimate how well-trained police are and underestimate how traumatized and afraid they are. This insight makes me want to hold the system more accountable rather than individual officers. None of this is to say there shouldn't be accountability at the personal level. I think it's perfectly reasonable any officer who uses excessive force is never put in a place where they have power over people again. I want to be very clear: I am no apologist for the police. I consider myself an abolitionist and believe policing is fundamentally flawed if our goal is to create safe communities. Nonetheless, with insight it becomes clear the call for more accountability applies just as much to the system that leaves officers woefully unprepared for what is legitimately a difficult, stressful, and traumatizing job.

Remorse

Years ago, we ran a weekly program at the San Bruno County Jail. Sean was in the first cohort to go through our intensive training to become certified as a Kingian Nonviolence trainer. The housing unit we worked in held mostly pre-trial men, and Sean was in the process of fighting his case. One day, he said he wanted to tell me what he did and apologize to the people he hurt. He was ready to show remorse and to hold himself accountable. But of course, that's not how the system is set up. Because he was still fighting his case, his lawyer advised him not to tell anybody anything and certainly not to talk about what he "allegedly" did. I could tell it was killing him to hold this in and that all he wanted to do was express the remorse written all over his face.

And there's our criminal justice system for you. You have a young man who wants to come clean, wants to apologize, wants to hold himself accountable, but has to play his role of "defendant" to get the best possible outcome.

Of course, not everyone who causes harm is like Sean. If someone doesn't feel remorse for a harm they caused, they can never really hold themselves accountable for it. And again, if we're busy attacking and shaming people, it's a very human response to put up walls and get defensive. So how do we bring out a sense of remorse from people who refuse to acknowledge harm?

Around the time I began writing this book, my friend and colleague Chris Moore-Blackman participated in an action in North Carolina where he and his community of activists occupied the governor's mansion in an effort to confront him about the construction of the Atlantic Coast Pipeline. It was actually during the planning of this action that someone threw out the words "fierce vulnerability." Because they had a strong sense of the healing energy they wanted to cultivate in their action, they decided not to hold any signs, and they agreed not to do any chants.

A protest without signs and chants? What on Earth would that look like? And why? Isn't that what you're *supposed to do* at a protest?

When the governor's staff came down to the lobby to meet with them (the governor was out of town), they didn't yell or scream. Instead, they sat in circle and invited the staff in. Each person shared why they were there. Many were moved to tears as they expressed their concerns and grief over how this pipeline impacts the communities it goes through and how the climate crisis will impact the future of their children. Chris could see tears forming in the eyes of the staff. This was an experimental action not tied to a long-term campaign, so it didn't lead to any concrete changes. It was simply an attempt to organize an action that had the fierceness to shut down the governor's mansion and the vulnerability to open up remorse.

In personal conflicts, it's when I stay away from finger-pointing and accusations and vulnerably share the impact something is having on me that I reach the other person. In movements, how can we lead with the same spirit? What human impact do the issues have on us, on our hearts? If we lead with vulnerable truths about the ways we experience harm, could this support the awakening of remorse?

Amends

Sometimes wisdom emerges from the most unexpected places. One day I was watching a basketball game being called by one of my favorite analysts, Jeff Van Gundy. A referee made a call he disagreed with, and he went off on the poor ref. He said refs are always calling for players and coaches to be accountable, but the refs need to be held to the same standard. In the midst of this wild rant, he said, "Accountability isn't something you take, it's something you give." I love that.

Accountability requires the person who caused harm to actually give something to try to repair as much of the harm as they can. It's about getting to a place where they *want* to make amends. But if accountability isn't something you can forcefully take, how do you get people to *want* to give? Helping people have insight into the harm and begin to feel remorse is a start.

In the United States, I believe part of the path to our healing is reparations for stolen land from Indigenous peoples and stolen labor from Black people. This can be an example of making amends. Someone can be forced to give reparations, and that can be seen as a victory in a zero-sum, win/lose conflict. But if we want reparations to be healing, what elements need to be in place? Reparations given in the true spirit of healing don't come out of a sense of obligation or coercion. Reparations aren't something white people give to Black people so white people can release their guilt and Black people can get some cash. They are part of a transformational relationship that brings both sides closer to healing, reconciliation, and their own liberation.[*] Ultimately, it's less about the money and more about the relationship (though the money *really* goes a long way).

---

[*] Shoutout to my friend Morgan Curtis, who does amazing work coaching white people with wealth to redistribute it through reparations. Her work is not only about moving resources, but about healing ancestral legacies. Check it out at *www.morganhcurtis.com*.

If we understood accountability and the amends it calls for as an act of love based in insight and remorse, how would we approach conflicts differently? How might we organize our movements differently?

Healing Shame

Shame is a *huge* barrier to healing, so I want to spend a bit of time breaking it down. Brené Brown has done a lot of great work around our understanding of shame. Guilt says, "I *did* something bad, and *I* know it," whereas shame says, "I *am* something bad, and *they* know it." According to Brown's research, shame is a focus on self, while guilt is a focus on behavior.[9]

There is redemption in guilt—you can hold yourself accountable for something you did. But if you feel you *are* something bad, unworthy, unlovable, there is no redemption in that. Shame is debilitating. If we feel like there's something fundamentally broken about us and we have to prevent more people from finding out, we're constantly sapping our energy hiding something we believe to be true about ourselves. Quoting Brown again, "Shame derives its power from being unspeakable."[10] According to her research, shame is the emotion people least want to talk about. But the more we ignore it and the more we try to hide it, the more power it has over our lives.

When we create spaces where we feel safe enough to speak about what we are most ashamed of and trust there is belonging on the other side of these conversations, we can facilitate transformational healing. Whether in the circles I've witnessed in prison or the first time I spoke about my own shame at the Jam, such spaces are among the most liberating I've ever been in. They require a strong container with expert facilitation, trusting relationships, and the fierceness of vulnerability.

The work we need to do to heal our societal wounds requires us to open up conversations about the legacies this country is most ashamed of, because that's where the healing can begin. It would make sense for the United States to feel ashamed of its legacy of slavery and genocide. It would be understandable if it felt ashamed of its current practices of incarceration, war, and immigrant detention centers. The United States and its people may pretend the country isn't ashamed of these legacies. But having worked with so many people who caused harm, I know that as interdependent beings, we cannot harm another being without it impacting us negatively. I've talked with plenty of people who felt their crime was justified, but once we held conversations that created space for them to be fully themselves, shame for having caused harm always surfaced. Once people have insight and can be seen for all of who they are rather than just the worst thing they did, they can begin to have remorse and move the shame into guilt.

These conversations are happening in small, progressive pockets. But that's not enough. The urgency of this moment requires us to scale up the healing. The shame we hold collectively may be part of the reason this nation has refused to have these conversations in any genuine way. It's tricky, initiating conversations about things the nation may have shame around without shaming the people. There's a fine line between "shaming someone" and creating space for them to speak about their shame. The former is about putting shame into someone, while the latter is about helping them release it. Shame should never be weaponized.

If we can create a space for that shame to be surfaced and released, though, healing can happen.

CHAPTER 6

Matching Escalation

Resolving a conflict is about fixing issues, and reconciling a conflict is about repairing relationships.

BILJI VERGHESE

We need to have a movement that has the courage to have a relationship with our heartbrokenness.

REV. LYNICE PINKARD

NORMAL LEVELS OF conflict are minor conflicts that occur every single day and are completely unavoidable—having to wake up earlier than you want, having to pay bills, figuring out who takes out the trash. But as multiple normal conflicts add up, a conflict might escalate to the **pervasive level**, and you begin to feel the tension in the air. Voices are raised, people start to call each other names, body posture begins to shift. And if the conflict isn't successfully deescalated, it may reach the **overt level**, where the conflict is in full bloom and there is active harm occurring.

Levels of conflict are an important thing to study because in nonviolence, we're taught as conflict escalates, your nonviolent response has to escalate with it.

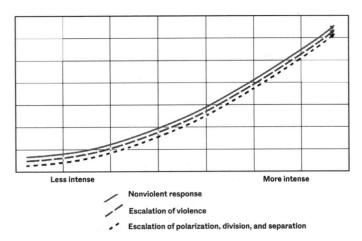

Less intense   More intense

✓ Nonviolent response

✓ Escalation of violence

✓ Escalation of polarization, division, and separation

The three levels of conflict are a foundational teaching in Kingian Nonviolence

If a person is experiencing a normal level of conflict, you may be able to give them a hug and tell them to take a deep breath. That may be an appropriate response, because the person is most likely still in their comfort zone or barely outside of it. You may be able to give them advice or offer a different perspective on things, because they're still able to take in new information. However, if you go to someone experiencing an overt level of conflict, they are more likely to be in their panic zone. Telling them to take a deep breath or trying to convince them to see things from a different perspective may not be an appropriate response, and it may backfire.

Let's zoom out on the fractal. On a social scale, a normal level of conflict might look like a busy intersection that could use a stop sign because of frequent accidents. As a response, filling out a petition and bringing it to your city council may be an appropriate strategy. It's a low-level response to a low-level intensity of conflict. Filling out a petition, though, may not be the appropriate response to, say, the climate crisis, since that is an *extremely* escalated form of harm. Responding to the climate crisis means you are engaging in a conflict directly responsible for the extinction of countless species, the destruction of irreplaceable ecosystems, the deaths of countless human lives, and the possible mass extinction of life on this planet as we know it.

So, what could an appropriate response to an overt social conflict look like?

Nonviolent responses to overt conflicts often look like shutting down a highway, occupying a government building, or organizing a general strike. Escalated responses to conflict are, by nature, disruptive. But one thing I have noticed is oftentimes, the more we escalate our *tactics* of nonviolent action, the more we escalate polarization: a black/white, us/them, right/wrong worldview of division and separation. And remember, a black-white binary perspective can be a sign of the panic zone—othering becomes the dominant worldview; we become the "good" side, and they become "bad." We're here to shut them down and defeat them so we can win and achieve justice.

Unfortunately, I believe the black/white, us/them worldview *is at the heart of what is destroying our planet.* Many psychologists say separation and isolation are at the core of trauma. It's our inability to remember our interdependence that allows us to cause harm to each other. I don't believe we can heal our wounds by continuing to perpetuate this binary worldview of separation.

In organizing circles, we're often taught to bring injustice to the surface and force people to pick sides, essentially polarizing the public. But there's a big difference in asking people to choose between justice and injustice and asking them to choose between *us* and *them*, thereby forgoing our interdependence to one another. We will never get to liberation if we build movements that may be able to win short-term gains on various issues but move us further away from each other on a relational level.

Shut It Down versus Open It Up

It's tricky. When I talk about needing an "escalated" response to harm, we too often end up envisioning strategies that move us away from the healing of relationships. For some reason, the more we imagine "escalated" responses to conflict, the more it begins to look like separation, like digging the line between "us" and "them" even deeper. When you see violence and injustice in the world, it's often evidence of the delusion of separation. The *response* I want to see heals that separation; it doesn't deepen it. What we want to escalate is not violence, but our antidotes to violence.

When a conflict is escalated, there's naturally going to be more energy, more tension, more urgency, more at stake. This leads to a sense of less spaciousness, less time, less choice, less possibility. As we enter escalated spaces, it's hard for us to not be affected by that energy and move toward panic. And that's the dilemma, one of the million-dollar questions of fierce vulnerability: How do we engage in the most escalated conflicts—perhaps the most escalated conflict in the history of our species—while remaining grounded? How do we remember to breathe in the face of the biggest crisis we have ever seen? How do we protect ourselves against operating purely from our survival mechanisms in the face of a possible mass extinction?

This explains why many activist movements are grounded in an "us versus them" worldview. Most activist communities struggle with very escalated issues. In that space, it can be hard to stay connected to the neocortex that helps us see nuance and interdependence. Many direct actions lead with an energy of "shut it down." We're here to shut down factories, pipelines, and corporate board meetings that cause immediate, direct harm. We do need to stop injustice.

> What if our intention is not only to fix issues but to repair relationships? What if, even if we are tactically choosing to shut down a government building or a coal-fired power plant, the spirit that

guides us into action is not one of "shutting things down," but of "opening things up"?

What if, even as we use our bodies to block a bus filled with people getting deported, we try to open up our hearts and the hearts of those around us? What would it look like if we were clear our intention was to open up possibilities for connection and transformation? To open up a conversation we've been afraid to have about the root causes of injustice? To open up our vulnerability as a way to help people *feel* something? To open up space for genuine healing and accountability?

When I'm in panic and operating from trauma, I'm not capable of slowing myself down, regulating myself, holding myself accountable for harms I may have committed, and moving toward healing and transformation. If, at that moment, you try to "shut me down . . ." well, I'll probably shut down and get defensive.

To me, the work of nonviolent action is about asking society to look at, and to open up to, conversations about a deeper truth than we may feel ready for. As we do that, we have to ensure our messaging and energy avoid reinforcing or intensifying an "us versus them" worldview, and refrain from using fear or intimidation to force people to change. Whether it's anti-abortion activists using images of aborted fetuses or animal rights activists using images of animals being tortured in slaughterhouses, I wonder if these images may actually put people into panic and make introspection harder for them. I wonder if the tactics are too aggressive, making people defensive and less open to healing.

This is complex, because I do believe we need people to wake up to how critical of a moment we are living in. Sometimes shock can be effective in ending our complacency. But I wonder if we can do it in a way that supports people opening up, as opposed to forcing a scary message down their throats. I haven't figured out exactly what that looks like. I know crying in front of a police officer isn't going to stop police violence. Sharing our heartbreak at the destruction of our environment isn't going to change the mind of oil company executives. Reading a vulnerable letter in front of my family might help to shift the dynamics in my family, but it probably isn't going to make a politician live up to their campaign promises.*

My mind may not be able to articulate it yet, but my heart knows there's a way to escalate the depth and sincerity of our nonviolent responses while doubling down on connection. My soul knows there's a way to organize actions that lead with vulnerability and tap into the possibilities it opens up without losing the power and assertiveness that fierceness gives us. I am convinced that ultimately, we cannot shut down injustice any more than we can shut down trauma.

As violence escalates, we need to escalate its antidote—connection, healing, empathy. Perhaps during direct actions, our bodies do the same things (blockading, resisting, intervening) but instead of yelling we ask questions and listen. Instead of chanting slogans we sing songs. Instead of trying to drown someone out with noise, we sit in silence.

How do we organize movements that not only create the leverage we need for change, but embody the things we long for in the world: beauty, magic, mystery, relationship, life? How do we, as the elders at Standing Rock taught us, remember direct action is ceremony? How can direct action become a modality of collective trauma healing? How do we shut down a highway while opening up our hearts?

Leading with Vulnerability

When Anuttara and I first started to work together, she shared a music video called "Rise | Vulnerable Rally" by an Oakland,

---

* There are, of course, rare exceptions to this where an act of vulnerability *did* move someone enough to make real changes. But for the most part, they don't lead to actual *systemic* change.

California–based musician named Mikey Pauker. In the video, Pauker invites people to write something about themselves that they would normally want to hide on a large piece of cardboard and then to stand there holding the sign for onlookers to see. Participants wrote signs like "I'm afraid I'm not doing enough with my life," "I drink to hide the pain of life," "I am afraid to be trusted," and "I feel I don't make a difference."*

I was struck not only by the power and simplicity of this act and the conversations it sparked with onlookers, but by *where* they filmed this: on the corner for 14th Street and Broadway, in the middle of downtown Oakland. Anyone who's been around Oakland knows 14th and Broadway is *the* intersection where shit goes down. It's where all the major protests happen. I've been there countless times over the years for rallies and demonstrations about every issue under the sun. On that exact corner, I've been tear-gassed, I've watched people smash bank windows and set fires, and I've witnessed wild acts of police violence against protesters. And yet, I feel like nothing I ever did there is as courageous as what the people in this music video did: stand there and share a deeper truth than we're used to seeing in public. "I am hurt." "I am alone." "I am scared." These simple truths spoken from the depths of their hearts opened things up in complete strangers who walked by.

When I'm in conflict, I quickly enter my panic zone, build up a wall and create a "me versus them" worldview. The one thing that tends to break down that wall very quickly is one of us moving away from the place of blame and into a place of feelings and impact. When one of us can home in on what we are feeling—hurt, alone, scared—and speak from that place, it tends

---

* The Vulnerable Rally was the brainchild of Gabriel Diamond, a filmmaker from the San Francisco Bay Area. Gabriel and his partner Candice Holdorf, who eventually attended one of our Fierce Vulnerability workshops, started organizing Vulnerable Rallies throughout the Bay and beyond in 2016. You can check out their work at *www.vulnerablerally.org*.

to melt down our walls, and compassion can enter.* And when compassion comes in, it activates the PNS and we begin to regulate again, making connection possible.

> What lessons could we learn from that to take into social movement spaces? What would happen if this "vulnerable rally" took place with masses of people while shutting down the White House? What if, instead of leading with messages of "fuck the police" or "shame on you," our collective voice expressed our pain, our fear, our grief, our vulnerability? What would the reaction be, not only from those who hold power, but from the onlookers who witness our actions? Could space be created for them to touch into their own vulnerable truths? In addition to sharing our vulnerable truths, could we hold space to listen to theirs?

Imagining these sorts of actions feels like fierce vulnerability. Combining the fierceness of asking others to wake up to the crisis with the beauty and possibility of what it looks like when we are deeply vulnerable with each other.

When I look at the reality of the world around us, it breaks my heart. When I see images of children in cages on the US-Mexico border, when I watch videos of animals trying to get away from the wildfires on the West Coast, when I read details about the latest police killing, and I actually allow those images and stories to penetrate my heart, I can barely contain myself. Those feelings are scary. And yet, we need to be able to feel them and to lead with that heartbreak. These issues *should* break our hearts and *should* scare us. And we cannot have courage without fear. We need to have the courage to be real with our heartbreak.

It's not about trying to make someone else afraid and forcing vulnerability onto them, but about offering up our own fear and vulnerability as an invitation. As the compounding crises of our times escalate fear, separation, and violence, we need to escalate our capacity to open up our hearts.

---

* "I feel like you're being an asshole" or "I feel like you are wrong" aren't feelings. They are thoughts, projections, judgments, and evaluations.

CHAPTER 7

A Crack in the Matrix

Even in some of our most successful movements, our demands are often to get the state to do something for us.

CARLOS SAAVEDRA

In a world of falsehoods, truth is inherently confrontational.

MICHAEL NAGLER

SPOILER ALERT: in the movie *The Matrix*, human beings are no longer born organically as a result of a natural process. Instead, we're harvested by robots and spend our entire lives asleep inside of capsules. Our only purpose is to serve as batteries to power our artificially intelligent robot overlords. To keep us in a state of calm and prevent us from rebelling against the reality of our lives, the robots created the Matrix: a computer simulation system all humans are plugged into. Inside the Matrix, our consciousness lives in the late twentieth century with all the luxuries and conveniences we could dream of. We spend our entire lives asleep inside this simulation, going about our day never realizing the reality of what our life has become.

Of course, all of it is a delusion created by the Matrix. None of it is real. And some of us can sense it. We can't quite put a finger on it, but some characters in the movie live with a suspicion *something is off.*

Neo, our main protagonist, played by Keanu Reeves, is one of those people. He has long lived with a suspicion something is amiss. He's eventually recruited by Morpheus, the leader of a renegade band of resisters, and given a choice. He can take a red pill to see the truth behind the Matrix, or a blue pill to forget everything and go on living as if all is well. Of course, he takes the red pill and is shown reality as it is. He joins the resistance. After a period of training, he's plugged back into the Matrix, back into this delusional world, to run various missions. Toward the end of the movie, he becomes "awakened"—even from inside, he's able to see the Matrix for what it is. As real as the simulations around him seem, he's able to see all of it is made up of binary 1s and 0s, the coding behind the Matrix.

I've always found it ironic that Reeves also played the role of the historical Buddha in the 1993 movie *Little Buddha*, since *The Matrix* is essentially the story of the Buddha—if the Buddha were a badass action hero who wore a black leather coat and used violence to save the world. Prince Siddhartha Gautama of the Shakya clan, the historical Buddha, was not a god or a prophet. He was a normal human being like you and I.* But through years of practice, he awakened. The term "Buddha" means "awakened one." He didn't become a god or a prophet, he simply gained the ability to see beyond the delusions that cloud our ability to see things as they truly are.

In his first teaching after enlightenment, the Buddha taught us about the "four noble truths." The first truth is about the reality that our lives are filled with unsatisfactoriness.† The second truth is that this unsatisfactoriness has a cause. The third truth

---

* Well, technically he was a prince so maybe not *exactly* like you and I. Unless you're actually a prince reading this.

† The Pali word *dukkha* is most traditionally translated as "suffering," but because the word *suffering* has so many different connotations in the West, many teachers believe "unsatisfactoriness" may be a better translation.

is that there is a path out of the endless cycles of unsatisfactoriness. And the fourth truth points us toward that path—what Buddhists call the noble eightfold path.

If one had to expand on the second noble truth, it may go something like this: the cause of our suffering, our feeling of unsatisfactoriness, is ignorance and the delusions that arise out of ignorance. We tend to walk through life with big ignorance goggles over our eyes, tainting everything we see. We can't see things for what they truly are, and we believe our delusions are real, so we cling to them. It's our clinging to delusions that causes suffering.

Once Neo saw the world the Matrix created was a delusion, he was free of it, even as he was inside of it. Nothing inside the Matrix could affect him in the real world. The same thing happened to the Buddha. Once he saw the world for what it was, he escaped the endless cycles of suffering, and nothing could affect his calm and inner peace. From this place of unshakeability, he could fully and wisely engage to transform suffering in the world.

We are all, in more ways than we sometimes want to admit, Neo before he met Morpheus. The Buddha before his enlightenment. We are swimming in a sea of delusions so thick it renders us incapable of seeing the world for what it is. We cling to these delusions, which create untold suffering. And the suffering that grows out of being stuck in the delusions prevents us from being able to engage in liberatory work. A big chunk is not our own doing. It's the Matrix. It's all the distractions constantly bombarding us, trying to take our attention away from the things that really matter. It's reality TV, shopping sprees, social media, celebrity gossip, the never-ending wheels of capitalism demanding every hour of our free time. It's modernity.

We *do* live in a Matrix. There *is* a world beyond the superficial world created by capitalism and materialism, beyond partisan politics, beyond surface-level identities, beyond our ideas of "beauty," "success," and "happiness" defined by a system that only exists to feed itself in an endless cycle of perpetual growth. There *is* a world where you are already enough. Where you already belong. Where every life is sacred and there are enough resources for all of us to thrive. If we're not able to at least get a glimpse of this, we'll be stuck forever. I imagine even within the simulated world of the Matrix, activist groups fought "the man." But nothing they did ultimately got them closer to true liberation, because even "the man" they were supposedly fighting was part of the delusion. Any "injustice" within the Matrix was part of the plot line created by a computer. Like Neo and Morpheus, we need to step outside of the delusion to see reality with clear eyes. Then, and only then, can we figure out a way out.

Truths and Untruths

In the development of the fierce vulnerability workshop, Anuttara introduced us to an activity called "Truths and Untruths." It helps us get a sense of how deeply we have accepted some untruths and the power of reclaiming truth.

She starts the activity with two quotes from Napoleon Bonaparte:

"A soldier will fight long and hard for a bit of colored ribbon,"

and

"Give me enough medals and I'll win you any war."

These quotes speak to how deeply rooted concepts like nation-states and patriotism are. A stripe on a military uniform signifies rank and a medal shows their bravery in battle. They're earned through years of loyalty and sacrifice. Earning them is, for many people, one of the great honors of their lives. But at the end of the day, what are they but a piece of fabric and some metal? Their value and meaning are completely made up—they hold no practical, real-world value beyond what we put into them. They're valuable because we say they are. They hold meaning because we decide they do.

Of course, for the people who receive them, they symbolize something real. They acknowledge their service to their country and honor the very real sacrifices they've made, which I'm not discounting. But as human beings, we *choose* to place value in some things over others. In reality, things like "rank" are made-up concepts. The fact that you may rise to the level of lieutenant or sergeant means nothing to the universe. What is considered "brave" and "honorable" is subjective and far from universal. We, as people, decide. The military may consider risking yourself to kill countless enemies brave and worthy of a medal; I would consider brave a conscientious objector who serves prison time for refusing to go to war. It's subjective, and not "real" in the universal sense. We've come to believe some things are as real and as true as the Earth being round or water being wet, when in reality they're completely made up human constructs.

Look at how our entire global economic system relies on our faith that it's a real thing. The "value" of multinational corporations is assessed based on what investors decide they're worth. The fact that money is valuable isn't "real" in the way gravity is real. Science can prove gravity over and over again, but there's nothing about the economic system that can be "proven" to be "real." And yet, because our world is so reliant on these illusions, they end up having very real impacts on our lives.

Unbridled capitalism and an unregulated housing and banking system contributed to a global collapse of the marketplace in 2007–2008. Overnight, millions of people lost their jobs, their homes, and their savings. In the United States as many as 800,000 people lost their jobs every month. 3.8 million homes were foreclosed. Lives were destroyed. Trillions of dollars just . . . disappeared. And yet, the Earth still had the same amount of people, air, water, natural resources. Food didn't disappear, land mass didn't shrink, workers didn't perish into thin air. The housing crisis didn't happen because homes simply vanished. People were kicked out of them because the numbers in their online accounts no longer had enough zeroes after them.

Many of our delusions are not neutral. Often, they set up one group to benefit at the cost of another. Race is real. Gender is a binary. Beauty standards are universal. Men aren't supposed to cry. Only bad people to go prison. Racism is over.

Delusions, lies, untruths.

Trauma is one reason we have so many delusions in our lives. Trauma makes us think something's there when it's not, that something is dangerous when it's not, that something that happened twenty years ago is happening now. Trauma puts us into survival mode, where our minds crave anything that might seem stable, safe, secure—things the Matrix can offer us. In addition to increased trauma responses, we're living in a world where there are simply more methods for spreading delusions.

I remember seeing a meme on social media featuring a picture of four people standing in line looking at their phones, ignoring each other. The caption read, "The zombie apocalypse is here." I giggled, then realized I was looking at this meme *on my damn phone!* The zombies had got me! We're constantly bombarded by social media, a twenty-four-hour news cycle, billboards, and advertisements. Many of us actually contribute to spreading and reinforcing delusions.

It's no wonder we're so confused and polarized. It's no wonder everyone believes "we" are right and "they" are wrong. Both stories are fed by a system built on delusions. If we can't see things for what they are, we'll never be able to work our way out of them. Attempts to solve our collective problems are hampered by the depth of the many delusions our world is entrenched in.

In the World

Do you remember the Hillary Clinton email controversy? In October 2019, the State Department submitted a report to Congress after a multi-year investigation into the scandal. On October 18, I browsed Google News and saw these two headlines right on top of each other:*

> *State Department probe of Clinton emails finds no deliberate mishandling of classified information*
> —The Washington Post

> *State Department report on Clinton emails finds hundreds of violations, dozens of individuals at fault*
> —Fox News[†]

Isn't that crazy? Regardless of our politics, most of us can agree the US has two medias—left-wing and right-wing. And for most of us, it's not just the difference between left and right, but between right and wrong. If you listen to liberal media, there is constant discussion about how racist and homophobic conservatives are, and if you listen to conservative media, there is nonstop conversation about how closed-minded and fragile liberals are.

Two Truths

The world is a complex place, and the Buddhist Doctrine of Two Truths—that we're constantly living inside two levels

---

[*] You don't? Honestly, I don't really either. It doesn't really matter for the point I'm making, but you can easily Google it if you'd like.

[†] I swear this is real. Both those articles are still up online if you google them, and I also saved a screenshot of my Google News feed here: *https://bit.ly/3Qzlhxa.*

of truth—helps me hold that complexity. The conventional, relative, mundane, or provisional truth is the reality we can see with our eyes and touch with our fingers. It's the reality that describes our daily interactions with the concrete world. Things are predictable, linear, and stable. Then there's the ultimate or absolute truth. This is the world we can see when the veil of delusion is lifted from our eyes. It's where Newton's law no longer applies and the quantum realm takes over, where nothing seems to make sense when we look at it through our conventional lens. It's where you have to give in to mystery and surrender.

KEY ELEMENT	CONVENTIONAL REALM	ULTIMATE REALM
Reality	Dualistic, binary	Non-dualistic, infinitely complex
Perception	Based on ordinary sense perceptions	Insight into true nature of reality
Existence	Things exist independently and inherently	All phenomena are inter-dependent and are empty of an inherent self
Time	Real and linear	Seen as constructs. Timeless and formless

In the conventional world, I exist as a separate, individual being named Kazu. In the ultimate realm, the idea of me existing as an independent being is a delusion. In this realm, there's no separation, no up or down, no right or wrong, no black or white; everything exists in deep interdependence.

Despite the two truths being described with words like "conventional" and "ultimate," it's said that we shouldn't create a hierarchy between the two; they exist side by side. One truth is not "more" true. They're different expressions of truth. Nāgārjuna, the second-century monk credited with expanding on the Doctrine of Two Truths, wrote:

> *Without a foundation in the conventional truth*
> *The significance of the ultimate cannot be taught*
> *Without understanding the significance of the ultimate,*
> *Liberation is not achieved.*[11]

The two truths exist in interdependence with each other; one cannot be understood without the other. Kazu *does* exist. My fingers are typing these words into my laptop. That *is* happening. The delusion is in thinking conventional truth is *all* that exists. If I am wearing a dirty pair of goggles, they obscure what's in front of me. This doesn't mean the dirt on the goggles isn't real, just that it may keep me from seeing beyond it. The goggles and the dirt are there. The delusion is in believing the entire world must be dirty.

In the conventional world, there is war, poverty, and injustice. We're hurting, suffering, and traumatized. However, in the ultimate realm, time isn't linear, and we're already free. Separation doesn't exist, and we already belong to each other. We're already whole. As Ram Dass taught, "You need to remember your Buddha nature and your social security number." In the ultimate realm, each of us has the innate potential to become fully awakened. Meantime, in the conventional world, we *do* have social security numbers!

We've lived in and prioritized the conventional realm and ignored the ultimate for too long. The changes many movements fight for have mostly been in the conventional realm. But life moves in waves. In breath, out breath. Expansion, contraction. We live in times when the ultimate realm is emerging more and more, and it's in this realm transformation will not only be possible, but inevitable. The work we must do now is to try to be with change in the less logical but more magical ultimate realm.

The Delusion of the Binary

When I'm in a heated argument with someone, I *know* I'm right. Let's be real, it doesn't even need to be that heated. Whenever there's conflict, I usually *know* I'm right. And if I'm right, the other person must be wrong.

Or so the delusion goes.

Usually, when I calm down and get back into my comfort and stretch zones, I can take in different perspectives and be more introspective. Sometimes it turns out I was simply wrong. But most times, it wasn't that I was *wrong* per se, it was simply that I didn't have the complete picture.

Our lack of ability to see complexity and nuance often comes from the fact that many of us were raised in a culture that sees everything in black and white. The foundations of the institutions many of us grew up with are grounded in Abrahamic religious traditions that always saw our lives as a battle between good and evil. There was no nuance. It was God or the Devil.* From folklore and superhero movies to comic books and cartoons on TV, the world has been presented to us as a battle between the "good/right" side and the "bad/wrong" side. And remember, being in our panic zones also impairs our ability to see complexity.

The delusion of the binary—the idea something is either one or the other—prevents us from seeing the complexity of truth. It creates enemy imagining and tribalism, where we begin to see entire groups of people as the problem. It creates false binaries between those deserving of healing and liberation and those who are not. This black/white thinking manifests on every political issue. We convince ourselves we're right and view the other side as stupid, immoral, and not deserving of compassion. It's not just about individual issues either. We pick a team, and

---

* At least this is how many people have interpreted the Abrahamic religious traditions.

then we're supposed to go along with our team on *every* issue under the sun.

I have my own strong feelings about many issues. But with practice, I have also found the complexity of all issues. Oppression exists. Within oppression, there are very real dynamics of power and privilege. One side is harmed by oppression, and another side benefits from it. There is a binary. But that's only a relative truth. In the ultimate realm, oppression hurts everybody. No one is free from the violence of oppression. Everyone is oppressed when we live in a delusion of separation and supremacy, and the simplistic binary of "oppressor" and "oppressed" belies the complexity of oppression. White people need to heal from the trauma of white supremacy and men need to heal from the trauma of patriarchy.

Again, this isn't the *only* truth. It's *also* true power and privilege exist, and we play different roles within the dynamic of oppression. But healing from oppression isn't a battle between the oppressor and the oppressed. It's a battle between oppression and humanity.

In my experience, restorative justice at its best begins to blur the line between who caused the harm and who was harmed. As Transformative Justice activist Mariame Kaba says, "No one enters violence for the first time having committed it." The deeper reality is simply that harm exists. And once we can see that, we can move forward toward healing. It's hard, because the nature of social change work can look very black and white. When we're on the front lines of change, putting our bodies on the line against the forces of injustice, it's a battleground. "There" is where the violence happens, and "here" we call for justice. Using tactics like nonviolent direct action as a healing modality can feel like a paradox. But that's part of the work ahead of us: to be grounded enough to hold the complexity that there are at least two truths operating in even the most escalated spaces. Both levels of truth are 100 percent true.

In the ultimate realm, truth isn't a zero-sum game. It's non-dualistic: one thing can be 100 percent true, and a contradictory thing can *also* be 100 percent true. Living with the delusion that only one thing can be true or that it all has to add up to 100 percent is stressful. If everything has to either be "right" or "wrong" in a world that's actually incredibly complex, you can develop a lot of anxiety trying to "figure it out."

In 2019, I spent a month traveling through India with members of the Ahimsa Collective, facilitating Restorative Justice workshops, visiting young people in jails and sitting in ancient meditation halls. I felt such a deep sense of belonging during that journey. And I'm aware this deep sense of belonging came partly from belonging to a clearly defined "in" group. I was part of the Ahimsa Collective, and other people were not. When I attend the annual Asian Diaspora Jam and am among others who share an Asian identity, I feel a deep sense of belonging. I felt belonging as part of Mass Resist, a small but powerful affinity group I was part of in my early twenties. I felt it when I participated in the first-ever James Lawson Institute in Nashville, and a group of us went out barhopping one night, taking over whatever establishment we walked into with our dancing and energy.

For someone trying to create a world where *everyone* belongs to each other, it seems contradictory to feel so much belonging by creating an "in" group and an "out" group. It is a contradiction. And there's nothing to solve. It can be 100 percent true there are times when we need to be in a small group with clearly defined boundaries to feel belonging—especially as we live in conventional truth. It's *also* 100 percent true our liberation will come from seeing all people belong to each other. These are complex truths, and whenever we use language to try to communicate the core nature of reality, it's going to be incomplete: an expression of partial truth.* The

* I would argue, though, that poets and songwriters can use language to access a deeper truth.

notion our truth is the *only* truth or the *complete* truth is one of the largest delusions we must overcome. All of it can be true, all at the same time.

Life is sacred, and I will do everything I can to protect and affirm life. Every life matters. At the same time, I truly believe we are all specks of stardust in an infinitely large universe. Even if we survive this current climate catastrophe, at some point our own sun will burn down and all life will cease to exist on this planet. It was written from the moment our solar system came into being. Nothing in this universe—our lives or the life of our sun—is permanent.

The problems we face as humanity are larger than we can possibly imagine. The issues are so big and complex there's no way to truly name them. At the same time, in the grand scheme of the universe, it's not all that big of a deal. What we do at this moment in human history will have an enormous impact. It means everything. What we do tomorrow truly matters. And, in the vast tapestry of the cosmos, no matter how sacred our lives are and how large and expansive our planet may seem to us, everything is destined to be gently swept away by the relentless current of time. Our ability to hold paradox is what will allow us to continue to move forward in these complex times.

CHAPTER 8

We Are Okay

It is no measure of health to be well adjusted to a profoundly sick society.

ATTRIBUTED TO JIDDU KRISHNAMURTI

Not everything that is faced can be changed, but nothing can be changed until it is faced.

JAMES BALDWIN

SOME OF THE DELUSIONS we need to unravel are bigger than others. One of the biggest delusions we need to pierce through is the idea that "we are okay."

We are not "okay."

The world is burning. Our social and ecological systems are on the brink of collapse. Things are falling apart. You're not crazy for thinking this. That has to be okay for us to say out loud.

I often feel a deep loneliness, and I've come to understand much of it is rooted in the experience of my mother being disowned from her family and having to move to the United States. At that moment, I lost my extended family as well as a relationship to my homeland, my language, my culture, my lineage. It's one of the earliest times I began to lose my sense of belonging.

I have countless beautiful memories of spending time with extended family in Japan. A lot of them were with my mother's youngest sister, Shigeko, and her American husband, Marcus. I remember harvesting wild mushrooms around Shigeko's house, making spaghetti together, and Marcus swinging me around in his arms. Earlier, I wrote it was deeply confusing to me each time I later received a gift from them. That entire period was deeply confusing for me. It was obvious something had shifted in our family. I imagine it was some combination of my parents trying to protect us from the painful truth that they had been rejected by their wider family and trying to protect themselves from having to explain this vulnerable truth to three young children. But children are incredibly intuitive, and I could *feel* the pain emanating from my parent's bodies.

If we could do it all over again, I would have liked to have known what was happening. I was too young to fully comprehend the complexity of adult relationships, of intergenerational trauma, of the ways in which deeply held Japanese values of honor and pride as well as a culture of shame impacted so much of what happened. But my comprehension of the details of what happened isn't what would've mattered. It's the transparency. It's me knowing I'm not crazy. It's me not feeling alone with this sense of something not being right. I would have been confused, but at least I would have been confused *together with my family.* I would have been scared, upset, and lost, but at least I could have been those things with my family. Instead, I was confused and scared alone. It seems paradoxical: in some way, being able to say out loud that things are not okay actually helps make them a little more okay. The simple acknowledgement of the hurt makes it hurt a little less. If we don't have the courage to say it out loud and we just go along pretending when our bodies know the truth, it only adds to the pain.

If our house were burning down and our family was inside of it, what wouldn't we do to try to protect them? That's essentially what's happening at a global scale. Yet, for the most part, we ignore this reality and continue to go along with business as usual. Of course, it's not healthy for us to always be in crisis mode. But it's also not healthy for us to ignore there's a crisis going on.

The delusions help us feel safe, or at least help us ignore the fact that we don't feel safe. We ask ourselves as a species, "How are we doing?" And the response we get is, "Oh, you know, it's been a hard couple of years, but we're all going to be okay. Things are starting to return to normal." Fierce vulnerability is about having the courage to say we are not okay. It's about being vulnerable enough to be honest with ourselves and fierce enough to not collapse.

Chris often wonders out loud: "If we really took stock of where we are at this moment in human history, what would a meaningful gesture in defense of life look like?" What would it look like to act to protect the sanctity of life when our home is burning? If we're honest about where we are, so many things we do in our lives feel arbitrary and inappropriate. Is organizing another permitted march downtown so we can all listen to a bunch of speakers about things we all already agree with what we really need?

The reality that we are not okay can be a scary one, but it can also be incredibly liberating.

The Enormity of It All

One of my earliest memories is from a trip I took with my family when I was about four years old. We still lived in Japan, but we'd traveled to Arizona. Really, we weren't in "Arizona" or the "United States." We traveled to the sovereign lands of the Hopi people to meet with an elder named Thomas Banyacya.

In 1948, the Hopi elders named Thomas as one of four spiritual ambassadors of sorts tasked with taking the spiritual teachings of the Hopi people, specifically the Hopi Prophecy, to the general public. My parents befriended Thomas through some friends who supported his work in Japan years prior. The Hopi Prophecy, until 1948, was kept secret among the Hopi people and passed down from generation to generation through oral tradition. It was a big deal when the elders decided to share it with the world for the first time.

In a speech Thomas delivered to the United Nations, he said:

Today, December 10, 1992, you see increasing floods, more damaging hurricanes, hailstorms, climate changes, and earthquakes, as our prophecies said would come. Even animals and birds are warning us with strange change in their behavior, such as the beaching of whales. Why do animals act like they know about the Earth's problems and most humans act like they know nothing? If we humans do not wake up to the warnings, the great purification will come to destroy this world, just as the previous worlds were destroyed.

According to the Prophecy, humanity is approaching the days of a great Powateoni, or purification, through social and ecological disruption. We face this period of great hardships because we've lost our way. We have abandoned a way of life in balance with the beyond-human world. During this time, humanity has the opportunity to make a choice. If we continue down the path laid out by technology, separate from natural and spiritual law, it will lead to chaos and destruction. However, if we remain in harmony with the natural law, we will be able to create a world of beauty and lasting peace.

Later in my life, due to relationships my then-stepfather had, every summer we went up to the Kitigàn-zìbì reserve* of

---

* The Canadian version of a Native reservation.

the Anishinabeg First Nation peoples in northern Quebec. We stayed in the basement of the home of Chief William Commanda, who served as band chief for close to twenty years. He carried several traditional wampum belts, including the Seven Fires Prophecy Belt. The seven fires prophecy tells us we're in the time of the Seventh Fire—in this time, we have to make a choice between the material and spiritual world. If we pick the material world, it will lead to destruction. If we pick the spiritual world, it will lead us to the time of the Eighth Fire and lasting peace. Either way, the Earth will go through an intense purification where many people will suffer, and few will survive.

These two prophecies were very present in my early upbringing. We even traveled to Japan with William when I was a young teenager so he could bring the Seven Fires Belt to warn Japanese people about the looming choice we have to make. At the time, to young Kazu, these prophecies felt like hippie new-age spiritual BS my mom was into. I didn't think much of them. But in retrospect, I'm deeply grateful these are the teachings I grew up with and that I had the gift of hearing them directly from these elders my entire childhood. Because when I look at the science, or when I close my eyes and listen to my own intuition, they both tell a story similar to these prophecies: we are entering a period of climate catastrophe, and we will witness suffering on an unimaginable scale.

Anybody paying attention will have noticed this has already begun, and the pace will only increase. The last ten years have seen countless "historic" floods, earthquakes, tsunamis, wildfires, mudslides, heatwaves, blizzards, and hurricanes. Words like "historic" and "record-breaking" have become so commonplace they have almost lost their meaning. I also believe, as these prophecies say, we have a choice—even with all the catastrophes on their way, it's possible to create beauty and community on the other side. Lasting peace is possible if we can find our way toward each other and toward wholeness again.

The scale of what we're up against is ginormous. We must undo things that have been around for so long they feel like part of human nature: capitalism, patriarchy, white supremacy, materialism, a separation from the natural world—the things Vanessa Machado de Oliveira Andreotti, author of *Hospicing Modernity,* simply calls "modernity." Let's be honest. It's not just the status quo that's afraid to really look at the possibility of this transformation. It's us. It's those of us working on the alternatives, trying to shut down coal-fired power plants, reading and writing about abolition, and living a life in line with our deepest values. We're scared too. We haven't experienced what's on the other side either, and the unknown is always going to be scary. Philosopher Frederic Jameson once said, "It's easier to imagine the end of the world than it is to imagine the end of capitalism." As scary as it is, that rings true for me. I can easily imagine a hundred different ways the world might end. But what would the world *actually* look like post-capitalism? We need science fiction writers, artists, poets, and songwriters to even begin to imagine it.

Given the scale of the transitions we face, our responses to them, our capacity for creativity, and the audacity of our visions have to be equally large. We have to think so much bigger than three-year grant cycles, four-year election terms, and five-year strategic plans. We have to think beyond a Green New Deal that allows us to continue driving in more efficient cars that still rely on fossil fuels, beyond banning assault rifles when we know the majority of guns in the United States are handguns, beyond abolishing the death penalty but keeping prisons, beyond fighting for a $15 minimum wage so people can make $30,000 a year, beyond instituting universal health care so we can wait to get sick from polluted environments and poisoned foods and then be taken care of by a for-profit medical and pharmaceutical industry.

Talking to my friend sujatha baliga once about the dire situation in Palestine, she asked out loud what "freedom for Palestine" even means for someone who believes the very notion of a nation-state is an act of violence that perpetuates the delusion of separation. Regardless of whether we fight for a one-state solution or a two-state solution, if we fight for a "vision" firmly entrenched in a state-solution, we continue to base ourselves in a worldview of separation, domination, and violence.

These are transformational times. The visions we're fighting for have to be dreamt up outside the delusions we've gotten so used to. We're not trying to live better lives within the Matrix. We're trying to break out of it. Joanna Macy talks about our time as the Great Turning—we have the choice to stay in the Industrial Growth Society or choose a Life Sustaining Civilization. Zen teacher Norma Ryuko Kawelokū Wong Roshi calls it the Great Reset. Others call it the Great Awakening. The New Story. The Great Remembering. Powateoni. The Seventh Fire. Whatever you want to call it, countless wisdom traditions (including ones guided by Western science) speak of this moment as a huge turning point. That excites me. And scares the shit out of me.

Opportunity in Crises

I wish it were true because it sounds so cool, but unfortunately, the adage so many people repeat about the Chinese characters for "crisis" and "opportunity" being the same is not true.* It was probably made up by the guy who created fortune cookies.† But no matter, because it still speaks to what I believe is an important truth: in every crisis is an opportunity. And for better or for worse, there are no shortages of crises in our lives.

---

* Well, it's not *entirely* true. The Chinese word for "crisis," 危機 (wēijī) has the character 機 (jī), which is also used in the Chinese word for "opportunity," 機會 (jīhuì). But to say the character 機 (jī) on its own means "opportunity" is a bit of a stretch. It turns out John F. Kennedy used to mistakenly say the Chinese characters for crisis and opportunity are the same, so we can blame JFK.

† Also not a real Chinese thing. Though not invented by JFK.

Generally speaking, social change happens really, really slowly. The movement to abolish legal slavery, for example, took well over a century, and our cultural norms around slavery took even longer to shift. The underlying philosophy of white supremacy that justified slavery is still around. The Overton Window describes the range of ideas or policies the general public might be willing to consider as progress is made. This window is often pretty narrow, which is why change takes so long. Several things can dramatically expand the Overton Window and change our understanding of what is possible. Social movements have always pushed the boundaries of what is possible, widening the Overton Window and forcing changes that may have been unthinkable just a few years prior. Before the Civil Rights Movement took to the streets, legislation like the Civil Rights Act was thought to be nonviable. The movement made it viable by shifting the cultural tide and pressuring those in power.

Unexpected crises and disasters can also very quickly widen the Overton Window. Part of what movements often do is to try to create a state of crisis to expand the window. But unexpected crises can also have the same effect. For example, the *Exxon Valdez* oil spill in 1989 released an estimated 11 million gallons of crude oil into the Alaskan sea and resulted in the Oil Pollution Act of 1990. The 1996 Port Arthur mass shooting in Australia led to immediate changes in gun controls laws, as did the mass shooting in Christchurch, New Zealand in 2019.* While none of these changes created fundamental social transformation, they're still important examples of progress that may not have been possible if not for the preceding crises.

Each one of these crises and disasters caused an incredible amount of suffering. I wish they didn't happen. But they did. And they will continue to. Not only that, but their pace will increase.

---

* I'm not even going to *touch* the sad state of affairs in US legislation after mass shootings.

It's now inevitable the climate crisis will escalate. We'll continue to see more and more climate and weather catastrophes. This will lead to compounding crises such as increased migration of climate refugees, economic instability, and food insecurity. Things are going to continue to get harder for us in the coming years. If a movement is ready to respond, our understanding of what's possible can expand. The Earth is supporting us in widening that Overton Window, giving us opportunities to reimagine what's "politically feasible." We just have to be ready with a vision bold enough to be worth it.

The Earth as Our Ally

Our understanding of what is "politically feasible" will continue to shift as the Earth continues to cry out loud. Even as we suffer the consequences of treating our home planet so poorly for so long, we need to continue to look to Earth as our ally in transformation.

Our work is to build resilient movements that are close to the Earth. It's only through connection and relationship, not only with other humans but with the beyond-human world, that we can be fully alive in this time—separation from the natural world is one of the root causes of the crises we are in. Someone once told me "Nature is the only thing big enough to hold our grief." Francis Weller encourages us to do our grief work by a large body of water whenever possible. Drawing on the natural world matters in every element of our work to transform the world.

How are we in relationship to nature? What are we learning from the natural world? How are we considering the impact of our actions on our non-human relatives? I've often wondered out loud what it would look like for our organizations, campaigns and movements to align our work plans with the seasons and the alignment of the stars. In every aspect of our work, how can we be in closer relationship with the rest of the cosmos?

It's also important to include fun, joy, silliness, celebration, and gratitude in our work. We see this mirrored in the way animals play and plants flourish. Healing is not only about looking at the darkest places. We have to pendulate—to move in and out of the hardest things and the most joyful things. This isn't about ignoring the darkness, but honoring the balance in the true nature of reality—if we're not careful, pain is all we see, yet it's never all that exists. We need to continue to bring it back to spirit, to remember the miracle that we are walking on this Earth at all, to be continually humbled by the reality that we're small specks of dust in a universe bigger than we can possibly comprehend, to be in awe of it, to be inspired by it.

We must continue to remind ourselves that while the conventional world we can see is scary and seems to be burning and collapsing all around us, this is not the only truth. We also live in a deeper, ultimate truth.

Liberation isn't only possible, it's already here, available to us at each moment. We just need to remember to breathe into it. Jewish elder and peace activist Michael Lerner encourages us "to respond to the universe with awe, wonder, and radical amazement." Cultivating awe and being inspired by the grandeur of the creation we're part of is a spiritual practice. And this practice will help us accept the reality of the times we live in. Because when we struggle less, when we suffer less, we can act from a place of stability and openheartedness that has the potential to truly transform the way we live, as individuals and as a whole.

The Liberation of Surrender

A relatively small intervention can impact an entire ecosystem. We've seen this in the years since a small number of wolves were reintroduced to Yellowstone National Park in 1995. There's a beautiful video online that tells us about the "trophic cascade" (an ecological process where changes in one species have wide-ranging ripple effects that transform the entire system) this small intervention caused.* Though many impacts of the reintroduction—a decrease in the deer population, widespread plant regeneration, increased biodiversity—were expected, there were also unanticipated impacts. The presence of the wolves changed the behavior of the rivers. Regenerating vegetation stabilized riverbanks, narrowed channels, and created pools that helped the river's course stabilize.

This is a reminder that natural systems are so complex, it's impossible to know the full impact of any intervention we make. When the Earth decides to make a change, there's no way for us to fully "know" what that change will look like. This is the era we are in. While human beings may be responsible for climate change, the changes happening across the Earth are no longer up to us. While we may have tipped the first domino, the momentum is no longer in our control. We are no longer the agents of change.† The Earth is. There's nothing we can do to control the changes we'll witness over the next ten, twenty, fifty years. We can only be in relationship with them.

There's no way for us to know exactly what the changes will be, when they will happen, and what the world will look like after. Science can give us some sense, but we'll never know exactly when the next climate disasters will happen, which species will go extinct next, and what trophic cascades may result. Often, because we don't have control, because we don't "know" everything that will happen, we're afraid. A lot of the training and preparation we need now works toward giving up control and surrendering to the changes that are inevitable and uncontrollable. And that's scary. It may even feel demoralizing. As activists,

---

* The video, called *How Wolves Change Rivers*, is less than five minutes long and available on YouTube. If you can watch the video before moving on reading this book, I highly recommend it.

† Were we ever?

we've always been taught to have a bold vision and develop a strategy to get there. To realize there's no plan and little we can do goes against so much of our training. But the worldview that underpins much of our current methods of engagement—that we're able to predict the future and control our outcomes, that human beings are the biggest drivers of change, the conviction that we can manage the Earth—has been handed down to us by modernity, the same system that got us into this mess.

When I lived in a monastery in my late teens, almost every hour of my life was scheduled. Chanting from 5:00 to 7:00 a.m. Breakfast from 7:00 a.m. Labor from 9:00 to 5:00 p.m. Chanting from 5:00 to 7:00 p.m. Dinner from 7:00 to 8:00 p.m. Lights out at 10:00 p.m. In the free moments, we had to find time to bathe, do our laundry, and take care of any other needs. Breakfast was the same puffed rice cereal every morning, lunch *and* dinner were rice, a simple dal, and a cauliflower potato curry. Seven days a week. I had very little control. And you know what? These were some of the freest days of my life. It turns out there can be great liberation when choice is stripped away and you don't have the responsibility of "figuring everything out." *Surrender* isn't about "giving up." At least, it's not about giving up on life, purpose, or beauty. It's about giving up the delusion of control. To simply be in the flow can be incredibly freeing.

This moment isn't about giving up agency and letting the Earth destroy what we hold sacred through devastating climate events. It's about seeing the planet as our ally in healing and transformation and learning to be in relationship with the Earth's flowing energies.

CHAPTER 9

The Delusion of Individualism

We are not here to win and we are not here to tell other groups how they should do their work. We are here to be our true selves and to serve life.

THE FIERCE VULNERABILITY NETWORK HANDBOOK

We are not trying to save the earth. We are the earth trying to save itself.

RESISTENCIA INDIGENA/MUNDANO

WHEN I TALK to people about some of our most deeply held traumas, I've found almost all of them end up being some version of "I don't belong." *I'll never be loved. I'm always going to be alone. I'm not pretty enough, good enough, smart enough to be accepted.* Most of us have some experience with this feeling. As cooperative and relational creatures, the fear of not belonging is one of the most common and scary things we feel. Many psychologists agree a sense of isolation and loneliness is perhaps the most common source of trauma.

And it is a delusion created in the conventional realm.

In the ultimate realm, we live in an interdependent world. I believe this to be a universal law of nature, much like gravity. Yes, there are people who don't believe in gravity. But gravity is a universal truth, and even people who don't believe in it are governed by its laws. As common as the fear of not belonging is, the ultimate reality is we can't help but belong to each other. In our interdependent world, there is nothing outside of belonging. A redwood tree never questions its sense of belonging. It wouldn't even think to ask such a question—its body knows there's no such thing as *not* belonging. By virtue of existing at all, we are made up of and connected to everything around us, now, in the past, and in the future.

I'm talking about Belonging with a capital B. The kind of Belonging the redwood feels. The kind of Belonging where we feel like we can share our deepest self and be witnessed, express our deepest fears and be held, speak our most vulnerable shame and be in relationship. As much as we're a relational species, how many of us ever get the privilege of feeling *unconditional, unwavering, universal* Belonging? How rare is that? We've created such an incredibly isolating society that few of us ever really get to sink into that sort of community.

I believe creating a culture within movement spaces where people never even think to question their sense of belonging might be the biggest contribution we can make to social change. If we can be so grounded in the reality that we belong to each other, perhaps we can extend that sense of belonging to those who have lost their way.

The Reality of Belonging

Here's another way to look at the delusion that we are independent beings. According to research, as much as 90 percent of the cells in our body are made up of bacteria and other microorganisms. These microorganisms are so tiny they only make up 1–3 percent of our body's mass, but still, the majority of the cells in a human body are . . . not human.* Science educator Luis Villazon

---

* Here's one study from the National Institutes of Health that speaks to this— *https://bit.ly/3QvzSLX*. Some research suggests the percentage of non-human cells in our bodies is closer to 56 percent, but 90 percent is the most commonly cited figure.

writes for the BBC's *Science Focus*, "Like all multicellular animals, we can't easily point to individual components and say, 'This is part of me, and this is not.' Your body is like a city—it has a collective identity that goes beyond its individual inhabitants. The pigeons and squirrels who call London home are just as much part of it as the humans who live there."

I remember the moment I first heard the science behind the statement that we are all made of stardust. I thought it was just a pretty thing we say and didn't realize it was actually a scientific fact: every element we're made of, and the Earth is made up of, was fused inside of a star some unknown millions of years ago. Since we're made up of elements on Earth, our bodies are entirely made up of elements fused in a star. Every time I think about it, it blows my mind.

But where did the original elements like hydrogen and helium come from? As many of us learned in school, they've existed since the Big Bang. While there's still a lot we don't know about the Big Bang, it's said that before the explosion, everything in the universe existed on one singular point. Out of that singular point, the universe came into being, spreading the original building blocks for all that is and all that will ever be into our ever-expanding universe. In essence, the original building blocks for everything that is come from one, singular source. Not just the things you and I are made of, but the trees, the birds, and the bees, our automobiles, our mobile phones, our guns, our nuclear weapons, the moon, the stars, and the galaxies. We all came from the same source.

Most of us have come a long way from living in right relationship with the natural world. Due to colonization, slavery, forced migration, and so many other factors, many of our communities have actually become scared of the beyond-human world. Western notions about "conquering" nature or the capitalist view that nature is a commodity haven't helped. Even people who "love" nature see themselves as separate from it.

But everything that exists comes from nature. The reality is that there is nothing outside of it. The idea that human beings are somehow separate from nature is a delusion.

The idea that "we are all one" isn't just some silly hippie concept. It's a scientific fact we've forgotten. If the delusion we don't belong is one of our biggest sources of trauma, our path to healing has to be about reminding each other of this universal truth: we can't help but belong to each other.

There Is No Personal Liberation

Just as I wouldn't be who I am today if it weren't for the trauma my stepfather experienced, I also wouldn't be who I am today if not for the healing so many of my teachers, mentors, and friends experienced. I think about Jun-san, a Japanese Buddhist nun who was like a second mother to me in my late teenage years. Living in a monastery with her, traveling throughout South Asia, and walking all those miles with her made an enormous contribution to my own healing. Her own journey of growing from a rebellious young person into someone with decades of dedicated practice as a Buddhist monastic allowed her to mentor me.

But remember: fierce vulnerability is not about individual healing. The very idea of personal healing is a delusion. There is no such thing as individual liberation in an interdependent world.

Personal, individual work is part of the journey to collective liberation, because each one of us is part of the larger whole in this fractal world. If my hand is hurting, my body isn't well. But if I heal the wound on my hand and ignore my bleeding nose, I'm deluded to think I am now well because one part of my body is better. So yes, let's all continue to take care of ourselves in all the ways we need to. But let's never lose sight of the fact that in our path toward liberation, the extent to which we work on our own healing is the extent to which we can offer the world collective healing.

Healing, Not Winning

Shoutout to grandmas everywhere.

Nancy Ambrose was the maternal grandmother of Howard Thurman and a great influence on his life. Thurman, of course, would go on to become one of the most impactful mentors to Dr. King. One day, a young Thurman came home bloodied after a fight he had "won." His grandmother proclaimed, "No one wins a fight." Rev. Liza Rankow, producer of *The Living Wisdom of Howard Thurman*, wrote about this interaction between a young Thurman and his grandmother.

Reflecting years later, Thurman wrote:

There is something seductive about the quickened sense of power that comes when the fight is on. There is a bewitching something men call honor, on behalf of which they often do and become the dishonorable thing. It is very strange. How honor is often sacrificed in defense of honor.[12]

Most of us are raised in this black/white, binary worldview where everything is considered a zero-sum game. For us to be liberated, we need to "win." We need to win our campaigns and build more power so we can overpower our opponents. That's the story. But that's the old story. Today, we find ourselves in a different story.

I'm hyper-competitive. I always want to win. To this day, the biggest argument LiZhen and I ever got into was over a game of Monopoly Deal. When we play silly ice-breaker games in our workshops, I *really* want to win. I once accidentally tackled a high-school student during a game of "The Big Wind Blows."* But in the world today, there's no such thing as "winning," because we aren't in a game. Out of the delusion of individualism, the delusion of "winning" emerges. The story we're in now is that we are either going to learn to live in right relationship to each other and to Earth, or we're all going to lose together. As Dr. King once warned, "Today it is no longer a choice between violence and nonviolence: it is either nonviolence or nonexistence."[13]

In the conventional realm where things can be black and white, it's easier to measure "success." How many people signed up to our mailing list? How many people came to our protest? How much more power do we have then them? How much can we force our will? How big can we get? When do we win? In today's story, in the ultimate realm, the metrics are less clear. It's harder to measure the strength of a relationship or to quantify healing. Because healing is not about winning. No one has to lose in order for someone to heal.

I want to work toward a world where we see violence— including the violence of separation—itself as the enemy, a world that sees that any attempt at forcing our will over another will never give us sustained peace. I don't want to win anymore. I just want us to be healed.†

---

* This is a game where you sit in a circle and one person stands in the middle. That person completes the sentence, "The big wind blows for . . ." and says something true about themselves. It could be, "The big wind blows for . . . anyone wearing glasses. Anyone who has an older sibling. Anyone who grew up speaking a language other than English." Then everyone else for whom that is true gets up and runs to another empty chair until all the chairs are filled and one person is left standing in the middle.

† Unless we're playing Monopoly Deal. Then I'm coming for the win.

Privilege Isn't All Rainbows

Hot take. Sometimes, I feel bad for wealthy, heterosexual cis-gendered white men.

Let me explain.

I don't feel bad for them because I think they're being oppressed. At least in the conventional world, they aren't. However, recently we've heard a lot of white men talk about feeling like they are being oppressed.* I saw a social media meme once that said, "When you're used to privilege, equality feels like oppression." This makes a ton of sense to me and largely explains why so many white men are feeling oppressed. As social movements gain steam and more marginalized voices are heard, people who got used to having *all* the space feel threatened. They mistake equality with oppression.

I disagree that they're being oppressed, but I have some empathy for them. From their perspective, the reality that they're not actually being oppressed doesn't matter as much as that they *feel* like they're being oppressed. That does matter. But that's not even the reason I feel bad for them. The real reason is I believe we're living in a time of many emerging Truths with a capital T. From an expansive understanding of gender to the 1619 Project,† Truths are being revealed at an incredible pace. The veils of delusion we have been living with for so long are lifting. And wealthy, heterosexual cis-gendered white men have the farthest to fall to get back to Truth. In so many ways, the

---

* I listen to a lot of conservative podcasts, so I may be hearing this more than the average leftist. This is a pretty common sentiment among many conservative white men. And while I don't hear the word "oppressed" as much on the left, I have heard similar sentiments from white men there as well.

† The *1619 Project* is a book and an effort initiated by journalist Nikole Hannah-Jones to look to 1619—the year the first enslaved Africans arrived in the United States—as the birth of the nation.

intersection of all those privileged identities means they're the ones living in the deepest delusion.

The nature of privilege is that you don't have to see oppression—you've always been taught everything is okay and going according to plan, and you've rarely (if ever) witnessed anything that challenges that narrative. Communities who have historically been marginalized have known forever the police are violent. Poor communities have always known we need to depend on each other to survive. Black folks didn't need Hurricane Katrina to realize the state might not be there for them. Immigrant communities know capitalism is exploitative.

There's a movie called *Brother Outsider*, a documentary about activist Bayard Rustin. Rustin was a major player in the Civil Rights Movement. He mentored Dr. King and was the lead organizer of the March on Washington where Dr. King gave his famous "I Have a Dream" speech. He was also openly gay—for which he was often ostracized from the movement. The documentary features interviews with Walter Naegle, Rustin's longtime lover. Naegle, who was white and almost four decades younger than Rustin, recalls coming out to his parents. The conversation went like this. "I'm gay. He's Black. And he's older than you."

While I hope to one day live in a world where we celebrate love in all its manifestations, that's a lot of truth to drop in one conversation in the 1970s. I wonder if that's sometimes what it feels like to have been deluded by privilege your whole life—like having an elephant-sized reality check dropped on you. Out of the delusion of separation comes the delusion of supremacy. And out of the delusion of supremacy, we've built countless narratives and institutions that have blinded the very people who created them.

To navigate the transitions we'll soon face with grace, we must come to terms with many long-hidden truths. As we engage with that work, historical privilege may work against you. In the relative world, some people are absolutely privileged and continue to benefit from that privilege. But in the ultimate realm, as long as we're swimming in the dynamics of oppression, we're all oppressed. It's important for us to remember this, because that whole collective healing thing includes everybody. Collective healing isn't about collectively healing only the people we love.

CHAPTER 10

The Delusion of Knowing

The right view is no view.

THÍCH NHẤT HẠNH

We tend to only legitimize what makes sense (in articulated meaning): what we can understand through chains of words. As a result, a whole world of unsayable possibilities is dismissed as meaningless.

VANESSA MACHADO DE OLIVEIRA ANDREOTTI

WHEN I GET into conflicts with my partner, my habit is to try to "fix it" as quickly as possible. Despite my work in the world, I have a natural tendency to be conflict avoidant, so I try to "figure it out" so we can get back to "harmony" at all costs.* My mind runs 1,000 miles a minute trying to think of what I can say to make her feel better. Over time, I realized my desire to "make her feel better" wasn't actually about her. It was about my own discomfort with being in conflict. I wasn't trying to make her feel better as much as trying to get her to stop expressing difficult emotions that trigger mine.

When I'm regulated, I can recognize this as a pattern I have. But when I'm in panic, my amygdala kicks into gear and

---

* I'm a nine on the Enneagram. That will make sense to some people.

I desperately try to figure out the one thing I can say to fix it all. This rarely works. In fact, it usually makes things worse. It's when I can stop trying to "figure it out" and slow down enough to listen to our hearts that we can begin to reconnect. It's when I can get out of my head and into my body that I can contribute to moving us back toward relationship.

When we zoom out of the fractal, I see a similar dynamic playing out in our world. The compounding crises put us into our collective panic zones, and we retreat to our heads, trying desperately to figure out how to "do" racial reconciliation, how to "fix" climate change, how to build a campaign strategy that will save the world. This is another delusion keeping us from liberation: the idea that if we think hard enough, we can figure our way out of this mess.

The compounding crises we live in are far too complex for us to "figure out" using our intellect alone. There's no work plan big enough to encompass our current situation. There's no campaign strategy to liberation.

In *Reinventing Organizations*, Frederic Laloux quotes Jean-François Zobrist, the former CEO of a French car parts manufacturer, explaining the difference between something being *complicated* versus *complex*.

> *An airplane like a Boeing 747 is a complicated system. There are millions of parts that need to work together seamlessly. But everything can be mapped out; if you change one part, you should be able to predict all the consequences. A bowl of spaghetti is a complex system. Even though it has just a few dozen "parts," it is virtually impossible to predict what will happen when you pull at the end of a strand of spaghetti that sticks out of the bowl.*

Our mistake is thinking our world is a complicated place. I mean, in the conventional realm, it's definitely *also* complicated.

But the larger problems we face as a species involve living systems that are *complex*, and we can't think our way out of them. Yet we live with a delusion that we're smart enough to understand it all—if we study hard enough and map everything out, we can put it all down in a book with fancy charts and graphs. In our attempts to solve the world's problems, we often end up creating strategies worse than the thing we're trying to fix.

We can't think our way out of complex problems, but we can intuit our way through them. As Laloux writes, we can move from a "command and control" worldview to a "sense and response" way of being. The path to liberation is less about *making* change and more about being in relationship to it. We're not working on transformation; we're walking with it. We're no longer leading this process. Earth is. The challenge is we live in a culture that values rationality over intuition at all costs, causing many of us to lose touch with our ability to listen to or trust our own instincts.

Every time I've been involved in building a campaign strategy for some issue or another, it looks similar to how I imagine a corporate business meeting would. We sit around a table with charts, graphs, reports, and lots of data. We create power maps, spectrum of allies analyses, strategic plans. I'm not saying there isn't a need for those things. But I have a deep sense the world in this moment *also* needs wisdom found somewhere other than our intellect. In addition to strategic planning sessions, perhaps we need to sit silently in nature together, to look out at the stars, to ask our ancestors for guidance, to sing together, to make art together, and to slow down enough to listen to the voice of emergent wisdom in our bones.

There's no manual for this moment we are in. We try way too hard to create one, as if we can map out every bit of complexity of our universe. We can't.[*]

[*] Says the person who helped to create the nearly 300-page *FVN Handbook*. Multiple truths.

Listening to the Tao

I have a tattoo of Winnie the Pooh carrying a backpack full of fireworks.

When I was seventeen, during some of the most tumultuous and harmful years of my life, I was tripping on LSD and hanging out with a bunch of friends on the roof of some abandoned shack, smoking weed and setting off fireworks. At the time, I had a beautiful hand-blown glass pipe that was the envy of all my friends. We would often get lost just gazing into its intricate designs. At some point, my friend Josh jokingly yelled across the roof, "Yo, Kazu, I'll trade you this for your pipe." In his hand was a small strip of blue rubber—a piece of trash he'd found lying around on the roof.

I was getting ready to leave for the Interfaith Pilgrimage of the Middle Passage, a six-month walking journey from Massachusetts to New Orleans retracing the footsteps of the transatlantic slave trade.* It was a drug- and alcohol-free walk, so I knew I had no need for a pipe. Josh was one of my closest friends, so I thought, *Why not?*

"Sure," I hollered back. To which my other friends erupted in anger.

"Why would you trade away your pipe? I would've paid you for it! What the hell is that thing he gave you anyway?" they shouted.

Looking down into my hand at this blue strip of rubber, I randomly blurted out, "It's the meaning of life!" I was tripping on acid.

"What do you mean?"

Of course I had no answer, so I murmured, "It just *is*, man . . ."

And I kept saying it. "It just is." "It just is." "It just is."

---

* I wrote a bit more about this, and the impact this journey had on my life, in *Healing Resistance.*

And at some point, I started to believe it. Like, *really* believe it. This may or may not have coincided with the peak of my acid hallucination, but I was convinced I'd discovered the meaning of life. An hour later, I was literally on the floor of my friend Than's kitchen in tears at my discovery. At some point I convinced my other friend Jacob this strip of rubber represented the meaning of life (he was also tripping on acid). My first convert! We spent all night walking, smoking more weed, lighting off fireworks and waking the neighbors, and repeating our newfound mantra, "It just is."

Something funny happened, though. When you're on drugs, you have all sorts of insights that usually sound silly the next morning. This one, however, kind of stuck. *Everything just is.* It is what it is. It's not good, it's not bad, it simply *is.* Our problem is we try to explain things too much and we lose touch with the simplicity of that truth.

Six months later, I found myself in a bookstore in Japan. Browsing through some books, I saw *The Tao of Pooh* by Benjamin Hoff. I'd never heard of it before and knew nothing about Taoism. But it sounded interesting, so I grabbed it off the shelf and turned to the back cover.

"While Eeyore frets . . . and Piglet hesitates . . . and Rabbit calculates . . . and Owl pontificates . . . Pooh just is."

I was blown away. I read the whole book that night. From that moment, Taoism became one of the great influences of my life, the *Tao of Pooh* one of my bibles, and Winnie the Pooh one of my great spiritual guides.

Hence the tattoo.

Shortly after this incident, I read *The Electric Kool-Aid Acid Test* by Tom Wolfe. The book talked about using LSD as a catalyst to open the door to different perspectives and realities, but at some point, one needs to move beyond mind-altering substances to find true liberation. These substances can open a door, but you need to step through.* I deeply resonated with this, and after coming away from that evening with the answer to life, I stopped taking LSD. I no longer smoke marijuana and haven't taken LSD in over twenty years. While some people use these substances as part of their spiritual practice, I realized at some point they were getting in the way of mine.

Back to the *Tao of Pooh*, where Hoff writes:

> *earth was in essence a reflect of heaven, run by the same laws—not by the laws of men. These laws affected not only the spinning of distant planets, but the activities of the birds in the forest and the fish in the sea.... According to Lao-tse, the more man interfered with the natural balance produced and governed by the universal laws, the further away the harmony retreated into the distance. The more forcing, the more trouble ... What he saw operating behind everything in heaven and earth he called Tao (DAO), 'the Way.'*[14]

I love science. When I listen to a great teacher talk about bio-mimicry, cosmology, or quantum physics, my mind fills with awe. It's no different than when I'm awed by a deep spiritual teaching. Science and spirituality are both attempts to understand truth; scientists and spiritual sages have spent centuries trying to understand the laws that govern the universe. One of the dangers of science, however, is our tendency to seek understanding so we can find loopholes and bend the laws of nature

---

* In the last fifteen or so years, we have seen a huge surge in the use of various substances in psychedelic-assisted therapy, as well as the growing recognition of the wisdom of Indigenous plant medicines. Both have shown to be effective in supporting people through trauma healing, navigating addictions, managing anxiety, or simply communing with a larger power. However, both of these practices are supported by experienced guides—therapists, ceremony leaders, and others. They are a far cry from the days of using substances simply to get high.

to our will. Science has given us a deeper understanding of why certain fruits grow in certain areas in certain seasons, for example. So, we genetically modify them, spray them with harmful pesticides, create artificial environments for fruits to grow in, and then we transport them thousands of miles so we can enjoy a mango any time of year.

Science in this way can be deeply disembodied. It's about trying to understand the laws of the universe strictly through our intellect. There's no end to this quest. Given enough time and scientific advancements, the story goes, we'll know *everything*. In believing this, we lose the ability to simply be in awe of the mystery of it all. We lose humility and grow ever more attached to the constant consumption of knowledge.

One of my favorite things to read about is the farthest edges of our scientific understanding—the things scientists don't yet understand. Did you know over 95 percent of the universe is made up of "dark matter" and "dark energy?" While scientists know this is true, they have very little idea what dark matter and dark energy actually is, how they work, or what they're made of! That means only 5 percent of the universe—our bodies, our planet, all planets, the stars, all matter and energy—is made up of atomic matter we're familiar with. That amazes me! It's so humbling. While I'm curious about the mystery of dark matter, I'm also perfectly content marveling at what I don't understand; that dark matter just . . . is. There's wisdom in letting go of the constant need to understand.

In our endless battle to figure things out and bend nature to our will, we've lost our ability to listen to the subtle voice of the Tao. We've lost our ability to listen to the wisdom in our bodies, to hear the meaning of the songs of the birds, to understand the lessons in the movement of the stars. We've lost our intuition, our connection to the spirit world, to our ancestors, to emergence.

While Taoists caution against using words—a tool of the intellect—to describe the Tao, well, you're reading a book, so words are what we got. In our current age, the word "emergence" is something I often associate with the Tao. In a lecture at the California Institute for Integral Studies in 2004, cosmologist Brian Swimme said emergence is the "Single energy that begins 13.7 billion years ago [at the Big Bang] and sweeps through to our moment. It's a single energy. It's one process." Everything happening in our bodies—from your brain processing the words on this page to the chemical reactions happening inside you at the molecular level—is a continuation of this process, of one single energy dating back to the Big Bang. That's the Tao.

Emergence is remembering how to jump back into that stream. And that's hard for those of us who have spent our entire lives being taught to trust science exclusively, ignore intuition, and take control of our lives.

Swimme reminds us that since the moment of the Big Bang, the universe has created stars, planets, life—all the natural beauty that exists in the galaxies, every moment of birth, every second of laughter, every tear—without hands, a brain, or a plan. The process of creating "everything that ever was" hasn't followed an "inherent plan that works out the way you'd work out an engineer's plan and build a building." The power of creative emergence involves profound confusion, wandering around, and getting lost. Swimme explains:

Creative emergence loves ambiguity. Even ambivalence. It's the ability to embrace the situation and not have a clear idea of how to move forward. One clear idea is not good enough. You need millions and millions of ideas. Try them out and see which one finally takes off.

Part of why we're in this mess is because humanity stopped listening to emergence; we've spent the last several millennia largely going against the flow, too long letting our intellect lead and trying to control things beyond our understanding. The path forward is about letting go of our attachment to understanding and control, accepting that we're lost, confused, and don't know what lies ahead, but continuing to move anyway, walking slowly enough to hear the subtle voice of the Tao. The path forward is not, as we've been taught, about *forward progress*. The path forward is about going backward and remembering—remembering we're part of something much greater, remembering our ancestors knew they were part of their larger ecosystem, remembering we can live in accordance with the eternal laws that put us in right relationship with everything that is.

Tao. Emergence. God. Nature. Intuition. Your heart's true calling. The voices of your ancestors. Whatever you want to call it, there is a deep wisdom that cannot be fully understood by the intellect. I believe our most skillful next steps as a species will become clear in this wisdom.

Training for Emergence

Because so many of us have lost our ability to listen to emergence, we need to reorient ourselves to it. The universe has built-in feedback systems constantly telling us what is working and what is not. If we listen carefully enough, we can hear these voices.

In 2013, I started an organization that existed on the Gift Economy for ten years. This means many things, among them: we had over 10,000 people come through our programs, and we never charged a single dime to any of them. We barely did any fundraising and stopped applying for foundation grants unless there was a relationship and we were asked to apply. We didn't wait for funding to start a new program. We listened for feedback. We put our faith in our work and trusted if our work was valuable, it would be sustained. If funding didn't follow, that was feedback telling us to find something else to do. We could only grow to the extent our community and the universe allowed. We didn't paint a fundraising target and develop a complicated strategy to try to meet it. We simply did our work.

In our world today, this isn't how we're trained. In the nonprofit sector, we're trained to create a budget and develop a strategy to raise it. We're trained to constantly grow. If we're under budget, this isn't viewed as feedback from the universe. It's simply a challenge to overcome with more fundraising; we're meant to survive at all costs. The "survive at all costs" and "constant growth" worldviews are borrowed from free-market capitalism. Because we think we must always "figure it out," we stop asking questions and listening for answers. We're too busy trying to figure it out to listen.

Sometimes, the questions we ask are too superficial. We spend the entire year asking ourselves things like, "How do I meet my fundraising goal for the year?" and "How do we recruit more donors?" while our ecological and social systems are torn apart all around us. Other times, we get too overwhelmed by the scale of the crises and can only ask ourselves questions that aren't really questions, like "WTF?"

> The questions I'm asking myself these days: How do I get back into right relationship with earth? How do I remember my belonging and interdependence? How do I cultivate right relationship? How do I invite beauty to emerge? How do we heal together?

One of the greatest gifts of my life is that I'm a resident of a community called Canticle Farm, a multiracial, multigenerational community of fortyish people committed to being agents of healing amid this Great Turning, the transitional time we live in. We often discuss modeling racial healing, how to honor our commitment to restorative conflict engagement, how to raise our kids together, and how to live with shared economics.

I've had these conversations with many different communities for years, but grappling with them while living on the same land together has brought my commitment to a whole new level. I'm often humbled by the *immense potential* I feel in our collective experiment. When I ask myself *how* we might fulfill all this potential, it's very clear to me *I have no fucking clue.* That not-knowing excites and inspires me. The fact that I sense immense potential and have no idea how to realize it tells me I'm asking questions big enough for these times. I don't need to know, because there's no way to know. The point isn't to "know." The point is to ask the right questions, to grapple with them, and to take the next step our hearts lead us toward.

As David Cooperrider and Diana Whitney, two pioneers of Appreciative Inquiry, often say, "Human systems grow toward what they persistently ask questions about." If our questions are about how we win the next political campaign, we may "figure it out," but it won't lead us to liberation. That question—with all due respect—is too small. In this moment, we need to grapple with questions too big to be knowable. The responses to these big questions come through the voice of emergence, and they can be really subtle. Reality TV shows scream at you. Commercials and advertisements yell at you. Social media grabs you by the throat and doesn't let go. These are distractions that get in the way of me noticing the wind gently blowing in my ear.

Of course, not everything about emergence is subtle. The effects of the climate crisis aren't so subtle. Racial uprisings aren't subtle. Political upheaval, corporate corruption, and war aren't subtle. These are all forms of feedback the universe gives us. But we're so deluded we're not able to interpret them as such. We don't listen deeply enough to understand the messages behind each crisis.

While these forms of feedback that scream in our ear "HEY! This isn't working! Do things differently!" aren't so subtle, my sense is the guidance toward repair will be. The instructions on how to move forward won't be so loud. As we move through these times of urgency, how do we learn to be still enough to hear the subtle voice of emergence? How do we listen to this voice even while we mobilize into the streets? We can't be slow like "we have fifty years to figure this out" slow. We need to be out in the streets tomorrow. But as we move, our hearts need to be grounded and our breathing needs to be slow. Ironically, one of the great pieces of wisdom on this comes from an incredibly violent institution: the Navy SEALS, who teaches their soldiers that "slow is smooth and smooth is fast." In the midst of urgency, we need to learn to slow down our responses. In the increasing pace of our world, we need to find stillness.

Much of our ability to do this lies in our own healing. The more unintegrated trauma we have, the more easily we enter panic—where everything speeds up. As agents of change, the more healed we are, the more we can contribute to a grounded collective nervous system. Being in our panic zone doesn't allow us to slow down enough to listen for the voice of emergence. It doesn't allow us to access the creativity needed for these times. Our thinking becomes more linear, and the need for the "order" of command and control takes over. My *thinking* keeps me from *being*.

In 2018, when I attended my first FVN training (then the Yet-To-Be-Named Network), we had a pretty extensive list of assignments to prepare ourselves. One included spending an evening without electricity—no phones or computers, no electric lights, just candlelight. Part of the intention was to bring awareness to our carbon footprint—some members of the Network live completely off grid and without electricity. But this practice gave me so much more than awareness of my carbon emissions. When I spend an evening under candlelight, I move closer to the person I want to become. Without the distractions of technology, I read, write, meditate, make art, rest. Above all, I slow down. I can hear the voice of emergence. Sometimes, when I slow down enough, I can see a crack in the veil. I can see the coding in the Matrix. Knowing my ancestors spent evenings in the light and warmth of a flame for so much longer than electric light and gas heaters have been around connects me to the wisdom of countless generations. When I'm under candlelight, I can literally only see what is directly in front of me. I can't see the busyness of my calendar, the books on my bookshelf, the pile of paperwork on my desk. Only what's right here.

That's so much of what emergence is: listening to what's right here. This candlelight practice is something I've adopted since and try to do on a regular basis.* While this particular practice may not resonate with everybody, I believe it's crucial for all of us to relearn how to listen. Truly listen.

Practices to Listen to Emergence

- Spend an evening under candlelight. Grab some candles, light a fireplace, or find an oil lantern. Turn off all electricity, and simply be human.

- Go for a walk in nature in silence. Don't listen to music or a podcast, and don't talk on the phone. In fact, leave your phone at home. Listen to the sounds of nature. *Listen.*

- Visit a tree, a stone, a river, or some other being in nature. Make an offering. Ask it a question. Listen. Do

---

* Full confession: I used to do this one night a week, but the NBA season, the Marvel Cinematic Universe, and new episodes of *The Challenge* have taken over.... Not to mention a small child. But this is something I hope to get back to doing. I have never regretted spending an evening in candlelight.

this practice with a friend. Each of you can find a spot in nature to spend a few minutes and then share with each other what you heard.

• Even if you live in an urban environment, nature is all around you. It may be a house plant or some weeds growing through a crack in the concrete, a patch of grass in a city park, or even the breeze outside your door. Begin to bring awareness to what comes up for you as you recognize nature is everywhere, without ignoring the reality of the obstacles to accessing more wildness.

• Grab a notepad and a pen, start writing, and don't allow yourself to stop. Simply let your hand write whatever it wants to, without thinking about it. This kind of stream-of-consciousness writing can bypass your intellect and access a different intelligence.

• Keep a journal next to your bed, and journal about your dreams every morning. The more you do this, the more you will begin to remember your dreams. Look for patterns. Begin to ask yourself a question before bed.

• Create altars. This doesn't need to be spiritual, but creating a space in your home specifically for centering and creating beauty can be supportive. Visit it often. Make offerings of food or wildflowers. Make altars in nature with whatever you find around you.

• Move your body! Practices like yoga asana, t'ai chi, qi gong, Theater of the Oppressed/Living, somatic practices, or even intuitive dance can unlock the wisdom of your body. Try holding a question in your mind as you move, listening to your body.

• Utilize divination tools such as tarot cards or I-Ching. If you're not familiar with them, find a friend who knows!

> You don't have to believe these tools have some sort of magical power. A lot of the wisdom is simply in the practice of learning to see meaning in things and to interpret what they tell you.

The First Strategic Step

Practicing emergence is about the vulnerability of not knowing and the fierceness of trying anyway. It's about moving forward without a strategic plan and a million contingencies in place. It's surrendering to the unknown without being debilitated by it. I long for movement spaces where our "strategy sessions" happen sitting in circle around a candle as opposed to staring at a Power-Point presentation of Power Maps.

After weeks of debate about our mission and vision statements, we decided on this language for the FVN Handbook:

We long to see what life wants to do through us. We resist the temptation, therefore, to predict or to attempt to shape the outcomes of this experiment by way of fine-tuned mission or vision statements. We simply hold trust the teams we assemble—if true to the DNA described in these pages— will offer beautiful and sacred gifts to the continuing struggle for justice and wholeness.

I find myself laughing as I read this. I feel like we're doing *everything* "wrong" according to traditional ways of thinking about how social change happens. We're going against every best practice.

If I'd listened to my mind alone, I may have chosen to work with an organization that has a strategic plan and an Instagram account. It's how I've always been trained as an "activist." But if

I'm real with myself and really listen, really make space for emergence, I know in the very pit of my stomach something is fundamentally flawed about continuing to organize social movements in the same old ways we always have. We certainly don't have it all figured out—part of the refreshing nature of FVN is that we're *very* clear we don't know. By the time you read this book, FVN may not even be around. As inspiring as my time with FVN has been, it hasn't always been a smooth process, and multiple people have left our work with feelings of hurt. But something about the *way* FVN operates inspires me.

The reality is no one knows how to do racial healing at scale, because it's never been done before. No one knows the best way to respond to the climate crisis, because it's never been done before. It's not about knowing every step and turn that will get us to our North Star. It's about sensing the general direction we need to walk in, being clear about our deepest values, leaning softly into what feels right, sensing the feedback, and adjusting slightly to stay in the smoothness of the current.

If you're kayaking down a river, it's not like you know the *exact* path you're going to take. You simply try to find the smoothest part of the river and adjust as you go. You know what direction you're headed, and you know your immediate next step. The direction you need to paddle your kayak three minutes from now will only become illuminated once you're there. Sense and respond.

When I had that initial conversation with my family about our childhood experiences, I had no idea what was going to happen next. But I had a vision of our family healing and a deep faith that reading my letter would move us in that direction. It's the same faith I have in this thing we are calling fierce vulnerability. I have a vision of healing our collective wounds. I have deep faith if we show up with our own vulnerability where harm is happening and muster the fierceness to stay there, some magic could move us in the direction of collective healing.

The Smallest Interventions

Through my own experiments in fierce vulnerability, I'm starting to see new possibilities. As I come to more acceptance about the enormity of our crises, the inevitability of collapse, the suffering that will follow, and the sheer complexity of these problems, I'm humbled. And out of that humility, I wonder if the best thing we may be able to do may be much smaller than my previous fantasies of worldwide revolution.

Someone still needs to figure out the most effective campaign strategy to get oil companies to completely divest from fossil fuel. I *do* still think that's necessary. But it's not the work I am feeling called to, and it may not be the work of fierce vulnerability. The problems are *gargantuan*. And maybe, just maybe, the appropriate response is to be small. The crises are incredibly complex. Maybe the right thing to do is the simplest thing. Maybe all we can do—all we need to do—is to continue to affirm life, create beauty, cultivate connection, and move toward healing even in the midst of collapse. Maybe all we can do is speak our deepest truths by leading with our hearts, hoping to connect with others and to help them feel something—perhaps to release unprocessed grief or fear.

Somehow, as "small" as these goals are, they feel like an appropriate response to the escalation of the crises. Russian-Belgian chemist Ilya Prigogine once said, "When a system is far from equilibrium, small islands of coherence have the capacity to shift the entire system." If we remain humble, acknowledge we have no idea what it's ultimately going to take to transform society, and focus on things we know we can impact, the results may be bigger than we can imagine.

In space, and in ultimate reality, there's no up or down, left or right, forward or backward. Maybe our binary way of measuring things like "big" and "small" is skewed. Maybe this is another characteristic of "quantum organizing." It's a path that definitely feels fiercely vulnerable.

In the World

One time, I was on the phone with a friend of mine who had just come out of a really difficult court hearing that did not go well for her. She was clearly in panic, speaking really fast about everything that had happened.

At some point in the conversation, I stopped her and asked her to take a deep breath. She paused and immediately started to cry. She quickly went from spitting out the "facts" of what had happened to releasing the emotions she was feeling.

This didn't change the difficult situation she was in, but it changed how she was orienting to it. It got her out of her panic, and after being able to say, "I'm scared and don't know what to do," she was able to think about what might be next from a more grounded place.

My asking her to take just one breath was a small, simple intervention. But it affected everything about how she was responding to the moment.

Perhaps all we can do is get the world to take a deep breath. It won't solve all our problems, but it may allow us to respond to this moment of crisis from a more grounded place. From a place where creativity, empathy, and visioning are possible. From a place where we can hear the Tao. Who knew washing your hands might prevent the next global pandemic? Or that something as small as the movement of a fox or the drop of an acorn could cause a massive avalanche? Or that the splitting of tiny atoms inside minerals like uranium would trigger a nuclear explosion?

Traditionally, a theory of change is about understanding inputs and outputs. If we do A, B, and C, then X, Y, and Z will happen. The X, Y, and Z of the movement I want to be a part of is about creating lasting peace and beauty by fundamentally restructuring everything we think we know about how to be alive on this planet. In this complex, emergent world, there's no way to predict what inputs will get us there. The theories we need right now are not theories of change so much as theories of being. We can't control the impact we'll have on the world, but we can control how we show up. We can have faith that if we show up embodying a certain way of being, something beautiful can happen.

In a fierce vulnerability workshop, Chris told us one metric he uses to measure the success of actions he participates in these days is, "Was *I* personally transformed by participating in this action?" Not, "Did we change legislation?" but "Did this action change *me*?" With metrics as small as that, we may never "win." But perhaps we can transform ourselves.

When I think about how to save the planet, I collapse under the pressure. When I think about how I want to show up, my mind eases, my body relaxes, and I feel a burden lift from my spirit. There's space for creativity. This is part of the paradox of our work: holding the tension between the bigness of our hopes (to change *everything*) and the smallness of our intentions (to simply show up). Our work is to go to the places where harm and destruction are happening, to face injustice head-on, and to be reminders that affirming life, creating beauty, and centering relationship is possible, even in the midst of social and ecological collapse.

CHAPTER 11

Healing Is Not Enough

Protest is like begging the powers that be to dig a well. Direct action is digging the well and daring them to stop you.

DAVID GRAEBER

In order for me to write poetry that isn't political I must listen to the birds and in order to hear the birds the warplanes must be silent.

MARWAN MAKHOUL

I ADMIT IT, the name of this chapter is a bit clickbait-y. Or page turner-y. (Not sure what the book equivalent of clickbait is.) The title is a little facetious, is what I'm saying.

Healing is central. It's everything. For me, it's the North Star of my life. Yet I worry that, despite my attempts to constantly talk about systemic change, people will read this book and walk away thinking if we work on our own healing and support others through their healing, that will be enough to turn this ship around.

If we had another five hundred years, maybe it would prove to be enough. But we don't have that kind of time. The urgency of this moment cannot be ignored. Because of systemic injustice, the resources needed for healing aren't accessible to many. If you live in an impoverished neighborhood or a war zone, things like therapy, meditation retreats, transformative workshops, or even access to nature are simply not an option. Even if those resources were available to every individual, the momentum toward destruction is too heavy to be turned around by individual healing alone. In recent years, brilliant minds have come up with countless modalities for trauma healing that have made wholeness possible in a way my parents' generation couldn't have imagined. Creative minds are building the new systems we need: alternative economic systems, new village-style living systems, systems of responding to harm in ways that center relationship. And a political awakening has reminded many of us that many communities—particularly Indigenous peoples all over the world—never lost touch with such "technologies"— which in reality are not new but ancient.

But none of this is enough for us to create a thriving world. At least not on its own.

Fierce vulnerability was initially envisioned as a direct action workshop. Years into this experiment, I've come to see fierce vulnerability as way more than direct action. Fierce vulnerability is our yearning for a fundamental transformation in every aspect of our lives and experiments on how to get there. On the way, it's critical we don't lose our commitment to processes in which we gather, step outside the comforts of our groups and communities, and face the large forces of injustice without backing down. We must continue the long legacy of nonviolent activists who took risks, put their bodies on the line, and said no. No more. Enough. Things need to change.

Yet one of the challenges in my work has been to figure out how to mobilize spiritual communities to engage in frontline work in a way that fully activates their gifts and vocations. It's not necessary each individual engage in direct action. It may not be their vocation. But if someone is clear direct action is not their work, how can they utilize the gifts they have to support work happening on the front lines? Spiritual communities have so much to offer to frontline movements, even if they themselves might not engage with direct action: practices that open our hearts, support in staying connected to the greater collective, reminders to breathe and honor the sanctity of all life, or ceremonies and rituals that ground us.

Years ago, I had the privilege to meet and receive training from Rev. James Lawson—considered by many to be the godfather of nonviolence trainings in the United States. Rev. Lawson was called on by Dr. King to conduct some of the earliest trainings in the Civil Rights era, and his trainings led to the development of countless leaders, including one of my mentors and coauthor of the Kingian Nonviolence curriculum, Dr. Bernard LaFayette Jr. During the week I spent with Rev. Lawson in Nashville, Tennessee, he told me something that always stuck with me: "Don't train for the sake of training. Train people to engage in action."

A lot of our trainings these days feel more like collective healing spaces than traditional nonviolent action trainings. I don't want to facilitate healing just for the people in the room. If I'm to truly embrace the teaching of interdependence, I can't ignore the suffering of countless people who will never attend a workshop I facilitate. Interdependence reminds me any healing will ultimately contribute to a more healed world, yet this is not an excuse to turn away from the suffering outside of our workshops. I have to continue building the courage to initiate difficult conversations with my own family, because that's where my earliest hurt lies. LiZhen sometimes talks about going to the places where we're hurting, because that's where healing is possible. The harm is where the medicine is. Yet I'm doing this healing work to be in the world. As I engage with my family, I train myself to initiate conversations with the larger human family, because that's where the hurt lies. It is, therefore, where the healing lies.

This is another example of 200 percent truth. It's 100 percent true my healing isn't dependent on what anyone else does, including my own family. I can become whole no matter what happens between us. It's also 100 percent true my childhood traumas are a relational harm, and if we aren't able to heal in relationship, there's a part of me that will never be whole. In the same vein, we have to continue building the courage to be present in the societal places where the biggest harms are happening. Healing cannot happen if we don't open up conversations about the harm.

When trying to heal the legacy of racial violence in the US, where in our collective body do we feel the pain? Perhaps it's in prisons, or in urban low-income communities. When working to heal the separation between us and the Earth, perhaps we feel the pain on sacred sites and Indigenous lands. I don't feel the pain of my childhood in my pinky, so focusing my energy there won't bring healing. The pain of collective violence isn't felt in fancy retreat centers and workshop spaces. Those are places where we can build up our capacity to go into the places of hurt, but they're not ultimately where the pain is felt.

The long legacy of nonviolence, of which I consider myself a part, has never been about seeing violence and looking the other way. It has always been about going directly into situations of violence and offering our bodies as a way to bring about transformation. Fierce vulnerability is not about direct action. But direct action remains a critical component of how fierce vulnerability understands changemaking. Fierce vulnerability can help guide us into actions that can mobilize the power to stop injustice while cultivating the love to heal it.

Reimagining Direct Action

In today's world, the systems responsible for the greatest harms—and the people behind those systems—aren't always willing to come to the table. I've yet to see a good faith effort from power holders to have conversations about healing and accountability. This is why direct action becomes necessary. In many nonviolent movements, direct action stops immediate harm and forces society to enter a long-needed dialogue.

Gene Sharp, one of the most well-known theorists on nonviolent resistance, defined direct action as:

> *methods of protest, resistance, and intervention without physical violence in which the members of the nonviolent group do, or refuse to do, certain things. They may commit acts of omission—refuse to perform acts which they usually perform, are expected by custom to perform, or are required by law or regulation to perform; or acts of commission— perform acts which they usually do not perform, are not expected by custom to perform, or are forbidden by law or regulation from performing; or a combination of both.*[15]

Kurt Schock, another scholar on the subject, describes direction action as:

> *an active process of bringing political, economic, social, emotional, or moral pressure to bear in the wielding of power in contentious interactions between collective actors. Nonviolent action is noninstitutional, that is, it operates outside the bounds of institutionalized political channels.*[16]

In essence, direct action is a way of engaging (sometimes through omission, as described by Sharp) with people or institutions that hold power and are using that power in abusive ways. It involves strategies outside of those same institutions and utilizes tactics not sanctioned by those in power. If you're working toward transformation, Audre Lorde's famous quote that "The master's tools will never dismantle the master's house" speaks directly to why it's critical to cultivate power using tools not sanctioned by the very institutions you're trying to transform. Voting, petitions, and town halls may be powerful ways to make change, but because they are all sanctioned by the state, they aren't considered forms of direct action by most practitioners.

And...

The more I engage in experiments with fierce vulnerability, the more I write about it and talk about it, the more I realize we need to radically reimagine what we think about when we use the words "direct action." Most people think of activists shutting down city hall meetings, occupying public spaces, and disrupting the construction of pipelines. Those are the examples of direct action I've mostly been writing about, because they're the models I myself am most familiar with. And I do believe these kinds of tactics will continue to be necessary in our journey to Beloved Community. At the same time, I can't help but feel the traditional forms of direct action are lacking *something*. Fierce vulnerability is about trying to figure out what that something is and then offering it into the diverse ecosystem of movements.

In the fall of 2016, I had the privilege to spend time on traditional Lakota/Dakota/Nakota land at Standing Rock. Among the many lessons I took away from that place was a reminder we kept hearing from the elders there:

When you go into town to that direct action, remember you're going to ceremony.

This teaching has helped me reimagine direct action. When I'm involved in a protest, direct action, or civil disobedience, I rarely feel like it's ceremony. And I want to feel that sense of sacredness and mystery. It's the depth of transformation and connection I feel when I'm in ceremony the world is craving. When it feels impossible to bring about the massive scale of change our world so desperately needs, being in ceremony shatters my notions of what's possible.

> What would it look like to see the work of direct action as cere-
> mony? What is the spirit and intention we bring to ceremony?
> What if we could bring that same spirit and intention to escalated
> actions?

Do we bring signs to ceremony? Do we yell and scream in
ceremony? There may be chants and songs, but what's the spirit
and intention of those songs? What if the next time we took over
a highway in the name of justice, we saw it as an act of healing?
What if we took the same energy, the same spirit, and the same
intentions we bring into restorative circles onto that highway?
What would that look like?

Every time I'm part of a group that takes over a highway, I
feel some amount of inspiration and empowerment. But another
part me feels like that inspiration is coming from the adrenaline
rush of "shutting things down" and rebelling rather than from
the depths of my soul. If I'm honest, after taking over highway
after highway, it begins to feel routine: an injustice happens. We
occupy a highway. Maybe some arrests are made, or maybe we
all scatter when the police threaten us with arrests. The people
who were arrested spend a few hours in jail, pay a fine, and are
released. After a few hours, the crowd disperses and traffic
resumes. And all too often, it feels like nothing tangible changes.

During the days of the Civil Rights Movement, it was a revolutionary act to engage in mass-scale civil disobedience—to
have so many people arrested it packed the jails. Small cities in
the South had never dealt with anything like this, and they had
no idea how to respond. These days, police departments around
the world know exactly how to deal with mass demonstrations.
Locking up hundreds of protesters is not revolutionary. It's business as usual.

This is not a criticism of anyone's work. I truly believe we
need a movement ecosystem as diverse as any natural ecosystem. There will always be a need for straightforward, "shut it

down" energy. Folks engaged in more traditional direct actions have an incredible wealth of knowledge and skills that are necessary components of the changes we seek. However, despite all our actions, when I look at the scale of our compounding crises, I see them spiraling out of control. This is a statement of multiple truths. On one hand, social movements are the most powerful ways to create transformative change. And the ways we've been doing movement-building work aren't creating the depth of transformation we need.

When I hear communities planning direct actions, the conversations often sound too familiar. What are our demands? Who's going to be police liaison? Who will contact the lawyers? Who's going to be in an arrestable role, and who will the support people be? We've been doing the same things for decades, and my heart longs for something radically different to respond to a radically different time.

These radically different actions do already exist. It's not that they never happen. At Standing Rock, almost every action was grounded in ceremony and a commitment to upholding the sanctity of all life. I participated in massive silent marches, blockades created by massive altars, and showdowns with the police led by elders singing ceremonial songs. The Buddhist Peace Fellowship has experimented with "meditation blockades," where they engage in direct action while meditating. In 2020 for forty consecutive days, an anonymous group of white-identified people, dressed all in black mourning clothes, silently marched close to nine miles from the West Berkeley Shellmound (a sacred site of the Indigenous Ohlone people) to the site where Oscar Grant, a twenty-two-year-old African American man, was murdered by transit police in 2009. The Reparations Procession raised more than $100,000 to redistribute to Black and Indigenous organizations in Oakland.

There are countless historical examples of fiercely vulnerable actions. In the 1971–1981 Larzac movement in France, leaders

cooked meals for soldiers while organizing mass-scale civil disobedience actions to resist the expansion of the base at which
these soldiers were stationed. The 1950s Bhoodan Movement in
India led to one of the largest peaceful transfers of land in history simply by asking wealthy landowners to voluntarily give up
parts of their land to peasants. History is filled with movements
that led with a spirit of "opening up."

But we need so many more.

The work of fierce vulnerability involves carving out a space
within the vast movement ecosystem for those of us committed
to creating large-scale change that centers healing and reconciliation. Part of what I long to see more of in direct action is a
commitment to healing and reconciliation—using direct action
to harness power and fix issues while understanding how to heal
relationships once the action is over.

> We're taught activism looks a certain way and has a certain energy.
> It's militant and aggressive. But can we build actions that are
> assertive without being aggressive? Can we lead with vulnerabil-
> ity and still be fierce? Can direct action be ceremony? Can we view
> it as a modality of collective trauma healing?

One day after a fierce vulnerability workshop, LiZhen said
direct actions sound loud, like the sound of a gun or a bullhorn.
Can they instead make the sound of a bell? A bell can also be
loud, but it invokes curiosity. It pierces through noise and invites
us to pause.

In many Buddhist monasteries, large bells strike throughout the day. The sound of these bells penetrates every corner of
the monastery, and everyone who hears pauses and brings their
attention back to their breath and body in mindfulness. In this
way, we can train ourselves to be less on autopilot and more in
touch with the reality of each moment.

When I close my eyes and imagine direct action, I quickly see
images of activists yelling into a bullhorn. Instead of a bullhorn

trying to force messages down someone's throat, I wonder if we can embody the sound of a bell, if we can pause, pierce through our collective delusions, and awaken in the depths of our souls to the truth that healing and liberation are possible. There may still be times when a bullhorn is needed. If there's a fire in the monastery, I imagine the monastics may forgo the bell and pull out the bullhorn. However, I want us to be more selective in our use of a bullhorn and more proactive in our use of our bell.

What would it look like if, instead of occupying City Hall and chanting slogans,* we occupy City Hall to hold a public grief ritual? What if instead of holding signs that list our demands, we hold signs that speak of our deepest fears? What if instead of yelling at the police, we tell our stories and ask questions? What if a group of activists blockade a major intersection so ceremony leaders and artists can hold a public grief ritual in the middle of the street? And what if we have facilitators and healers experienced in trauma and grief work engaging in conversations with passersby and inviting them into the process? For a society so unable to grieve even amid so much pain, how could an action like that serve those who witness it?

Perhaps continuing to use words like "direct action" makes it harder for us to imagine what fierce vulnerability asks of us. Perhaps our minds are so habituated to seeing what a direct action is *supposed* to look like it limits our creativity. Perhaps terms like "public witness" or "creative interventions" would be better. "Direct actions" are almost always focused on systems of violence. They are the targets for our actions. But I'm beginning to wonder if the focus of fierce vulnerability is not systems, but *life itself*. This doesn't mean we don't organize public actions where

---

* I am so uninspired by chanting at protests these days, by the way. Political chants, while creative, are almost always reductive and often confrontational. They don't allow for complexity. And constant chanting can feel like an assault on our nervous systems as well as our throats.

the harm is, because that's also where life is—it's the people and the beyond-human world that experience the harm. But focusing on engaging with destructive systems saps my life-energy.

> I want actions that focus on people and the Earth, not on systems. I want actions that strengthen interdependence, not ones that paint people as "targets." I want actions that wake people up, that remind them they are sacred, and they belong.

Focusing on a corporation as the "target" or a piece of legislation as the "demand" channels our energy on a delusional, violent, and inhumane system. It may be subtle, but saying the company building the pipeline is our "target" feels *very* different from trying to stop the construction of a pipeline because the Earth is being harmed. We aren't there because of the pipeline; we're there because of Earth. This is why many Indigenous-led movements don't use words like "protesters," instead turning to terms like "water protectors."

When I go to a ceremony, I don't measure the metrics of its effectiveness. I go curious about how it will continue to transform me. Because we don't think often about how our actions make people *feel*, I've been to many actions that inadvertently create frustration, fear, or confusion—even if our demands are righteous. There has to be a way for us to engage directly with sites of injustice that centers life and relationship and brings about healing. The intention behind our actions matters, even if the things we do looks the same.

What Are We Inviting People to Do?

On Martin Luther King Jr. Day on January 18, 2016, the Movement for Black Lives occupied the San Francisco Bay Bridge. I had the privilege to support the action that day. While Black leaders of the movement built an altar honoring Black lives lost to police violence and locked themselves with chains to the bridge, I was part of a team that used our cars to slow down and then stop the traffic behind us. Once traffic had come to a halt, we got out of our cars to engage with the motorists—to talk to them about why we had stopped traffic, offer them juice and snacks, and to listen. We stayed on that bridge for well over an hour, until the police came and were finally able to cut the chains off of the activists who were locked down and arrest them.

In most actions I've been to, not a lot of thought is put into engaging with the public. Often the role of peacekeeper involves engaging with people if and when they get enraged at our actions and start being disruptive. But rarely are people outside the action proactively engaged. Doing so on the Bay Bridge made the action more invitational. People got out of their cars and joined us. Of course, some people were upset we were disrupting their commute, but we had a chance to talk to them before they got out of their cars and started yelling at us. This was far from a perfect action, but I long for us to think more about cultivating engagement and invitation in direct actions in this manner. Too often, we only think about ourselves and the police. Think about some of the most recent examples of direct actions you have been to, witnessed, or heard about. To what extent did you see beauty? Healing? Vulnerability?

Activism and direct action should model the best of humanity and invite others to join us. Instead, too often what is modeled is how much of a battle life can be. Too often, separation is created not only between "protesters" and "police," but also "bystanders." I rarely hear considerations about how our nervous system may impact the bodies of the police or of the public around us during actions. If we're not clear our goal is healing, we can inadvertently invoke fear, confusion, frustration, and separation. We can push people away.

Trauma workers sometimes use a "bottom-up" approach when working with people experiencing a trauma response, working from the body to impact the mind. "Top-down" approaches like cognitive talk therapy don't always work, because when someone is in their panic zone, the parts of the brain responsible for cognitive functions (the neocortex) aren't engaged. So, people are invited to check in with their bodies, to notice sensations and try to become aware of their breathing.

In direct action spaces, large groups of people singing a gentle song or taking long, visible deep breaths together can engage the neocortex of not only those participating, but the people around them. Movements like the new Poor People's Campaign, If Not Now, and Jewish Voices for Peace have done an amazing job bringing this kind of spirit into their actions. Their actions are filled with the kinds of song, spirit, and beauty that create a space open to the possibility of healing.

Trying to convince the world change is necessary through facts isn't effective; that's a "top-down" way to engage in a conversation we're all traumatized about. Be honest—when was the last time you actually convinced someone they were wrong on a political issue by debating them? We have to make people *feel*. And we can do that by reimagining what direct action can look like.

CHAPTER 12

Resistance as Spiritual Practice

When you were born you cried, and the world rejoiced.
Live your life so that when you die the world cries, and you
rejoice.

KABIR*

Mindfulness is creating the nervous system for Earth's
future.

LARRY WARD

SOCIAL MOVEMENTS that engage in direct action typically
have goals, from pragmatic ones like passing legislation to grand,
courageous goals involving a whole country, such as bringing
down a dictator. Large or small, in this era of collapse, these goals
fall into the realm of "fixing issues."

I'm afraid we're on the *Titanic*, though. What's the use of rear-
ranging furniture on a sinking ship, of pushing for changes that
will do nothing to shift our long-term outlook, or of demanding
something from the people in power that none of them have any
control over? On the deck of the *Titanic*, people ran around like
mad trying to figure out how to survive. As scary as that moment
must have been, nothing good came of acting out of panic. On

---

* These words have also been turned into a beautiful song by Jodi Healy that
I love. Check out *https://thebirdsings.com/when-you-were-born/*.

Earth today, many of us live in a depressed freeze state under a cloud of anxiety or are desperately searching for ways out of our fear in a fight or flight state. Could the sound of a bell and a deep breath ground us enough to reengage our neocortex and lean us toward our most skillful next step?

In fact, on the *Titanic*, there was a bell of sorts. After the ship hit the iceberg and began to sink, the ship's band—an eight-member ensemble led by Wallace Hartley—played on the deck to calm everyone as people rushed into their lifeboats. They played until the very end. Lawrence Beesley, a survivor of the shipwreck of the *Titanic*, noted, "Many brave things were done that night, but none were more brave than those done by men playing minute after minute as the ship settled quietly lower and lower in the sea."

Playing music may not look like a traditional "direct action." The band wasn't harnessing power to enact legislative change. They weren't trying to take down the iceberg, nor were they trying to save the sinking ship. But they did engage in a public intervention, hoping their actions could cut through the passengers' fear and awaken them from the stupor of panic. They created beauty in the midst of collapse.

The *Titanic* analogy isn't perfect. On the *Titanic*, most people at some point accepted the ship was sinking. In our world, we're not seeing an actual ship sink into the water, so most of society continues to live in the delusion everything is okay. People are largely in denial because they're afraid, and yelling at them won't turn on their neocortex or bring them back into their comfort zones. We support people out of their panic zones by looking them in the eye, holding their hand, and assuring some sense of groundedness. The escalating disasters in our near future will cause a lot of suffering and the loss of countless lives. But 706 people survived the sinking *Titanic*. Who knows how many people will survive to see our new world?

How can we call on the courage of the musicians on the *Titanic*, on those who had the clear-eyed strength of purpose to accept their uncertain fate and their own mortality yet continue to create beauty in support of others? How can we make the sinking less turbulent so those who survive won't be held back by trauma as they create whatever comes next?

We must accept our own mortality. Nothing else in our future is guaranteed, especially in these times.

> Accepting the reality of where we are: on the verge of a possible mass extinction event.
>
> Accepting the things we have no control over: the escalation of the climate crisis.
>
> Accepting the smallness of what we can do: affirm life and create beauty.
>
> Accepting these things is nothing short of the work of liberation. In resisting delusion, it is a fierce and vulnerable spiritual practice.

Death Doula to a Dying Empire

A while ago, LiZhen turned me onto a TEDx talk by Deborah Frieze. In this talk, titled "How I Became a Localist," Frieze said something that really made me think.

> *You can't fundamentally change big systems. You can only abandon them and start over or offer hospice to what's dying.*[17]

She went on to explain that systems—our educational systems, economic systems, criminal justice systems—are nonlinear and incredibly complex.* These aren't machines but living systems. And as with anything alive, they go through a natural cycle of rise, peak, and decline. It's the nature of life. In breath,

---

* As opposed to complicated.

out breath. Expansion, contraction. Birth, death. The inevitable cycle of any living system. Frieze shared her belief that our big systems are on their death beds. I agree. Our medical systems make us sick. Our food systems create malnutrition. Our educational systems are failing our kids. Our criminal justice system makes our communities less safe. Our democratic systems are run by a select few. Our economic systems continue to create poverty. And, of course, our ecological systems are collapsing all around us.

Frieze's talk made me think about how we would design our public actions differently if we viewed part of our role as being death doulas to dying systems, empires, and worldviews. "Death doula" is a term consciously chosen to echo "birth doula" and bring attention not only to the fact that death, like birth, is labor, but that both are important transition points in life. Michelle Mondia, a death doula, told me her work "is about midwifery. We're preparing them for another world. It's the same work. It's the death of the physical and the birth of the spiritual. Some of us call ourselves death midwives."

I don't believe we're approaching the "end of the world." But I do believe we're approaching the end of *something*, and it's something *big*. Whatever it is, I think it's big enough that we're all starting to feel its decay. What would it mean for us, as movements, to play some role in helping ease the transition to whatever comes next, even if that "next" involves the death of something? As I was almost done writing this book, I discovered *Hospicing Modernity: Facing Humanity's Wrongs and the Implications for Social Activism* by Vanessa Machado de Oliveira Andreotti.* The book offers a framing I find deeply resonant:

---

* When I read her book, it almost made me stop writing mine. "Oh, the book I wanted to write has already been written!" I obviously continued to write my own, knowing every contribution to a life-affirming world matters. But I highly recommend everyone read *Hospicing Modernity*.

modernity as we know it is in its last days, and we can play a role in supporting its transition.

Just as our massive systems are failing, the governments and nongovernmental organizations we created to fill the gaps left by these systems are also going through extraordinarily difficult times. Many of our social justice nonprofits are falling apart. The exact organizations working on conflict transformation are collapsing under the weight of internal conflict, and groups working on racial justice have been pushed to the limit by internal racial strife. It makes sense, because nonprofit organizations are a part of modernity. As modernity is dying, all its tentacles are in the midst of collapse as well. We have to find ways to build movements where our relationships and shared purpose aren't defined by some corporate charter or bylaws.

When a similar idea—that large systems around us are dying and we would be wise to consider the role of hospice—emerges simultaneously from different sources, I feel like there is something to explore. I ended up having conversations with over a dozen death doulas and hospice care workers to better understand their work. One such person, Gwi-Seok, a yoga teacher and death doula based in Hawai'i, told me, "As a society, we've forgotten how to die." We've forgotten how to accept that death is inevitable and to go into it gracefully. Instead, our society grasps onto life at all costs. All sentient beings want to live. But this clinging—this attachment we have to something as impermanent as life—causes incredible suffering.

In all the conversations I had, the importance of normalizing death emerged as the most common theme. Death is one of the most natural aspects of life. We experience it every single day. As many as 50–100 billion cells die each day in our bodies alone. There is nothing more normal in life than death. I learned from Jeanne Denney, hospice worker and founder of the School of Unusual Life Learning (SoULL), that death is not in opposition to life. Death is an *integral part* of life. But in our death-phobic world, we're taught there's life, and then there's death. This false duality creates the delusion that death is not a part of life. Part of what we need is to remember not all death is undesirable: as I learn to undo the patriarchy that lives inside of my body, the part of myself that grew up with toxic messages of how to "be a man" is dying every day. As I entered into fatherhood for the first time, my identity as someone who had never been a parent died.

In the last couple of years, I've been around several people accompanying their own loved ones in their final days. I've seen the potential that opens up when someone looks at and begins to accept the inevitability of their own death. It is perhaps the hardest thing for us as human beings to do, but there's incredible liberation in the work of accepting our own mortality. Of course, this process can create complicated feelings. I've known people who accompanied abusive, hurtful parents and caretakers and been with people suffering so much it came as a relief when they finally passed. Because of our binary worldview, it can be hard to reconcile feeling love and anger or grief and relief at the same time. Even when accompaniment is complicated, people found it possible to be present with love and compassion.

Many of us have wildly mixed emotions toward the systems, cultures, and worldviews dying around us. Can we lovingly accompany and support these systems and worldviews in their final days, even if they've caused us so much harm?

When people don't accept their own mortality, their final days can be filled with great fear. This fear, often expressed as grasping, is a desperate energy that can lash out and cause harm. Our systems, empires, and worldviews *are* dying. Many of us are too scared to accept this reality. Fear blinds us, so we continue to live in the delusion everything is okay. But in that unacknowledged fear, our systems are grasping too, refusing to acknowledge the inevitable. And that grasping is leading to an escalation of harm, which we can see manifested in the increase in political violence, hostility toward those we see as "other," and growing apathy and indifference toward the horrors of war and the world-wide refugee crises. Throughout their life cycles, our systems have grown so massive and powerful that if we aren't careful, their grasping and thrashing could take down everything we love and hold sacred. We are called to become interventionist death doulas, to bring ease, skillfulness and wisdom to this transition.

In nonviolent resistance work, "pillars of support" is a common analysis tool. The idea is you're trying to take down a dictator (or CEO, politician, etc.), propped up by many societal pillars: the police, the military, the courts, the media, etc. The dictator is at the top of a pyramid held up by these pillars. If we can identify and knock down a couple key pillars, the entire house may come crumbling down.

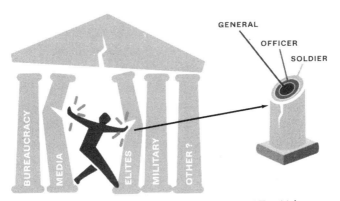

Pillars of support (image courtesy of Beautiful Trouble)

Movements need to be spirited, but they also need to be strategic. Tools like this will always be important. But look at this visual for a second. We're all still living under the systems we are trying to take down. If we simply topple these pillars and the whole house comes crashing down, it'll crush us all. The work of a death doula isn't to go to people who are dying and knock them down so they transition quicker. It's to accompany them, to help them be with what is inevitable, to breathe deeply through discomfort, to help heal any relationships while there's still time, to support those around them who are in pain, to ease suffering, and support dignity in a precarious time of transition. Even in the final moments before death, it is still possible to heal, affirm life, and create beauty.

The Gift of Grief

Gwi-Seok also shared that we're an "under-grieving society." Unprocessed and unnamed grief shuts us down. We bury our grief in the depths of our unconscious, and it ends up controlling us. The work of "normalizing" death can be tricky. In our society, we normalize death all the time. We normalize mass shootings, we normalize murder, we normalize war. But I don't get the sense this is what all those death doulas mean. We normalize *killing*; this isn't the same as normalizing *death* as an inevitable part of the life cycle. Birth is a gift, but death is considered a curse. Normalizing death includes accepting the grief that naturally comes with it. If we bury grief, we don't normalize death; we suppress it.

On May 24, 2022, a former student walked into Robb Elementary School in Uvalde, Texas, and killed nineteen students and two teachers. Eighteen others were injured, including his grandmother, whom he shot before heading to the school. The shooter himself was killed when the police finally raided the classroom in which he'd locked himself. I was in Southern California when I heard the news. I'd just finished facilitating a fierce vulnerability workshop and was on my way to another presentation, followed by a work retreat. It was a back-to-back-to-back week, and I didn't have time to process the news. When I finally got home a week later, I could feel the tension in my body. LiZhen was overseas, so I was alone when I finally had time to process the news. I sat down on my bed and, with intention, looked up the names of each of the victims and read their stories.

I looked at each of their pictures, printed them out, and placed them on my altar. I cried. I grieved.

There's a way in which it would have been easier for me to ignore the grief. But this would have meant normalizing their killings without acknowledging their deaths. I don't enjoy crying and thinking about the loss of almost two dozen children. Yet I needed to do this for myself to be able to move forward. I have to have some balance. When I read the news, there's something to grieve every day, and it could be easy to fall into a never-ending spiral. But if I don't take some intentional time to grieve every once in a while, grief builds up in my system and cripples me. Once there's built-up grief, it becomes harder for me to accept mortality. The more I suppress these things, the more I get buried under their weight and the more my awareness becomes muted and heavy.

Though I read the stories of the Uvalde shooting alone in my bedroom, I believe it's critical we do grief work in community. We need our grief to be witnessed and reflected back. We need to know we're not alone. Spaces for *collective* grief are transformative. When I'm around a community holding space for grief, it feels less scary. When I know I'm not alone, when I see grief modeled by others, when I know I'm in a space explicitly designed as a container to hold our grief, I can touch into it and find the richness there.

We're used to imagining the "end of the world as we know it" as this terrible, scary, dark thing, thanks to so many post-apocalyptic movies. Maybe it will be that way. But it doesn't have to be. We can create something more beautiful than we can possibly imagine. Accepting death is upon us may be the first step. Once we accept it, we can make *conscious* choices about how we want to accompany it. Grief is an emotion that, if left unattended, can live in your body for years and become debilitating. This is why I felt the need to read the stories of each child killed in the Uvalde school shooting and grieve their loss.

We need people activated at scale. It won't be enough for small groups of activists and progressives to hold grief rituals on our own, though that's an important start. We need public interventions—direct actions, if you still want to call them that—to bring grief to the masses. We live in a world filled with so much normalized violence and chaos. We don't realize our bodies need to grieve every time we hear a story of a mass shooting or a climate catastrophe. We just continue with our lives. We turn on Netflix and move on to the next thing. And at times, maybe that's what we need to do. Sometimes, the pain is just too much. It's important to give ourselves time to prepare for grief. But other times, the inability to allow ourselves to grieve is toxic.

Francis Weller talks about "grief muscles." Grieving is a practice, much like going to the gym. The more we grieve, the more able we are to grieve and to grieve deeply. Creating regular, explicit spaces for communal grief is like going to the gym and preparing our grief muscles for what is to come. Grieving, paradoxically, creates strength.[18]

Making a Grief Altar

When you're ready to grieve, making a special place for it is something you can do in your home to cultivate a connection to grief and the vitality an awareness of mortality can bring. A grief altar is a space for you to touch into deeper realities that can shake but also nourish us. Though everyone's grief altar will look different, here are some ideas to get you started:

- Find a space, if you can, where your altar won't be disturbed.

- What would you like to have on your altar? Pictures? Beauty or reminders of the cycles of life and death from nature?

- In addition to items that remind you of beauty and connection, what would support you in connecting to your grief? Pictures or stories of people who have recently lost their lives? Images from recent climate catastrophe? What images could support you getting into your stretch zone but *not* your panic zone?

* Adding a candle, incense, or sage to your altar can be a nourishing way to incorporate a visit into your day, for example coming to light and take a few breaths with it each morning after you brush your teeth.

* These things can also help clear heavy energy so you aren't stuck in your grief as you go about your day. It's important to connect with grief, but it's also important to protect yourself and not get stuck there.

This can be a beautiful yet intense practice, especially if you are new to it or engaging in it during especially difficult times. Be gentle with yourself, and check in to see if you think you have capacity to be with grief. Consider doing this with a friend or making sure you have people who can support you as feelings may emerge. Perhaps you can even do this with a larger community as a collective effort. If you don't have community with whom to engage in these practices, please see the organizations listed in the next section that do collective grief work.

And finally, before you start, ask yourself again if you want to engage with this practice, and give yourself permission to say no. Sometimes, there's too much going on to engage with grief. Other times, the support systems you need to dive in aren't present. Regardless of the reason, saying no to something can be an empowering decision that gives you agency. Celebrate the "no," and celebrate giving yourself space to take care of yourself. Go be in nature. Go get some ice cream. Go dancing. Go smile, laugh, and be with your joy. This is just as important as being with the grief.

Ecological Grief

The constant bombardment of bad news has made us numb
to the unprocessed, unexpressed grief filling our world today.
I believe one of the biggest causes is our unprocessed climate
grief, sometimes referred to as ecological grief. Ecological grief
is not a new concept. The American environmentalist and
writer Aldo Leopold wrote about it as early as 1949 in his book,
A Sand County Almanac, to give name to the emotional pain
of environmental loss.[19] But with the escalation of the climate
crisis, ecological grief is having something of a revival and has
recently become a hot topic of study among psychologists and
grief workers.

Two experts on the topic, Ashlee Cunsulo and Neville R.
Ellis, define ecological grief as "The grief felt in relation to experienced or anticipated ecological losses, including the loss of
species, ecosystems, and meaningful landscapes due to acute or
chronic environmental change." This grief is being felt everywhere. According to a 2020 study by the American Psychological Association, 54 percent of US adults say climate change is the
most important issue facing society today, while another study
from the same year shows 96.5 percent of young Americans sur-
veyed reporting being "very" or "extremely concerned" about
the future of their existing, expected, or hypothetical children
because of climate change.[20]

We experience ecological grief in different ways. Some of
us have experienced climate catastrophes ourselves and may
have lost homes or loved ones. Whether a wildfire, a flood, or
something else, living through such experiences can be traumatic. Others develop ecological grief in ways similar to chronic
or insidious trauma. I live in California, where "fire season"
is now an annual reality. For years now, smoke from wildfires
periodically fills the entire Bay Area, making it unsafe to go

outdoors—we learned what an N99 mask was long before the COVID-19 pandemic. Going about our days as our cities fill with smoke, knowing fires are raging all around us, and seeing people walking around with gas masks on is not normal; it can lead to chronic trauma or ecological grief.

Ecological grief can be harder than other forms of grief to process. For one, the scale of the calamity is so large it's hard to grasp. The climate crisis is an existential threat that may lead to the next great extinction! How do you process that? Despite the enormity of the threat, the danger isn't something most of us see daily. The crisis works its way through our ecological systems every day, but it's not in our face the way a car accident or a war might be. Human beings have always been adept at ignoring threats that aren't right in front of us. While there's growing awareness things are changing, that we're living in a time of transition, and things are only going to get harder, as a society we haven't reckoned with it, nor have we created spaces to express whatever feelings may come up as a result of it. We just keep moving forward as if everything's okay.

It's also difficult to grieve because it's not over. Far from it. Ecological grief is about grieving what has already happened— the species that have already gone extinct, the lives lost, the communities devastated—and grieving what is yet to come. We don't know when this "yet to come" will happen, the scale of it, what it will look like, how or even if it will affect us directly. This—what some psychologists call "anticipatory grief"—can lead to high levels of anxiety because so much is unknown. It's easier to grieve concrete losses that have already happened—you know exactly what you're grieving. But knowing the next threat may be around every corner and living with the anxiety of not knowing where or when can lead to illnesses like post-traumatic stress syndrome.

Part of the work of fierce vulnerability is to help people express what they may not even be aware they're feeling through public ritual, dance, art, creative expression, or ceremony. But it's not enough to hold grief rituals for people who voluntarily sign up to attend a grief ritual. We need a much bigger *us* to express this untapped grief.

> How can we use direct actions, public witness, creative interventions, whatever you want to call them, to help wake people from denial? Can we lead not with the same-old messages of "We demand this legislation" or "We demand you shut this power plant down," but with the truth that we are scared, saddened, and confused? How do we help a society unable to grieve lower their defenses enough to notice we are all feeling this loss?

Moirologists, or professional mourners, have been around for thousands of years in cultures around the world—particularly in Asia, Africa, and the Middle East. These mourners play three important roles.

First, they perform rites and rituals. They sing songs and put on theatrical performances to honor the dead, mark the transition, and help families mourn as well as celebrate the life of the person who has passed.

In China, families hire performers and musicians to act out scenes from the life of the deceased and play music that evokes certain emotions related to grief, guiding the family through ceremony. In ancient Egyptian rituals, two women who represented the Goddesses Isis and Nephthys were often present at funerals, symbolizing their roles as mourners and protectors of the deceased.

Second, professional mourners ensure families don't mourn alone.

The Arlington Ladies are a group of volunteers who show up at the funeral of every single serviceman buried at Arlington

National Cemetery, the US Army's largest cemetery. They've been operating since 1948, when the then–Chief of Staff of the US Air Force and his wife witnessed young service members being buried without anyone present.

The third role professional mourners play is supporting anyone who has been told, implicitly or explicitly, wailing loudly and outwardly expressing strong emotions like grief is not appropriate.

In the Indian state of Rajasthan, it was viewed as "inappropriate" for higher-caste women to cry in front of others, so they hired *rudaalis*, lower-caste women, to wail in their place. I don't want to discount the heavy casteism present in this dynamic, however, rudaalis play an important role in helping families grieve.

I envision public actions where we can perform rites and rituals, sing songs, and honor the passing of so many of Earth's species and ecosystems, where we can mark the fact that we're living through a major transition and support those who can't themselves grieve.

Too often, political die-ins and mock funerals feel performative. I wonder what it would take for us to lead such actions less as political theater and more as sacred ceremony. Can we create performance without making it performative? I imagine a lot of it has to do with how we prepare for these kinds of actions. Are we actually grieving as we prepare for them? Do we let our hearts break during our preparation, or are we just rehearsing for political theater?

The sanctity of the lives being lost to the climate crisis— human and otherwise—isn't being properly honored and grieved. We need more people to show up in public spaces to remind us life is being lost at an alarming rate. Someone needs to be there to grieve these losses. We need to create a culture of expressing ecological grief. For many of us, especially those of us socialized as men* or as members of the "upper socioeconomic classes," loud expressions of any emotion are looked down upon as "uncivil," "impolite," or "improper." This conditioning has taken away our ability to grieve. Andrew Bryant, a therapist in Seattle, talks about "disenfranchised grief": "A type of grief that doesn't have core cultural support or social acknowledgement in the general public." Having an army of activist-mourners might just help society break out of our shell. If we see ourselves not only as activists who train to shut down intersections and hang banners, but as death doulas to dying systems, as grief workers, and as healers, what new forms of training might we need? What new actions might emerge?

Movements need to partner with grief workers to hold regular grief rituals for ourselves. Groups like the Good Grief Network and Climate in Mind are already doing that work. The Work that Reconnects inspired by Joanna Macy is a large community working on grief tending within the context of social change work. The Re-evaluative Counseling world has committed deeply to this. And even on an individual level, the Climate Psychiatry Alliance can help people find climate-aware therapists who can support ecological grief. We need to do our own grief work, and we need to take grief work into the streets.

A lot of the public conversation about climate is focused on actions we need to take. And of course, there is *a lot* we need to do. But when people are in denial, when they're scared and feeling hopeless, it's not always skillful to try to get them to *do*

---

* In most traditions, only women were allowed to be professional mourners because men were supposed to be "tough" and not show emotions. I don't think I need to say much here about how toxic that message is. What I do want to point out is how prevalent that message still is, even in our movement spaces. When we started facilitating fierce vulnerability workshops years ago, people eagerly signed up. We typically filled a workshop within a week of announcing it. The vast majority of participants were women and non-binary people. I'm afraid something about the word "vulnerability" turns off male-identified folks. C'mon, men! We need to step up!

something. They simply need space to *be* with their grief—a grief they may not even realize they are feeling. Explicit spaces to honor our grief and rage are both necessary ingredients in fierce vulnerability. To create a sword, you need a red hot furnace to melt the steel. That's the power of rage. But once you shape the sword, you need to dip it into cool water to temper it. That's the power of grief.

To Serve Life

So many systems—human-made systems like governments and capitalism, as well as natural ecosystems—are in the midst of collapse. Demise is a natural and sacred part of the life cycle. Accepting death and helping others do so by playing the role of death doulas and public mourners is part of the work we are called to do in this moment.

And . . . throughout this book, I've continued to talk about the need to fight for, affirm, and honor life.

> Accepting death and fighting for life are not in contradiction to one another, because death isn't in opposition to life. It's a part of it. Only when we fully accept that reality can we honor the fullness of life.

Jeanne Denney helped me to see how much understanding and science there is around birth—there are so many related traditions, books to read, classes to attend, products for new and expecting parents to buy. But we don't study death in the same way. Maybe we don't think it's "worth" it. Because, well, we just die, and that's it. There's nothing more to understand, and there's nothing we can do to prepare. To the extent we study death, it's only to study every possible way to *prevent it.* That's not an honoring of life.

There are traditions that help us normalize death. The Mexican celebration of Día de Muertos, the Chinese Qingming

Festival, or the Japanese tradition of Obon welcome home the spirits of our deceased ancestors, giving us a closer relationship with the dead on a regular basis. Other cultures have a much stronger honoring of elders and of *eldering.* Many cultures celebrate not only the rite of passage of a young person becoming an adult, but of adults becoming elders. Elders are viewed and honored in the same way an old-growth forest is—with awe and inspiration, as opposed to people just getting older and less productive and useful.

When a whale dies and its carcass sinks to the bottom of the sea, it's teeming with life within hours. When a giant tree falls to the forest floor, it doesn't just disappear. As it decays, it becomes a nurse log, a home for countless seedlings. The 100 billion cells that will die in your body today will be replaced by 100 billion new cells tomorrow. So much life surrounds each moment of death. In the conventional realm, the work of hospicing and midwifing may be different. But in the ultimate realm, becoming a death doula to dying empires means we're giving birth to a new one. The work of accepting death isn't about giving up on life. It's about honoring the fullness of it.

CHAPTER 13

A New Generation of Training

*We don't rise to the level of our expectations; we fall to the
level of our training.*

ARCHILOCHUS

*A healthy nervous system allows us to attune to others, to
create a mutual field of experience with others. To by fully
attuned means we are able and available to host within us
the energy, mind, and emotions of another; to allow the
other to feel felt by us.*

THOMAS HÜBL

I STARTED MY "career" as a nonviolence trainer at nineteen. I
cut my teeth in the anti-globalization movement, the movement
to close the School of Americas, and campaigns to free Mumia
Abu Jamal and Leonard Peltier. After leaving the monastery, it
was in these movement spaces that I found purpose and community. A few years into this work, I started to feel like something
was off. While I couldn't put a finger on exactly what it was, this
sense was strong enough that I quit facilitating. Not only did I
quit facilitating, I moved away from any relationship with the
word "nonviolence" for almost ten years.

That all changed in 2008 when I took a two-day workshop
on Kingian Nonviolence Conflict Reconciliation, and my earlier
sense of unease clarified. I realized when I'd started facilitating

trainings in the late 1990s, I wasn't facilitating "nonviolence" trainings in the most holistic sense of the word; in fact I was facilitating nonviolent civil disobedience trainings. Kingian Nonviolence, a more expansive approach to nonviolence than I'd been exposed to before, gave me a framework that felt true for how to engage in social change work, and my experiments with fierce vulnerability infused this work with a focus on healing. These two frameworks made me realize it's not enough to use direct actions to overpower "opponents," as I'd thought when I began. Kingian Nonviolence reminded me the very idea of "opponents" is a delusion. Fierce vulnerability showed me if we want to heal relationships, vulnerability has to lead the way.

Gail Davidson, a death doula, said to me, "We're taught it's okay to show emotions, but not to make yourself the center of the story." When you accompany someone through their death, of course it may also be emotional for you. But you're there to support someone else. Your own emotions and grief may be supportive to the person you're accompanying, but you're not the center. When I facilitate healing circles for men, I have to be very clear about my intention. Because so many men have been ripped from their emotional selves with decades of indoctrination that "men don't cry," I sometimes tap into my own vulnerability to reach their hearts. But in doing so, I have to be careful not to make it about me. These circles aren't created as spaces for my healing. So even when I open up, I don't share unprocessed, open wounds that might send me into my panic zone and create a situation where the men in the circle have to take care of me.

I used to lead activities to prepare people to form blockades, to respond to police trying to make arrests,* to prepare people to be arrested, and to support people who had gotten arrested. These kinds of trainings are a critical component of nonviolence

---

* I actually used to train people to point their fingers and chant "shame" at police officers moving in to make arrests. . . .

work and always will be. But I was only preparing people to engage in civil disobedience. I wasn't, in any way, preparing people to do the work of transformation and healing—a critical aspect of nonviolence. In addition to those hard skills, we need an entirely new generation of nonviolence trainings. The work we're called to at this moment isn't just about shutting things down. It's about opening things up—and that requires helping people *feel* things. We need to help people wake up from the delusion that everything is fine. We need to enable people to tap into the vulnerability to say we are not okay, we are in a crisis, and then to move out of their panic.

Much of this starts with us—those practicing fierce vulnerability—and our ability to model this for others—to take our grief and our fear as well as our acceptance and our hope into public spaces as we offer our cries and our deep breaths as bells to awaken a nation. This is scary, dangerous, and risky work. One definition of *vulnerability* is, after all, "capable of or susceptible to being wounded or hurt." The nature of direct action puts our bodies in potential harm's way. If we lead with vulnerability, we invite an additional layer of risk. If we lead with our pain, with our grief, with our fear, we open up a vulnerable place in our heart in addition to our bodies. If we aren't careful, harm can enter through this opening, and it can hurt even more than a physical wound.

Intentionally putting ourselves in situations where we face tear gas from the police or endure ridicule from counter-protesters while we express our sorrow for the world's suffering could inflict deep emotional wounds. But with the right training and preparation, we're capable of leading with vulnerability, accepting the possibility of potentially harmful impacts, and staying grounded through it all. We need to, as Rev. Nadia Bolz-Weber teaches us, "Preach from your scars, not your wounds."

Today, after years of processing the pain of my childhood, I'm equipped to hear a difficult response to sharing my story in ways I wasn't when I first began opening up. Back then, a less-than-supportive response felt like a threat to my worth as a human being. Now, I can share my story publicly in spaces where I'm not always guaranteed loving support, still hoping my story can benefit others. Years of healing have helped build a scar over my wound. That scar still connects me to my vulnerability. At the same time, it acts as a shield—it provides a layer of protection, and now my pain can be offered as a gift.

As we prepare to engage with a world in crisis, we have to get right with ourselves. Not only because the conversations we need to have are so difficult, but because the *places* we may need to have them won't always be the safest places. Whether we're preparing to go into direct action or preparing to go into a difficult conversation with a family member, being in escalated spaces makes it more likely our amygdala will sense danger and take over. The more we've healed, the less likely we are to go into our panic zone.

In this way, the words "training" and "healing" become almost synonymous. Our healing *is* our training for the work of fierce vulnerability.

The Privilege of Training

In the Civil Rights Movement, organizers were very clear about the commitments people had to make if they wanted to participate on the front lines. If people felt they wouldn't be able to maintain nonviolent discipline even in the midst of physical abuse, they were often asked to stay behind and find other ways to support the cause. But it's not just about desire, willingness, and capacity. To some extent, and perhaps to a large extent, it's about privilege.

How many of us have the privilege to do this work? How many of us have the privilege—the time, the resources, the connections—to do enough of our own healing work to be ready to engage in escalated sociopolitical work? People who grew up with privilege may have had less traumatic experiences in their lives and fewer sources of trauma in the first place. If you come from a privileged or dominant identity, there are likely to be less triggers and reminders about the ways in which you are marginalized. And, of course, the more privilege you have, the more likely you are to have supportive community, access to therapy, nature, meditation retreats—the things that help you recover from trauma. In so many ways, the more marginalized your identity is, the more barriers there are on the path to nonviolence. Yet nothing will change if the people who have been most negatively impacted by systems of violence can't have a voice and play leading roles in movements for change.

Our movements need to proactively grapple with this tension. How can we empower our communities to offer more healing spaces for the most marginalized of us? And how can we build these systems outside of the capitalist, market systems that have made them inaccessible in the first place? In addition to building teams of peacekeepers, street medics, and media savvy communications experts, how can movements be more explicit about empowering healers, therapists, artists, restorative justice facilitators, grief workers, and more to offer their expertise to those who need it? The more we can build alternative systems that give access to healing modalities, the less we need to rely on the dominant system.

Groups like the Kindred Southern Healing Justice Collective and the broader healing justice movement they helped spark are doing just that. Programs like Darkness Rising's REBUILD offer free therapists to formerly incarcerated people, while organizations like Black Therapists Rock mobilize mental health professionals to heal the intergenerational trauma of systemic racism. The Fierce Vulnerability Network envisions a thriving Internal Reparations Fund that can support BIPOC members of the network in a variety of ways. For some people, just the act of showing up can be an act of nonviolence. We need to ensure there are resources to support this, resources that so often were taken from the stolen land and labor of their ancestors in the first place.

Some communities have more steps to move through to get to their collective comfort zones; building systems of support is not an acknowledgement of some deficit on their part. It's an acknowledgement of the history of violence inflicted upon them and their ancestors, and it's part of the process of healing from that legacy.

The Field

In every moment, in every place, there's an energetic field. This field is always present. The things we say, the things we don't say, our songs, our cries, our tone, the way we move, our pace, our environment, the sounds that surround us, the abundance of (or lack of) technology, the imagery, our intentions, and emotions all impact this field.

A redwood forest, a busy construction site, the Department of Motor Vehicles office, your backyard surrounded by friends, a showdown between police at a direct action, a spiritual ceremony: all of these spaces have their own energetic field, cultivated by every aspect of what's present. Some factors aren't within our control (the size of the redwoods, the fact that the DMV uses fluorescent lights). But many of them (your pace through the forest, awareness of your breath, or the candles you light in the backyard) are. The more awareness we bring to the field as we do our work, the more we create spaces conducive to our goal of healing.

We can be affected by the field others create. And we can cultivate and tend our own field and invite people into it. If we aren't intentional about the field we tend, we can be influenced in ways that impact our ability to create spaces for healing. Practices like having gatherings under candlelight or beginning each meeting with silence are an attempt to cultivate a field conducive to our work. Whether organizing a meeting with two colleagues or a public action with 100 people, fierce vulnerability relies on an awareness of our relationship with the field.

The field impacts us so much partially because of something called co-regulation. Co-regulation describes a phenomenon wherein one person's emotions can impact the stability, calm, joy, or equanimity of another. Co-regulation is possible because of our mirror neurons, which are a type of brain cell that responds equally whether we experience an emotion or witness someone else experience an emotion. As infants, when we cry or are in distress, our caretakers may have held us, sang songs for us, or gently rocked us back and forth. The field they created with their sounds, their tone, their gentleness, and their touch helped us to regulate and stabilize. Our nervous system sensed the calm in theirs, and this helped us learn to calm our own.

While we learn this early in our childhood, we continue to experience it throughout our lives. Not only humans do this— most mammals co-regulate through facial expressions, body language, respiratory rate, and other non-verbal methods of communication. Of course, co-regulation can work in the other direction as well. If your caretaker is in a state of panic, it can put you in a state of panic. It doesn't matter if you know why they're in panic. You pick up subtle cues and co-regulate along with them. When we're around people who are happy, it can impact our mood. When we're around people who are annoyed, that can impact our mood too. When I watched the Celtics win the title in 2008, I was *genuinely* happy, not only for myself but for the players on the team.* Those were my mirror neurons firing. If we're not mindful of our mirror neurons, we can unwittingly co-regulate with someone in their panic zone, taking on their stress

---

* Am I using a book about the healing of the world to justify my fanaticism of the Boston Celtics? Perhaps. #noshame

and mirroring their patterns of tension. This can spiral danger-
ously, each person activating the other's panic.

Our capacity to imagine, to build, and tend to a field conducive to healing—and to maintain it in the midst of crisis—
depends largely on our own practice and the depths to which
we have healed our own pains. This is why giving people like
Donald Trump such a large platform can be dangerous. Seeing
someone operating from such a heavy trauma response can fire
the mirror neurons of both his supporters and opponents, and
the entire field gets thrown for a loop.

On the other hand, in 2007, I served as the convention coor-
dinator for the Gathering for Justice's first national convention.
We brought close to 1,000 young people to Oakland from around
the country. It may have been the busiest week of my entire life. I
didn't sleep for days. Instead, I ran around the Oakland Convention Center throughout the entire three-day event. After most of
the participants had gone home, I saw one of my mentors, Nane,
standing around in the lobby. My energy was still a bit all over the
place, making sure everything was okay and no kids had gotten
left behind. I went to give him a hug, and unexpectedly, I burst into
tears. It was largely because I was *exhausted,* and I felt an incredible sense of relief the convention was finally over. But it was
also because of Nane—because of the decades of work he'd done
around his own healing, Nane generates a certain field of gravity.

Being around him, I felt trust, safety, support, love. That's
what we need to be: Nane to the world.

If one person enters a tense situation with calmness, it impacts
the field. If enough people enter a direct action space with calmness, we can impact the collective field. And if enough of us
around the country enter this time of crisis with calmness, we can
impact the collective field. If healing is our goal, what kind of field
is most conducive to that? How can we cultivate it, even in the
most escalated of moments? How can we help to create the "settled collective nervous system" Resmaa Menakem talks about?

In fierce vulnerability, a common question we ask ourselves the night before an action is, "What are the qualities we long to witness in our action tomorrow?" Not "What impact do we want to have" or "What is our messaging going to be?" What are the *qualities we long for*? Healing? Slowness? Curiosity? Beauty? If these are the qualities we long for, how do we cultivate them in the field of our action?

In the World

Years ago, my friend and fellow Kingian Nonviolence trainer Lori LeChien broke up a fight outside her house by singing a song. She came home from work one night to see a man on the ground getting beaten by another. Being the musician she is, she ran inside her house, grabbed her guitar, ran back out, and started singing a song right next to the fight.

But her action didn't have an impact right away. She realized the song she chose was maybe a little too upbeat! It wasn't the right field. So, she changed it up and started strumming a slower, calmer song. This managed to break up the fight. The way she tells the story, the person on top looked up at her mid-punch like, "What is wrong with this crazy woman? Why is she singing in my face?" Confused and puzzled, he got up and walked away.[*]

No matter how much we work to cultivate a certain field, it can easily get disrupted by any number of things. If we're leading a solemn grief ritual, all it takes is one person yelling, "Fuck the

---

[*] Years later, I watched Awkwafina's character do the same thing in the movie *Shang-Chi*. "They're living it up at the Hotel California. . . ."

system!" to disrupt and transform the field. So, we also need to practice field triage: how to rebuild and tend to the field when it gets disrupted. I'm reminded of an action where an altar was built and then promptly destroyed by a frustrated local whose daily commute was disrupted by the protest. While a group of us talked to the person, another group slowly rebuilt the altar while singing gentle songs. It took a while to rebuild that energy, but it was possible, and made easier by the fact that we'd anticipated disruption and practiced responding to it.

> How and where are we focusing people's energy by how we show up? Are we trying to focus people's attention on violence or beauty? On separation or healing? If, instead of chanting slogans, we take slow, deep, and visible breaths during a demonstration, might that affect the police dressed in riot gear? Might that get their mirror neurons firing?
>
> If, instead of playing the endless game of cat and mouse with the police all night, we wore ceremonial clothes and moved slowly through the demonstration, might that help onlookers tap into a healing, creative frame of mind? Might their nerves calm enough that they get curious about our actions?

Short-Term Strategies

Healing takes time. Years and lifetimes. That's time we don't necessarily have. I'm not suggesting we wait until all our childhood wounds have healed before we engage in action. Healing isn't linear anyway. Some of our biggest fears about the crises may begin to melt away once we're in community, doing this work in public. This new generation of nonviolence trainings we're envisioning has to have short-term, medium-term, and long-term strategies. In the short-term, in addition to learning how to build blockades while cultivating a healing field, we need to bring awareness to our bodies so we can notice when we're going into panic and utilize emotional regulation tools to bring ourselves back. Quick, simple tools can be used in the immediate moment to ground ourselves and reconnect to our neocortex—our nonviolence brain.

Something as simple as a deep breath can help us regulate our nervous system. My friend Emma Schoenberg teaches, "There's always time to take a breath. Even when a police officer dressed in riot gear is running toward you at full speed, there's still time to take a breath." And while everyone reading this book has taken *a lot* of breaths in their lifetime, we aren't all experts on taking deep breaths—especially when we're in panic. For one thing, most people spend the majority of their lives breathing unconsciously. So, while we *are* breathing, we aren't *practicing* breathing.

I'd love to see more and more nonviolence trainings (and meetings, gatherings, Zoom calls, etc.) incorporate short meditation periods. While it's true "there's always time to take a breath," it's also true for me that, thanks to years of meditation practice, I can get a lot more out of one intentional breath now than I could ten years ago. With enough practice, even one breath can pack the slowness of an hour of meditation. And if meditation isn't your thing? That's great. There's no shortage of emotional regulation tools that can be utilized in the moment to help us regulate.

Singing songs together can be a great practice. In the Civil Rights Movement, freedom songs weren't a pastime or a hobby. They were a critical strategy to keep peoples' souls uplifted. They kept the movement connected to something greater, kept the people unified, and they kept peoples' nervous systems regulated. There's a story of ten children getting attacked by Bull Connor's fire hoses in Birmingham in 1963. These children faced the hoses with their fists in the air, singing one word over and over again: *freedom*. Even in the face of such violence, their songs kept them grounded in freedom. In the past ten years or so, I've been thrilled to see the reemergence of song culture in many movements. When I started doing social change work in the late 1990s, no one sang songs at protests. Now, our movements are singing our own songs of liberation.

Physical touch can also help emotional regulation in the short-term. Of course, we all have different relationships to touch, so spending some time at a training getting to know each other's comfort levels can help us support each other in an action. One person might feel supported by a big hug, while another may want to lightly tap their own body. Knowing who would be supported by touch, what kind of touch, and from whom are facts as important as everyone's phone number and who has cats who need to get fed if they get arrested.

Having water and snacks can also be supportive. When we're in panic, our digestive system gets shut down by our sympathetic nervous system. We can kick-start our parasympathetic nervous system by taking a small sip of water or eating a bite of food, as we practiced in chapter 3.

Therapist Esther Perel talks about how humming can help you regulate your emotions. "When you hum," she says, "you create a space between the thought giving you anguish and your nervous system. You can't hum and think at the same time." She recommends you gently hum a tune—out loud or silently in your mind—next time you're dysregulated to reconnect with yourself.

These are simple things we all know how to do. Even if you never learned them as "emotional regulation tools," these tactics come to us intuitively. But again, when we're in panic, we often forget we have access to them. The more we actively practice these regulation tools in our daily lives and our communal spaces, at times when we're feeling calm and safe, the more accessible they'll be when we need them most.*

---

* I swear this is a true story. I am sitting at a café as I'm finishing this section on emotional regulation when the fire alarm goes off and we all have to evacuate. When I step outside, I realize it's not just the café—an alarm is going off in the entire plaza outside the café. I'm not quite ready to go home yet, though, so I'm debating with myself whether or not to continue to write about emotional regulation sitting outside while a very loud alarm blares all around me.

Medium-Term Strategies*

Activism as Spiritual Practice

The first thing I'd love to see in the medium term is an ongoing commitment to and the integration of practices like meditation, Yoga, ritual, and spiritual practices in movement spaces. When I say "spiritual," I'm simply referring to practices that help us ground ourselves, stay aware of our bodies and nervous systems, and connect us to something greater than our individuality. Plenty of science speaks to the benefits of having a regular practice rooted in spiritual traditions.† These practices give a workout to the muscles surrounding your neural networks that allow your neocortex to stay engaged. The more mindful we can become through these practices, the more we build a collective nervous system that can support life continuing to thrive on Earth. Of course, spiritual practices, like any practice, have their shadows. They can lead to the delusion of individual liberation, and spiritual bypassing can lead someone to believe they're becoming more "enlightened" without cultivating a commitment to ending injustice.

"Moments of the whirlwind," a term I learned from my friends Paul Engler and Carlos Saavedra, describes moments throughout history when some incident led to millions of

---

* Screw it, I decided to stay. I've actually led emotional regulation workshops while showing videos of police violence and climate catastrophes. These workshops prepare activists to utilize these tools in loud, chaotic, and potentially disturbing places. It somehow feels fitting that I'm working on this section with the sounds of alarms going off all around me. This is fun.

† A 2011 study published in *Psychiatry Research: Neuroimaging* showed meditation can increase the size of your hippocampus and decrease the sensitivity of your amygdala. A 2017 review published in *Frontiers in Psychiatry* examined 23 studies and found Yoga can reduce depression, anxiety, and symptoms of PTSD. And in 2021, *Social Science & Medicine* found frequent religious attendance or private prayer were associated with higher levels of happiness and lower levels of anxiety and depression.

people—many who had never been to a protest—pouring into the streets. Think of the moments after the murder of George Floyd, the Occupy Wall Street movement, the days after Trump's 2016 inauguration, or the battle to stop the Dakota Access Pipeline at Standing Rock.* These moments show us things can happen quickly in our world, and millions of people can be immediately mobilized into the streets.

While there have been countless moments of the whirlwind throughout history connected to a variety of political issues, I've never heard of a moment of the whirlwind related to spiritual practice. There's never been a moment (that I know of) when millions of people poured into meditation centers, temples, mosques, churches, and synagogues. This shows me it has typically been easier to mobilize people politically than to mobilize people into spiritual practice. This is one reason I hope to see more and more integration of spiritual practice in activist spaces: it will change the foundation from which people pour into the streets during the next moment of the whirlwind.

This can also happen when spiritual communities become more inviting of activists by committing to social justice principles within their space. The East Bay Meditation Center in Oakland, California, Phillips Theological Seminary in Tulsa, Oklahoma, or the Plum Village Tradition of Engaged Buddhism with eleven centers worldwide are great models of this welcoming approach to activists. There are faith communities that see spiritual liberation is not possible without social justice and commit their existence to that cause. Dr. King's school of Christianity was an example of this. Other communities like the Buddhist Peace Fellowship, Community Peacemaker

---

* You can learn more about this in Paul and his brother Mark Engler's book, *This Is an Uprising*, through Carlos's organization the Ayni Institute, and the training organization Paul and Carlos helped to start, the Momentum Community.

Teams,* and Faith Matters Network put their bodies on the line as an extension of their faith. Groups like the Thrive Street Choir or the Peace Poets bring songs and poetry into movement spaces. Recent movements like the Movement for Black Lives or Standing Rock have always understood their work is more than "political." In the medium term, activists can recognize our work is ultimately about liberation and bring more spiritual grounding to it.

Grief and Rage

The second thing I'd love to see in the medium term is for movements to engage in grief and rage tending. When we hold onto strong emotions such as grief and rage without giving them healthy avenues for release, our ability for connection, creativity, and visioning gets cut off. I've talked about experimenting with bringing grief rituals into public spaces through direct action. I'm not suggesting creating outlets for activists to express *unprocessed* grief and rage in public spaces. The intention is for activists, after having done their own processing work beforehand in community, to create space for the public to witness what this sort of release could look like and potentially even to step into their own release. Having done the work themselves, activists will be prepared to hold a container for people who may not typically go to or have access to a grief ritual. This means we need to first create such spaces for ourselves, away from public spaces, where our own rage and grief can be expressed, witnessed, honored, and tended in a safe container.

Grief and rage are powerful emotions, and scary ones to express. I know for me, sometimes these emotions run so deep I'm afraid if I touch into them, I'll fall into a never-ending well

---

* Formerly known as Christian Peacemaker Teams.

I won't be able to climb back out of. But as scary as these emotions are, we can't turn away from them. We need to give them an outlet, because they're there. It's not possible to live in this world and not grieve, not be outraged. If we aren't creating safe containers for them to be expressed, we will only repress them in our bodies until they leak out involuntarily at a protest, against one other in a conversation, or in some online debate.

Because these emotions are so powerful, it's important to find community to do this work with. LiZhen once said, "Creating safe space isn't about creating containers where nobody gets hurt. It's about creating containers safe enough to engage with our hurt." By creating space that feels safe enough to invite, sit with, and honor these powerful—and sometimes painful—emotions, we prepare ourselves to hold space for healing our world.

Long-Term Strategies

All this training isn't just to prepare ourselves for public actions. It isn't just to hold space for other people and their grief. We're also preparing to live through the oncoming collapse. As we face more and more climate catastrophes, many of the systems we've come to rely on are collapsing. We'll face more famines, civil unrest will increase, more of us will lose our homes, and communities will be separated from one another. It will take everything to stay grounded and loving in this context. All our inner resources will be called upon. For us to have access to them, we need to commit now to healing as much of our own trauma as possible.

When one person in our community experiences a loss, others can be there to support them. But when the entire community suffers a loss, who's there to carry them? This is often the role of a death doula—someone not personally experiencing the loss who has enough resources to be an anchor of support for others. With practice, it can be possible to be this anchor and support even in the midst of your own losses. To play this role as our social and ecological systems collapse around us requires *deep* healing work. To touch our own fears about the collapse as a way to reach people's hearts without ourselves going into panic is *massive* work. Our own healing is important not only because we need to allow scars to build over our open wounds, but so we can know in our bodies what it means to heal trauma. If we don't have an embodied understanding of moving through shame and trauma ourselves, we won't be able to facilitate such a process for people in the world around us.

It doesn't take a lot of skill to open up a wound, but it requires great care and knowledge to dig around inside it, cut out the disease, and stitch the wound back up cleanly. Anyone can ask a person to talk about their most painful experiences from childhood. But it takes great care to move that conversation in the direction of healing. We don't all need to be licensed therapists. Having or not having a piece of paper from some fancy university says nothing about one's capacity to help others heal. But we do need to take this work seriously and invest in our own training and healing.

I still remember the first therapy appointment I ever had. After our session, my therapist looked at me and said, "You don't need talk therapy, you just need to learn to be in your body." This whole "learning to be in your body" thing? I've been working on it now for years. It's something I still struggle with. But practices like yoga, qi gong, and even singing as a somatic practice have helped me get out of my head, a little bit at a time. Early on, I thought I was doing it mostly for my own healing and that of my family. But as I went further and further, I realized there was more to it. The deeper I went, the more I realized I was learning what it takes to *create* healing. Not just in the Haga family, but in the human family and beyond. The more my own nervous system learned to regulate through difficult conversations, the more I could contribute to the regulation of Earth's nervous system.

There's no such thing as individual liberation and healing. There is only collective liberation and healing. The more I do "my own" healing work, the more I grow my capacity to practice fierce vulnerability and contribute to greater healing. My own ongoing trauma healing inadvertently trains me as a death doula for dying systems.

Moving Forward

There's a lot I don't know, but in the years I've been exploring fierce vulnerability and listening to what it tells me, I've arrived at seven hypotheses I continue to experiment with:

One—We need a fundamental transformation of society and everything we think we know about what it means to be human. Fierce vulnerability isn't about waging years-long battles to win one piece of legislation or change the face of who gets to sit on the throne of a broken system. To be honest, it doesn't even mean changing the system. It's about changing how we, as a species, relate to each other and to the rest of the cosmos. Our work, ultimately, is about healing. About belonging. About wholeness.

Two—A transformation is coming, whether we're ready for it or not. With the escalating climate crisis, an increasingly isolating society, and technological advances that give us the potential to destroy the planet 10 times over, we've reached a threshold and are living in times of major shifts that will fundamentally alter our social, political, and economic systems forever. Human-made systems and natural ecosystems are in the midst of collapse. There is no "stopping climate change" or "saving the world." The level of destruction and amount of suffering caused will depend largely on our readiness to accept the coming challenges. As Movement Generation says, "Transition is inevitable, justice is not."

Three—We can't think our way to an answer, and we can't control change. The crises we face are far too complex to "figure out" with our intellect alone. Change at that scale is not something we can control. We aren't creating the change, but we can be in right relationship to it. We can slow down and sense and respond. Our movements need to be guided by sources other than power maps, data analysis, and strategic plans. We need to learn to sit in silence, watch the stars, be with the wind and the birds, align our work with the seasons, sing and make art together, and, instead of trying to solve anything, simply listen.

Four—Without knowing, we need to act. Despite not having all the answers, we need to have the courage to take the next step, to step outside the comforts of our own movement spaces and use our bodies and hearts to intervene in the places where systemic violence and injustice manifest—through direct action, public witness, creative interventions. The goal of our actions isn't to change legislation, and the targets of our actions aren't inanimate systems. Our goal is to help society feel repressed emotions like grief so we can wake up from our collective delusions. Our "targets" are living systems—humans, non-humans, and ecosystems.

Five—There is an inseparable connection between personal and collective healing. The more I heal my own traumas, the more I get a sense of what it means to heal collective trauma. The more I heal, the more I can contribute to creating healed movement spaces. And the more healed our movement spaces are, the more healing we can offer the world. There's no separation between personal and collective healing. They're the same processes simply taking place at different scales.

Six—Social injustices and systemic violence are not political issues, but manifestations of collective trauma. These systems don't emerge in our world because certain people are simply "evil" and want to make others suffer. Deep down, we're *all* hurting, and that unseen, unhealed hurt humanity is holding manifests in the many forms of violence, oppression, and injustice we see in our world. The nature of injustice is not political. It's the manifestation of a deeply human experience.

Seven—You can't "shut down" injustice any more than you can "shut down" trauma. You can't go to someone acting out of trauma and tell them, "Stop it!" Yes, if you use enough force, it may work temporarily, but it's never a sustainable solution. Yet in our movement spaces, because we believe injustice to be a political issue, we try to "shut it down." We need movements. We need people who have the courage to put their bodies on the line and organize for large-scale change. But we need to do it radically differently than what many of us are used to. If injustice is a sign of collective trauma and healing is our goal, we have to find a more skillful and inviting way to stand up.

If we can continue to live into experimentations with these kinds of hypothesis, I have so much faith we can affirm life, create beauty, cultivate connection, and move toward healing, even in the midst of collapse.

Coda—
Remembering

*The people of the Seventh Fire do not yet walk forward;
rather, they are told to turn around and retrace the steps
of the ones who brought us here. Their sacred purpose is to
walk back along the red road of our ancestors' path and to
gather up all the fragments that lay scattered along the trail.
Fragments of land, tatters of language, bits of songs, stories, sacred teachings—all that was dropped along the way.
Our elders say that we live in the time of the seventh fire. We
are the ones the ancestors spoke of, the ones who will bend
to the task of putting things back together to rekindle the
flames of the sacred fire, to begin the rebirth of a nation.*

ROBIN WALL KIMMERER

IN 2015, I took part in The Long View, a week-long training
envisioned by Carlos Saavedra and facilitated by the Ayni Institute. In six days, we retraced 5,000 years of human history
to try to understand the story of domination. Or that's what we
thought was going to happen when we showed up. In reality,
we retraced the entire 4.2 billion year history of life on Earth!
We were reminded many of our ancestors spent lifetimes looking up at the night sky in wonder and awe, watching and listening
to the stars illuminate the darkness. With every passing night,
they carefully and painstakingly observed their positions and
movements. Every few days or weeks or months, they noticed
a particular star had moved to the north, or over the course of

an entire season a cluster of stars formed a particular pattern, or every year when a particular constellation was in a specific place in the sky, a certain plant was ready to harvest.

This was hard-won knowledge, gleaned over years and years of patiently looking up at the dark, silent night sky. Our ancestors spent decades collecting this knowledge and carefully passed it to the next generation, who continued to add to it, gradually building vast knowledge of the cosmos. With each passing evening, each season, and each generation, the knowledge grew, and people developed a deeper and deeper relationship with the stars. For our ancestors, the stars weren't just random points in the sky. They were guides, teachers, and storytellers. By spending decades listening to them, they learned to navigate the oceans, to track the passage of time and the changing of the seasons. Stars helped us travel to distant lands and build intricate calendars that determined when to plant and harvest crops and when to prepare for the harsh winter months ahead.

The stories the stars told also sparked wonder about the universe and our place within it. Our ancestors weren't only scientists but healers, wisdom keepers, and philosophers. They talked to the stars about the practical matters of life and about its greatest mysteries. With the stars, they were in relationship with something much greater than themselves.

Around the time I attended this workshop, I'd developed an uneasy relationship with the word "revolution." I associated it with the word "revolt" and was turned off by how some people talk about being "revolutionaries" to justify violence. I often felt a sense of vanguardism or machismo when I heard the word. But one night, I got curious about its etymology. I looked it up and, to my surprise, it turned out the word had nothing to do with the idea of revolt. In fact, the word "revolution" comes from the Latin *revolvere*, meaning "to turn or roll back," and entered the English language through the Old French world *révolucion*, which refers to the "revolution of celestial bodies"—the rotation of stars and planets. I've since come to understand being a revolutionary is about going back to our ancestral ways, looking up at the stars for guidance.

That is a revolution I can get down with. And I believe that's the choice ahead for us. The Hopi and Seven Fire prophecies both present us with a choice: Do we become revolutionaries and go back to our old, ancestral ways, or do we continue down the "modern" and material way toward destruction? This is the revolutionary moment we find ourselves in.

> Perhaps we are being guided to move with the kind of patience, slowness, and humility of our ancestors.
>
> Perhaps we are being shepherded back to being in right relationship with the natural world, nudged to take our guidance from it.
>
> Perhaps we are being reminded there is nothing we need to "figure out." We simply need to look up, to listen, and to remember.

I once learned an activity from Sonya Shah at an early workshop for the Ahimsa Collective that teaches people how to hold space for someone sharing something deeply vulnerable.[*] In it, one person—usually a co-facilitator—sits in the middle of a circle and shares a vulnerable story. Each person then says something in response that may come from a place of good intention, but is likely to shut down or re-traumatize the person in the middle.[†] "How could you have been so silly?" or "You should think about what the other person must have been going through," or "You need to just move on."

---

[*] Sonya adapted the activity from Lorraine Stutzman Amstulz.

[†] This is a role-play, and the person in the middle of the circle knows what is going to happen.

With each comment, we place a piece of cloth over the person in the circle. At the end of the round, after over a dozen "harmful" comments, the person in the middle is covered in cloth. The second round begins with each person in the circle sharing a different response to the story, now one intended to support the person who shared, for example a question that may invite them to share more. With each supportive, loving, and connecting comment, we remove a piece of cloth from the sharer's body until we can fully see them again.

In one debrief, a participant recalled that when the person in the middle was covered in cloth, they "looked like a monster." This is how trauma works. We end up covered in so many layers of pain and put on so many masks that we're no longer able to see the person inside. Too often, we're buried under layers so heavy we lash out, making us look like monsters. But this activity also models how healing works. Slowly, through connection, support, and the experience of having our story heard and validated, we peel away layer after layer of pain until our true, authentic selves are visible. Until we can see who we truly are.

Healing is about rediscovering our truest selves. It's about a deeply embodied remembering of who we really are, beneath all the layers of trauma. It is about coming back to being whole.

Touching the Sacred

In the past few years as I've been working on this book, I've had a lot of experiments in fierce vulnerability—things I've done that help me remember who I really am. Public grief rituals, vulnerable conversations with my family, prayer and ceremony. But surprisingly, one of the most impactful things I've done is to stop using our clothes dryer.

After fifteen years of living in an apartment, I now have access to land outside my home at Canticle Farm. So, LiZhen and I have been hanging our clothes out to dry. What started as an attempt to lower our carbon footprint has unexpectedly turned into a deep spiritual practice. There's something about taking the time to hang my laundry outside that somehow makes me feel . . . more human. Perhaps it's similar to spending entire nights in candlelight: drying clothes in the sun is something my ancestors did for so many generations that the somatic memory lives in my body and reconnects me directly to them—and to myself. I can feel the texture of the jeans in my hands, the weight of the shirt hanging on the line, and the warmth of the sun that will dry my wet clothes. In an increasingly fast-paced and technologically driven world, it feels like a small, yet graceful revolutionary act.

These kinds of individual lifestyle changes will never transform the world. In fact, this is exactly what corporations want you to focus on. To be very clear, I am in no way suggesting if we all install solar panels and drive a Prius, it'll lead to some sort of social transformation. This is simply a personal reflection. The more I unplug from the Matrix, the more I grow my own food or buy only from the Farmers Market, the more I can hear my own heart. The more I can hear my ancestors. The more I can hear the natural world. The more I remember who I am. Seeding the external work of fierce vulnerability from that place feels important. If the work we're called to do in the world is to remind us of our belonging to each other and to the Earth, we ourselves must have a deeply embodied understanding of what that means. Because we live in fractals.

When I think about "training," it makes me think about learning something new. But when I think about "training" for fierce vulnerability, it feels more important to remember, with my whole being, what it means to be human, what it means to belong to each other, and what paths our ancestors laid out for us. By removing layers of trauma and the distractions of social media, endless political debates, and the busyness of our lives, I find the space to listen for inspiration about what actions I need to be engaged in. Fierce vulnerability doesn't need us to learn anything "new."

The work of fierce vulnerability demands we leave the comfort zones of our homes, meditation centers, and training spaces. We need to be out in the world, engaging directly with people lost in delusion and playing active roles in systems of destruction. To, at times, put our bodies on the line to stop immediate harm. But the *how* of fiercely vulnerable actions requires us to come from a certain way of being. It requires us to remember how to walk gently on the Earth and to remember that every time we take a step, we touch something sacred.

Energy

About halfway through writing this book, I found myself on a work trip in Las Vegas. On my last night there, I went to a park to offer gratitude to the land. Looking out at the lights of the Las Vegas strip miles away as the sun set, I thought about all the energy it takes to power a city like Vegas. It reminded me energy doesn't just appear or disappear, it transforms. It made me think about how everything in our universe is made up of energy. You, me, the book or device you're holding in your hand. And because energy doesn't just appear out of nowhere, nothing in this universe is "new." Everything that exists throughout our vast universe has always existed, just in a different form.

I've talked about "creating beauty" in this book. But that's arrogant. There is no "creating" anything. All the beauty that's possible already exists in our world. All we can do is to become a vehicle to transfer the beauty into a new form.

Embarrassingly, there are aspects of Vegas I enjoy. I also believe it's an environmental catastrophe not likely to survive the transition. Later that night on the phone with LiZhen, she said, "Imagine all the energy that will be released when Vegas collapses." Like when a star collapses in on itself and explodes, releasing energy into space. That energy is what we're made of. It's what everything beautiful about this Earth is made of.

What unimaginable beauty might emerge from this collapse?

Death and destruction are never just that. Death gives way to life. Destruction gives way to creation. Grief gives way to joy. Suffering gives way to liberation. Collapse will inevitably give way to beauty. It might take fifty years, or a hundred. It might take a million years, or 4.5 billion years. But at some point, all the energy released through this collapse will reorganize itself into beauty, because that is the nature of our universe. It can't help it.

I for one can't wait to see it. Because no matter how long it takes, I'll be a part of it. We all will.

Dedication of Merit

IN MANY BUDDHIST COMMUNITIES, events and practice periods close with a "dedication of merit." This is a way to acknowledge that through our practice and our time together, we have cultivated some value or goodness. We dedicate this merit to others to spread the value and goodness as far as it can reach. Rather than acknowledging names out of obligation, I'd like to use this space to return the merit, the wisdom, and the inspiration I have received from so many people back to them. I know I've gained much value and goodness in the process of writing this book, and it's not for myself only that I do this work, it's for the benefit of all living beings.

The lineage of fierce vulnerability is still pretty new, but has already gone through many different formations. The workshop itself was developed by Chris Moore-Blackman, Anuttara Lakshmin Nath, and Sierra Pickett, and it was fine-tuned over years with feedback from countless individuals. In 2019, the Western Region of the Fellowship of Reconciliation invited us to turn their annual conference into a fierce vulnerability workshop for 150 people. Recognizing the need for a team of strong facilitators, we reached out to our local Bay Area community as well as the national Yet-to-Be-Named Network (YTBN) community for support. A team of twenty people gathered outside of Seabeck days before the conference, and we ran our first experiment in training facilitators in fierce vulnerability. The conference was a huge success. That team—Chris, Sierra, Sandra Bass, Thomas Clarke-Hazlett, Robin Crane, Morgan Curtis, David Dean, Shawn Gregory, Erin

Kassis, Nathan Kleban, Mara Marcum, Tim Nafziger, Anthony Rogers-Wright, Aimee Ryan, Emma Schoenberg, Karl Steyaert, and Cristobal Van Breen—helped to create a magical weekend I'll never forget.

Following that conference, YTBN voted to make fierce vulnerability the first mandatory step in the process of onboarding into the Network. For months, a group of us traveled the country with no funding, sleeping on floors, taking trains cross-country, somehow making it all work so we could spend countless days working on our movement DNA and sowing the seeds of the Network. I had so much fun with that DNA building team. I'll never forget how hard we laughed during a particular game of Codenames. In addition to the aforementioned Chris, Morgan, Erin, Marla, Tim, Anthony, and Emma, I'll always miss working with Andrea Novotney and Kritee Kanko. Special shoutouts to Okogyeamon, Justine Epstein, Justin Novotney, Imtiaz Rangwala, and others for making it all possible, as well as people like Carlos Saavedra, Leonie Smith, Rev. Lynice Pinkard, Miki Kashtan, and others who guided us. There are many people who contributed to YTBN/FVN long before I came along. Ethan Hughes, Tom Benevento, and countless others I'll never even meet.

The early members of the Bay Area FVN crew. Chris, Nirali/ Anuttara, Aimee, Morgan, Vickie Xiao Rong Chang, Sarah Herrera, astrid montuclard, Alvin Rosales, and Bonnie Wills. Agh, I just lost the game! The first ever Bay Area FVN Cohort, that lasted so much more than our cohort, lol! Chris, Xiao Rong, Sarah, LiZhen, Alvin, Olivia Barber, Lauren Chinn, Nakachi Clark-Kasimu, laura ann coelho, Kwame Eason, Sapho Flor, Melanie Gin, Rama Hall, Chase Hommeyer, Sandhya Jha, Wei-Li King, Niki Klaymoon, Forest Lin, Katie Loncke, Jesse Marshall, Jihan McDonald, Patricia Moore, Cole Rainey, Erika Ramirez, Kimberly Schroder, Oren J. Sofer, Dhara Uy, and Maegan Willan, as well as Larry Yang, Thanissara, and others who couldn't join us but showed us so much love. You all remember that

Emergence session? Man, did that emerge.... And I'm still grateful to all of our pseudopods! Thanks to Luis Miranda for being our pseudopod guide!

To those who have been central in my journey of healing. To my Asian Diaspora Jam crew! Nandita Batheja, BK Chan, Shilpa Jain, Amadeo Guiao, Hyoyoung Minna Kim, Forest Lin, Rishikesh Tirumalai, and LiZhen Wang, thank you for reminding me what home feels like. The OG Men's Jam crew of Roan Coughtry, Jovan Julien, Elias Serras, Chris Tittle, Austin Willacy, and Sky Yardeni: I still remember how good that water felt and how good that BBQ was!

To my Ahimsa OGs and Core Fam! I so deeply miss our times together. Dave Beldon, Richard Cruz, Alison Espinosa-Setchko (thanks for all the hours in the car!), Ana Maria Hurtado, Nuri Nursat, Nicole Pittman, Martina Lutz Schneider, Daniel Self, Sonya Shah, Julian Ward, Maegan Willan, Bonnie Wills, and of course the one, the only, the never-again-will-we-see-a-motherfucker-this-bright, Kashka Banjoko. To other teachers I've met through my work at Ahimsa: Samantha Bautista, Parker Chamberlin, Alba Contreras, Kimberly Gragston, Ty Lancaster, Duran Lyles, Sachi Maniar, Seth Nguyen-Weiner, Frank Robles, Dennis Scott, Earl Sotto, Mikey Stephens, AJ Urriza, Rev. Samantha Wilson, and so many more.

To my Canticle family. Living with you is truly the greatest honor of my life. What a privilege to know where I want to raise my child and take my last breath. I'm especially grateful to Anne and Terry Symens-Bucher for having this vision and inviting us all into it. Carin and Isa Anderson; Lu Aya and Niria Garcia and little Tlayo; Orion Camero; Robin Crane; Morgan Curtis and Travis Gibrael and little Sabine; Dyna Erie; Deja, Kai, and Amne Gould; Nikki Hicks and Leo White and little Clodagh; Alicia and Pamela and Paola and Sara Sanchez; Jacob Sandoval; Watani and Kishana Stiner; Edwin Tatague; Vick Torea; Kylie Tseng; Oona Valle; Rubin Williams; Troy Williams; my own family of LiZhen, our amazing beautiful cutest baby in the world (tu tu! peh peh!); Yexin and my mother Naoko Hitomi; our Earth Abides family; Hawk Palmer and Kait Singley and little Osi; Mikilani Kumu Young; and to all of our family members in the Sanctuary homes. God, we're a beautiful mess!

I've had simply too many incarcerated teachers to name them all, but I want to shout out all of the people I've worked with, especially at Correctional Training Facility, San Quentin, and Valley State Prisons. I'm so happy I've gotten to hug many of you outside of the walls, and I can't wait to see the others once you're home. Your day is coming.

Of course, my family. In addition to the ones I live with at Canticle, my sisters Erika and Megumi Haga, and my nephew Jett, who I miss everyday! My aunts Noriko, Shigeko, and Motoko, who I don't get to see nearly enough. My uncle Seiji. Thinking of you, wherever you may be. My new Hsu and Wang family! Especially my sister-friend Doreen! We miss you every day you're not here!

And, finally, to the entire family at Parallax. Especially to Hisae Matsuda for continuing to give me this opportunity to publish, to Katie Eberle for the amazing design work, and to Miranda Perrone for the countless hours of dedication to the manuscript and for mining the book I knew was in there somewhere! And to everyone else working to support this book being out in the world. I'm so grateful to work with a publisher in it for the same reasons I am: to get us one step closer to collective liberation.

To all of those I named, and to all of those I did not: this book is *years* in the making—I know in all that time, all the individuals who contributed must have developed a decent amount of merit.

I dedicate it all back to you.

May the merits of this work reach back to each and every one of you, and through you to every atom in the universe. May you find silence to hear the gentle breeze whispering in your ear.

May you find the stillness to remember that with every step you take, you touch something sacred and the sacred touches you back. May you find slowness to witness the unfolding of each moment, like petals opening to the sun. May you find courage to face the deep shadows in your heart and the clarity of mind to know your light is infinite. May you have the humility to remember you're a speck of dust, and the sense of grandeur to remember the dust you're made of was born in a star. May you find joy in the smallest of wonders, wisdom in the simplest of truths, and inspiration in the emptiness that surrounds you in each moment. May your sorrows be eased by compassion, your fears softened by hope, and your path illuminated by love. May each impossible moment be met with acceptance. May that be enough. May these words sink deep into your bones and remind you every day that you belong, that you are already whole. And may you remember, always, that you are held in the quiet embrace of the Earth, as ancient as time and as vast as the stars.

Notes

1 Stefan Stenudd, *Tao Te Ching: The Taoism of Lao Tzu Explained* (Arriba, 2011), 199.

2 Barbara Deming, *Revolution & Equilibrium* (Grossman, 1971).

3 Resmaa Menakem, *My Grandmother's Hands, Racialized Trauma and the Pathway to Mending Our Hearts and Bodies* (Central Recovery Press, 2017), 9.

4 J. Douglas Bremnar, "Traumatic stress: effects on the brain," in NIH National Library of Medicine, *https://pmc.ncbi.nlm.nih.gov /articles/PMC3181836/*.

5 adrienne maree brown, *Emergent Strategy: Shaping Change, Changing Worlds* (AK Press, 2017).

6 The US Department of Housing and Urban Development's annual report found 653,104 people experienced homelessness in the United States in 2023. That number represents a record-high tally and a 12 percent increase over 2022.

7 From a speech Dr. Martin Luther King gave on December 16, 1967, called "Where Do We Go From Here?" Available to read in its entirety on the Stanford University King Institute website: *https://kinginstitute.stanford.edu/where-do-we-go-here*.

8 Staci Haines, *The Politics of Trauma: Somatics, Healing, and Social Justice* (North Atlantic Books, 2019), 217.

9 Brené Brown, *Daring Greatly: How the Courage to Be Vulnerable Transforms the Way We Live, Love, Parent, and Lead* (Avery, 2015), 58. For this and other wisdom from Brené Brown, see her enormously popular talks on YouTube, starting with "Listening to Shame."

10 *Brown*, 67.

11 Nagarjuna, Jay L. Garfield, trans., *The Fundamental Wisdom of the Middle Way: Nāgārjuna's Mūlamadhyamakakārikā* (Oxford University Press, 1995), 296.

12 Howard Thurman, *Deep is the Hunger* (Friends United Press 1951), 11.

13 From Dr. Martin Luther King's essay, "Pilgrimage to Non-violence," published April 13, 1960. This is one of Dr. King's most famous pieces of writing, and can be found here among many other places: *https://kinginstitute.stanford.edu/king-papers/documents/pilgrimage-nonviolence#fn13*.

15 Benjamin Hoff and E. H. Shepard, *The Tao of Pooh* (Dutton Books, 1982).

16 Gene Sharp, *Social Power and Political Freedom* (Porter Sargent Publishers, 1980), 218.

15 Kurt Schock, *Unarmed Insurrections: People Power Movements in Nondemocracies* (University of Minnesota Press, 2004), 6.

17 Deborah Frieze, "How I Became a Localist," TEDx talk on You-Tube, *https://www.youtube.com/watch?v=2jTdZSPBRRE*.

18 Francis Weller, *The Wild Edge of Sorrow: Rituals of Renewal and the Sacred Work of Grief* (North Atlantic Books, 2015).

19 Aldo Leopold, *A Sand County Almanac: And Sketches Here and There* (Oxford University Press, 1949).

20 See the American Psychological Association's study at *https://www.apa.org/news/press/releases/2020/02/climate-change*.

About the Author

KAZU HAGA is a trainer and practitioner of nonviolence and restorative justice and a core member of the Ahimsa Collective and the Fierce Vulnerability Network. He is also a Jam facilitator and author of *Healing Resistance: A Radically Different Response to Harm*. He works with incarcerated people, youth, and activists from around the country.

He has over twenty-five years of experience in nonviolence and social change work. He is a resident of the Canticle Farm community on Lisjan Ohlone land, Oakland, CA, where he lives with his family. You can find out more about his work at *www.kazuhaga.com*.

Monastics and visitors practice the art of mindful living in the tradition of Thich Nhat Hanh at our mindfulness practice centers around the world. To reach any of these communities, or for information about how individuals, couples, and families can join in a retreat, please contact:

PLUM VILLAGE
33580 Dieulivol, France
plumvillage.org

LA MAISON DE L'INSPIR
77510 Villeneuve-sur-Bellot, France
maisondelinspir.org

HEALING SPRING
MONASTERY
77510 Verdelot, France
healingspringmonastery.org

MAGNOLIA GROVE
MONASTERY
Batesville, MS 38606, USA
magnoliagrovemonastery.org

BLUE CLIFF MONASTERY
Pine Bush, NY 12566, USA
bluecliffmonastery.org

DEER PARK MONASTERY
Escondido, CA 92026, USA
deerparkmonastery.org

EUROPEAN INSTITUTE OF
APPLIED BUDDHISM
D-51545 Waldbröl, Germany
eiab.eu

THAILAND PLUM VILLAGE
Nakhon Ratchasima
30130 Thailand
thaiplumvillage.org

ASIAN INSTITUTE OF
APPLIED BUDDHISM
Lantau Island, Hong Kong
pvfhk.org

STREAM ENTERING
MONASTERY
Porcupine Ridge, Victoria 3461
Australia
nhapluu.org

MOUNTAIN SPRING
MONASTERY
Bilpin, NSW 2758, Australia
mountainspringmonastery.org

For more information visit: *plumvillage.org*
To find an online sangha visit: *plumline.org*
For more resources, try the Plum Village app: *plumvillage.app*
Social media: *@thichnhathanh @plumvillagefrance*

PARALLAX PRESS, a nonprofit publisher founded by Zen Master Thich Nhat Hanh, publishes books and media on the art of mindful living and Engaged Buddhism. We are committed to offering teachings that help transform suffering and injustice. Our aspiration is to contribute to collective insight and awakening, bringing about a more joyful, healthy, and compassionate society.

View our entire library at parallax.org.

THE MINDFULNESS BELL is a journal of the art of mindful living in the Plum Village tradition of Thich Nhat Hanh. To subscribe or to see the worldwide directory of Sanghas (local mindfulness groups), visit mindfulnessbell.org.